Lucky Conversations

Visits With the Most Prominent People of the 20th Century

By Morris Wolff

With Karen Weber

©2021 Morris Wolff. All Rights Reserved.

©2021 Morris Wolff. All Rights Reserved.

ISBN: 978-1-62249-598-6

Published by
Biblio Publishing
Columbus, Ohio
Biblio Publishing.com

Table of Contents

Table of Contents iii
Dedications v
Acknowledgments v
Foreword ix
Introduction 1
Aim High and Receive 11
Write Something Every Day 13
Being an Individual and Non-Conformist 16
We Need Adlai, Badly! 27
Ten Dollars for a Tank of Gas 35
Eleanor Roosevelt 41
Expanding the Vision in Africa 51
Securing Water Rights with Moshe Dayan 62
Working with John F. Kennedy 67
There Will Never Be Another Camelot 74
Working for Bobby Kennedy 84
Senator John Sherman Cooper 103
The Chitlin' Circuit 115
Divine Providence on a Cold November Day 121
If You're Black, Step Back 133
Marching with Representative John Lewis 138
A New Day Was Coming 154
A Chance Meeting in a London Bar 173
Finding Love in Prison 180
Justice Denied for Wallenberg 193
After the Wallenberg Verdict 205
My Biggest Influence, Leo Wolff 255
Growing Up with a Tough Dad 264
My Final Conversation with Dad 279
Epilogue 291
Von Dardel v. Union of Soviet Socialist Republics, 623 F. Supp. 246
(D.D.C. 1985) 297
Sabotaged by U.S. Supreme Court chief Ex-Hill attorney still fighting for
Holocaust Hero 322
Ex-Hiller fights shameful U.S./Soviet coverup, Hero victimized by gov't
officials at highest level 325

Dedications

I dedicate this book to Patricia, my fantastic and loving wife. She knows more about me than I know about myself. To my two daughters, Michelle and Lesley, and my steadfast and loyal and loving brothers Carl, Richard, and David and their wives, and to my beloved sister Ruth and her family for their continual love and support of my efforts and helping me to meet celebrities and famous people.

Acknowledgments

I thank my mother, Carolyn, who took me on my first excursion to New York at age eight on a Saturday in 1944 to meet my first celebrity. She got me excited about meeting famous people when she took me to meet the world-renowned poet, Carl Sandburg. I was simply in awe and was at first tongue-tied. He loosened me up and we talked together for a half-hour. I enjoyed it immensely. We talked about poetry and how to become a writer. And so, I did. I can still see that moment in my mind's eye. It stimulated me to want to meet and talk with famous people of accomplishment.

I want to thank Karen Weber, my steadfast, brilliant, patient, and loyal co-writer of this book. Karen gives a new meaning to the word editor. She checked out all the facts.

I thank my beloved beautiful, stubborn, feisty, intelligent, and independent wife, Patricia, for our fantastic life together during these past ten magical years from my gracefully aging a decade from my entry to her life at age 75, and making it to 85 this coming November 30, 2021. We have had a lot of fun together and shared great moments of laughter and joy. We manage to stay positive and even laugh at moments of insanity in our present-day world of mass shootings and a year of the Covid 19 epidemic with millions dying around the world. It has brought us even closer as elderly lovers still in their prime.

It is 7:10 a.m. on Friday, May 28, 2021, as I rewrite this section of my book. Patricia has brewed a cup of black coffee and fixed a large white enamel cup of healthy oatmeal and raisins. I am busy writing and rewriting, and watching the dawn and sunrise. She is the manager of my good health, good manners, courtesy, and acuity. "Yes, Dear" are now my favorite words in our happy home. It is my favorite use of free speech under the US Constitution.

At 85, I am a happy man looking forward to my daily morning bike rides as the sun rises east on a beautiful Florida morning. I am a lucky man with many lucky conversations and blessed by God to be able to laugh at the world. We find it is better to laugh together than to cry. Her incredible kindness, honesty, love, and sense of humor have kept me alive and healthy. She is the light of my life. She has persevered in getting this book published so everyone can share in this experience.

Author Bio

In 1993, Morris Wolff received the United Nations Peace Award for Humanitarian Service at Carnegie Hall. In 1983, along with Rosa Parks, he was awarded the National Council of Christian and Jews annual award for humanitarian service for his work with Attorney General Robert Kennedy in helping to draft and write the United States Civil Rights Act of 1964.

Morris practiced international law and trial law in Philadelphia from 1970 to 1993, as a partner with the Honorable Harold E. Stassen, former Governor of Minnesota and one of the five original signers of the United Nations Charter. During that period, Morris was also a Professor of International Law and Ethics at the University of Pennsylvania Law School and served for two years as the Chief Assistant District Attorney of the City of Philadelphia. In March of 1983, Morris was asked by Guy von Dardel of Stockholm, Sweden, half-brother of Swedish diplomat Raoul Wallenberg, to sue the Soviet Union to force them to release his brother Raoul. This book tells the Wallenberg story of heroic lifesaving work in Hungary and reports on Morris's gutsy pro bono effort in US Federal Court in Washington D.C. to achieve this awesome task of rescuing Raoul Wallenberg after spending 39 dark, incommunicado years in prison and still found miraculously alive.

Morris Wolff was a distinguished trial lawyer, former Chief Assistant District Attorney, and Prosecutor of crime in Philadelphia. He fought corruption with a passion. He was appointed by the Mayor to investigate unlawful behavior and major felony crimes perpetrated by Judges Lewis Mongeluzzo ("The Mongoose"), Judge Ruth Marmon ("Rat Marmon") who were caught taking large cash bribes from lawyers and other miscreants in the City of Philadelphia. Neither one attended law school or college or went beyond 7th grade.

Wolff's citywide investigation of corrupt judges was historic, leading to Judges going "up the river" and "doin' serious time." Major anti-corruption changes in selecting judges on merit rather than political basis, careful screening and investigation of their ethics and record beforehand, rigorous screening in person by the Ethics Committee of the Philadelphia Bar took place.

For the record, Judge "Mongoose" Moongeluzzo had a fifth-grade education and quit school to become a numbers runner for the Mafia. Later, at age 36, he became the politically corrupt Ward Leader of the 5th ward in the same Italian neighborhood where singers Mario Lanza, Bobby Darren, and Eddie Fisher first got started. The legendary Mongoose Mongoluzzo sold favors for the Mob everywhere. Hence, he was known as "The Enforcer," which furthered his interest in due process and disposal of dead bodies at his South Philadelphia funeral home for the Mob.

During the first six months of probationary service, new judges were watched carefully. Then, after a full year without any written complaints filed by lawyers or the general public, they were elevated to full-time service. The system now touted fairness, due process, and justice.

At the University of Pennsylvania, in Philadelphia, Morris was appointed Professor of Ethics and International law. He published many law journal articles on both subjects.

Morris is a cum laude graduate of Amherst College and of the Yale Law School, where he studied international law under Sterling Professor Myres McDougal and Federal Judge Guido Calabrese, of the U.S. Second Circuit Court of Appeals. Morris currently resides in Florida where he continues his career as an Associate Professor and Director of the Bethune-Cookman University Wild Cats Write! Program for entering freshmen.

Foreword

Life sometimes seems to zigzag around us, taking us on paths which we might have never expected, dreamed, or hoped for. While we travel on our way, we encounter unexpected surprises that nurture us to grow, learn, and to be better, kinder individuals within our families, co-workers, and our community.

In February 2018, I went to a synagogue in Brandon, FL, and heard an articulate, humble, and charismatic, idealistic man speak about Raoul Wallenberg, a Swedish hero of the Holocaust who went to Hungary to save 100,000 Jews during World War II. As a Holocaust student, I was familiar with Wallenberg's story, and I wanted to learn more. The man giving the speech was Morris Wolff, and the book he spoke about is, *Whatever Happened to Raoul Wallenberg?*

Before the speech, after I bought the book from Morris, I was standing around doing nothing when Morris waved me over. He asked me what I did for a living, and after telling him I'm a writer, I said that I had a strong interest in social justice, and perhaps he could help me follow that path. We clicked intellectually and socially.

Morris started telling me about his next book, this one. We came to an agreement that I would edit his manuscript. What an exciting opportunity and a lucky conversation! After that came a wonderful collaboration where we tossed ideas back and forth, where I questioned the truth of a story, and he always came back with a simple and verifiable fact. Morris is one of the most down-to-earth men I've ever met. He strongly believes in fighting for the rights of others, and the challenges of doing so became his life's work. This unexpected opportunity to edit Morris's book helped me grow as a person, writer, and editor.

Today, as I write this, the United States is confronted with escalating civil rights issues like those of the 1960s. We face an increasing wave of injustices against people of color that we must continue to fight against. I hope these stories help you, dear reader, work towards equal justice for all by not being afraid to stand up and speak out against racism and discrimination of any kind.

The story Morris tells is all about how to walk up to people, introduce yourself, and have a conversation. During editing, I sat in awe as Morris walked through his life in the corridors of history and the experiences that luckily came his way. Each of us gets a front-row seat to that astounding past. I hope you enjoy, learn, and grow as you read this amazing book.

Karen Weber
Websharp Writing & Editing
https://www.websharp.info
May 2021

Introduction

This book is about famous people with significant accomplishments whom I have met on street corners, in the halls of Congress, on the Rhine River, in Accra, Ghana and in the corridors of my life. I love meeting people. I learn so much from hearing their life experiences. I try to adopt some of their pearls of wisdom as a sensible and usable part of my own life going forward.

We find something in common from the outset, allowing us to develop confidence, trust, and interest in getting to know each other from step one. I talk a lot, but I have learned how to listen quietly, ask the next question, and allow the other person to enjoy having the floor. As a youngster in second grade, I began to learn how to listen quietly. Miss Marian Eckert, my second-grade teacher at Shoemaker School in Elkins Park, had me stay after school one day and write the word "listen" 100 times, in three straight columns. She taught me how to spell and listen. I loved her as I loved all my elementary school teachers right up from Miss Cornet Armstrong in kindergarten through Mrs. Grieb, always smiling, and the very stern and unsmiling Mrs. Wilson in the sixth grade.

At times, as I was reaching forward for a new conversation I was met with hostility. I learned something of value anyway from their rudeness, bad manners, and hostility. That includes Louis Farrakhan, who called Judaism a 'gutter religion' and Mohammed Ali, who, with an air of disdain, wiped his hand on his trousers twice after shaking my hand. Ali's rudeness was in front of a crowd of people in an assembly or reception line. That was not courteous, I was scared he was about to hit me.

I felt like punching Ali. I could have punched him, but since he was the heavy-weight boxing champ, after careful consideration, I decided not to do so. He said, "I thought the civils rights movement was an all-black civil rights movement." He apparently was not aware that there was room in the civil rights movement of the 60s for good white men of honor, like President John F. Kennedy, and

Robert Kennedy (my former boss), John Sherman Cooper, and Jack Greenberg, the white, Jewish legal counsel to the NAACP.

They were all there with me that night on the stage in Atlantic City in 1980 when I received the National Council of Christians and Jews Award for my sustained work as a teacher and lawyer fighting for civil rights and helping to write the Civil Rights Act of 1964.

Rosa Parks was awarded the same night, and believe it or not, Mr. Muhammed Ali, after an apology, handed me my award and gave me a bear hug. It was a great night with great people and many lucky conversations.

Jack Greenberg Esq., legal counsel to the NAACP, John Doar, and I worked day and night during 1963 as civil rights advocates. We know the truth: "all lives matter." In the protected sanctity of the U.S. Department of Justice, Office of Legal Counsel, 5th floor, we wrote the Civil Rights Act of 1964. I wrote Title II, which opened the doors of places of public accommodation' (meaning restaurants, hotels, swimming pools, movie theaters, and so on.) and housing and employment without discrimination for all people. I helped to write Title VII, dealing with fair and open housing, and employment without discrimination for all people.

Our goal was to achieve equality of opportunity for all of God's children. I have learned a lot through "lucky one on one private conversations" with Martin Luther King, Roy Wilkins, head of the NAACP, and Malcolm X, whom I met by chance on the steps of the Justice Department in D.C.

Martin Luther King and Malcolm X were like philosophical bookends, two ends of the argument with King advocating non-violent, peaceful persuasion and Malcom X advocating violence, anger, and looting.

I learned a great deal from meetings with Attorney General Robert F. Kennedy. We chose our words for the new law carefully. He taught me how to stay focused on the task at hand and to keep my eye on the prize.

My first early childhood experience with someone famous was with the shaggy white-haired poet laureate Carl Sandburg, at a National Book Award luncheon in New York at the Waldorf Astoria one spring morning in 1945. He greeted me warmly. He leaned down to my height and spoke to me. I was not very tall. "I want to know about your poetry," he said. "What do you choose to write about?" It was a warm and positive early experience, with a love of writing short poems. I remember his warm, enigmatic smile, his rimless glasses, his warm hand on my shoulder, and how he parted his abundance of soft white hair right down the middle.

I was a starry-eyed, sensitive, and precocious eight-year-old child who loved to write children's poetry, a unique genre I invented and carried forward until I transitioned and began writing poetry for adolescents at age 15. I started collecting poets as friends. I met with Pulitzer Prize winner Eudora Welty, a gentle bright soul known to her friends as "Miss Eudora" in 1995, during the year I taught constitutional law at Morehouse College in Atlanta. I felt like I was meeting another Emily Dickinson with the same soft brilliance and sensitivity.

I once served as a guide, chauffer, and chaperone for the brilliant poet Dylan Thomas. I picked him up at the trains station one spring day in Springfield, Massachusetts following his trip from New York, through New Haven, CT, and then to Springfield. I drove him 28 miles to the college. By the time we met on the well-worn platform at 2:00 p.m., he had already "had a few," as he put it, and was "three sheets to the wind" as I put it, but not to him. I was too polite, but Dylan Thomas reeked of booze and wanted to continue drinking.

I drove him back to campus, ostensibly to give a lecture at 5:00, but we took a detour. He insisted on having "just a nip." I sat down for a few beers, at Barsellotti's Bar and Grill in the little town of Amherst, with the world-renowned poet Dylan Thomas, the year he was invited by the English Honors program to give a talk to students about poetic style.

"A little drink before my talk won't hurt anyone," he quipped, as I arrived to pick him up again. At Barselloti's we focused on his great poem *Do Not Go Gently into that Good Night*. I questioned him about the third line in the poem, which read, "Rage, rage, against the dying of the light." This gave me insight into the suicidal character of the man. Thomas said, "The second line is full of anger; I hate to think about death." Dylan Thomas drank and drank. He was great fun sharing stories and anecdotes with me at the bar. He cost me a small fortune, and he never did make it to his public lecture. He actually fell asleep on his bar stool at Barsellotti's. I walked him back to the Lord Jeffrey Amherst Inn and tucked him in bed. He sang a bunch of Welsh songs, loud and strong, as we stumbled arm in arm over the lush green grass lawn of the Amherst Common on the way back to his room. They were beautiful Welsh songs or airs. I had never heard them before. He was great fun to be with at the bar. Dylan Thomas at Amherst became a joy-filled lucky conversation. I loved his Welsh accent, his delivery of songs and words, and his wisdom. But I missed his lecture, and so did he.

Alfred Kazin of "Native Ground" and the great historian Henry Steele Commager were my two favorite professors at Amherst. My conversations with them were great conversations, one-on-one alone. Later on, I met Daniel Hoffman, the 22nd Consultant in Poetry to the Library of Congress in 1973, and spoke about poetry with Elizabeth Bishop and Robert Frost at Amherst. A chapter in this book is devoted and dedicated to Mr. Frost.

My mother cultivated my ability to listen and learn from others by being patient, humble, and honest. She taught me, "Morris, you can learn an awful lot just by listening. Don't puff out your chest too much or tell your own story. Let the other person speak. That way, you will learn something of value." My mother gave me many books to read. She taught me how to walk up to people, introduce myself politely and engage them with a sense of humor. She developed my curiosity about life and a desire to chat with other people. As my chief mentor, John F. Kennedy, once said, "I am willing to face any challenge to meet new people."

She encouraged my passion for music, learning new things and meeting new people, and how to gracefully break into existing conversations. She taught me how to be tactful and diplomatic at a young age. Tact, diplomacy, and cunning are vital in gaining access to spontaneous conversations. I was born outgoing and remain willing to put myself forward modestly and obtrusively and, at times, obnoxiously to meet special people in any crowd. I was willing to pay any price, and bear any burden.

Gatecrashing at diplomatic cocktail parties in Washington D.C. and into a World Series can be great fun. In 1980, the World Series in Philadelphia was sold out. Scalpers were hawking tickets at $800 apiece. I couldn't and wouldn't pay that kind of money for one ticket. So, I invented a strategy for attending.

I got to the ballpark two hours early. Soon I saw a group of men all dressed alike in London Fog raincoats stepping down from a large yellow bus and walking slowly towards the stadium. Rain was predicted for around the 5th inning. I thought to myself, Hey, I got a London Fog in the back seat of my car." I said to myself, "Get out of the car, walk over and insinuate yourself in the middle of that crowd, that school of fish." They turned out to be the reporters there to cover the game. We shuffled together slowly to the Press Entrance and joke together. I saved $800 and crashed the Phillies National League Ballpark in Philadelphia and made my way to the press box by wearing the same London Fog raincoat that other members of the press wore that night.

After the first game, the press members enjoyed the joke and gave me passes to the press box for the rest of the series. I had prime seats plus an invite to attend the victory party with all the stars in the locker room after the final out. The Kansas City Royals went down to defeat 4 to 2 in an unexpected fireball of flames in five games. At the victory party after the last game, I ended up receiving as a gift a full Phillies game uniform. I was honored with an entire Phillies outfit. I had the gray batting glove of All Stars shortstop Larry Bowa, future Hall of Famer Mike Schmidt's shirt, and pitcher Tug McGraw's red, warmup shirt. This "honor" was accomplished with the explicit permission of the players involved. Each piece was left on the floor, abandoned by those men not realizing the eventual value 50 years down the road. I met and interviewed each one of these men along with CBS sports commentator Red Smith for television on the Sunday night show, *60 Minutes*. That was quite something.

I have a flexible and pragmatic personality with an opportunistic bent. I witnessed chance meetings about to happen before my very eyes, and I grab onto them. It is a combination of improv and chutzpah. I love playing games. I feel comfortable speaking to anyone, ranging from President John F. Kennedy to President Kwame Nkrumah, and Premier Patrice Lumumba to the washerwoman doing the floors at the Waldorf Astoria or the Ritz doorman in the Belgian Congo. Some of the lesser-known folk are at times even more interesting than the puffed-up world leaders. I am comfortable speaking to anyone on a global basis. Celebrities can be fun, informative, or dangerous. I have met my share of interesting personalities, as you, my dear reader, shall soon see. They taught me many things in four different languages — French, German, English, and Spanish. Knowing a second or third language is a good icebreaker. People warm up to a stranger if they hear their own language spoken back to them. At times you must have a catchline that stops the celebrity or icon in their tracks. They are usually in motion, going somewhere. The chapters on meeting President Kwame Nkrumah in Accra, Ghana, and the chapter on meeting Jackie Kennedy in Central Park are examples of this skill at work. Sometimes we make our own luck. It rarely happens by chance. Timing and presence are everything. You have to be there to meet someone famous.

Why should they want to speak to you? A particular curiosity and politeness prevail.

Take the poet laureate, Robert Frost, for example. He loved playing games. There was a price of admission to pay for a one-hour visit, which turned out to be the greatest literary hour of my life. I had to memorize a long poem to get in. Robert Frost, always the puckish egotist, required me to learn *Birches*, so I might meet with him alone at the quaint and famous Lord Jeffery Inn the spring of my senior year at Amherst College in May of 1958. It was worth it, and he cut me off after the first five lines anyway, claiming, "Oh, I have heard that poem before."

I love meeting and talking with famous people in different countries and in other languages. I like trying to "walk in their shoes" and to empathize and have compassion for language differences. This book is about some of the best meetings in Europe, Asia, Latin America, Israel, and America with sports and political celebrities, including one on one meetings with three different Presidents in the Oval Office. I also played singles tennis with U.S. Supreme Court Justice Antonin Scalia in Hawaii. We became good friends, and through him, I was invited to attend a luncheon at the US Supreme Court with Justice Ruth Bader Ginsburg. She was shy, but brilliant, with a warm smile and a great trailblazer for women's equality. May her memory be a blessing.

During my formative school years, I was trained at home to be selfless, giving, and a kind humanitarian. I deeply care about the wellbeing of other people. I am a peaceful person. I love to reason things out amicably, and I hate bullies and cowards — both ends of the weakness curve.

Stephen Cary and other leading Quakers encouraged me to become a humanitarian, a civil rights fighter, and an advocate in the halls of Justice. They trained me at school in the classroom at GFS to devote myself to becoming an active change agent and leader. Do not accept social conditions as you find them. Change them! So, they sent members of our high school class of 1954 downtown to a weekend work camp in the poverty sections or slums of Philadelphia to learn what it is like to be poor. We worked to rebuild worn out buildings and rat-infested homes. We attended the corrupt

Magistrate's Court of Philadelphia on Sunday mornings. That's when I decided to become a civil rights lawyer and promised to come back to reform the court. There were no legally trained judges on this kangaroo court, and people were treated like crap and without due process of law or decency. They were ridiculed and humiliated in open court and told to put a quarter in the Heart Fund. Was this justice in downtown America? I did precisely that as Chief Assistant District Attorney of Philadelphia in 1965. I came back just eleven years later and prosecuted the magistrates.

These brave Quakers taught me from Henry David Thoreau's "Theory of Civil Disobedience." The lessons taught me about fairness, justice, due process, and fighting for the powerless and standing fast for what is right and not giving up an inch of ground when you are fighting for what you know to be right. And "to stand tall" and speak truth to power — a Quaker maxim.

They helped me create tactics of lively political responsibility and to lead without fear or anxiety. They reiterated, "Speak truth to power," no matter what the cost. My English teachers, David Mallery and Edward Gordon, at the Germantown Friends School, prepared me to advocate for the less fortunate. They also taught me to stand up for human rights and to fight for world peace.

I played tennis with Don Budge and Hank Greenberg in Jamaica in 1969. In 2017, my Taiwanese partner, Leng Chung, and I won the Florida seniors state championship. We also got to play in the nationals in Birmingham and reached the quarterfinals.

I walked up to Malcolm X in front of the U.S. Department of Justice in 1963, and I debated civil rights with him in front of 1,000 people. I stopped President Kwame Nkrumah, the President of Ghana, and Congo President Patrice Lumumba on the tarmac at Accra Ghana airport in 1961. I spoke with them about international peace for 20 minutes or so. Together, in a conversation, we changed the course of history.

I met with President John F. Kennedy alone in the Oval Office for an hour on April 11, 1963. I shared with him my thoughts on AIESEC, a massive international student exchange between all nations. We talked about using AIESEC as a strategic program for finding world peace. I also urged the President to promote and sign the nuclear test ban treaty with Russia, which he discussed in his speech at the American University in Washington D.C. a few months later in September of 1963.

I worked with Robert Kennedy at the Department of Justice early in my career, drafting Title II of the Civil Rights Act of 1964. The act is dedicated to ending discrimination against blacks in hotels, restaurants, public swimming pools, libraries, movie theaters, and other places ordinarily open to the "general public," where you can relax. Places where life can be enjoyed without hassle, fear, or humiliation. Hard to imagine these places were closed to blacks at that time.

Yes, black lives mattered even back in the dark ages of 1960, 61 years ago. We embarked on a historic and courageous journey, working with Martin Luther King in a peaceful, legal battle towards equality. We are still on that journey with more work still to be done. But at least we started out on the trail towards equality with Bobby Kennedy as our leader. As a team, we wrote Title II, the section called "Public Accommodations." It opened up doorways for everyone in public places to be treated with decency and respect. I did that work for three months with my pen and my heart, engaged in the collaborative writing of the Act with Attorney General Robert F. Kennedy, and five members of the Office of Legal Counsel.

I walked and talked with Jackie Kennedy Onassis by chance on my 57th birthday, November 30, 1993. My law partner, Stephen Beck, pointed her out to me as we were walking through Central Park. He pointed and said, "Look, there is Jackie Kennedy!" Like a fool, he continued on to our law office and did not stop. Such people, like my law partner, never fail to miss a great opportunity. I stopped her in her tracks. We had a good time together, reminiscing.

Was this meeting by chance? Was this a "lucky meeting" with an icon? The timing was exactly right. Two minutes one way or the other, and our paths would have never crossed. We would never have spoken. Was this a birthday present?

I met many of the people in this book by chance meetings. I walk up and say hello, and then find something we have in common. Mentioning this common thread right away is to try and put the other person at ease. I never met a stranger. Each human being had something good to share.

Were some of these meetings destiny or fate? I worked intimately and professionally for two years for the Kennedy family. Was the meeting with Jackie many years later meant to be a kind of reward or gift?

Were all my encounters by chance or by good fortune? Were some of them destined from the very beginning of my life? Did God have a plan for me? I believe he does as for everyone. At times, I have a thorough awareness of his direction for me. Some of my encounters seem divinely planned and wholly spiritual, a coming together guided by a more delicate hand than mine.

Read on and decide for yourself. Most of all, remember and enjoy these moments in history.

Morris Wolff
Author

Aim High and Receive

My parents installed an "Aim High and Receive" reward system early. I was the third son, but the first to receive the high expectations program. I was my mother's favorite, named precisely by her in honor of my maternal grandfather and her brother, both named Morris Hirsch. I had a wonderful mother who knew how to make each one of her children feel as if we were all her favorite, quite a diplomatic balancing act.

Grandpa Moe Hirsch, until he died when I was eight, was my favorite person on the face of the earth. He was grandfatherly and non-judgmental. He bought me a chocolate cake for my seventh birthday in 1943. He was also my best friend and confidante. He always insisted on whatever subject that "It Can be Done." And that inspirational sign in large letters hung above his desk in his third-floor apartment at 2601 Parkway in Philadelphia.

I traveled by Broad Street subway downtown with my brother Richard to spend every Saturday afternoon with Pop Pop at his apartment in the posh new building across from the Philadelphia Art Museum. He knew famous people.

He introduced me to heavyweight boxing champ Joe Louis and Philadelphia Orchestra Director Eugene Ormandy. Still, all I can remember is the graciousness of Ormandy and his smile as he pronounced his name and the shyness, silence, and humility of heavyweight boxing champ Joe Louis. My granduncle, Sol Hirsch, was the doctor for the Pennsylvania Boxing Commission and the Philadelphia Orchestra. We got free tickets to prize fights and symphony concerts on Friday afternoons.

"It is valuable to meet famous people," Pop Pop counseled. "They can teach you important things about life," said my mother. She was my inspiration to reach out and say hello without being shy. She also set the bar quite high for my own achievements.

She played the piano, with a focus on Chopin. I sat alongside her at age seven, my hands tucked under my thighs, looking up at her soft brown hair in the lamplight. I watched her graceful white hands, and long fingers slide gracefully over the black and white keys and smiling down at me, as if I was the only person in her world. She was skilled at staying in the now and being present. She played Chopin, Schubert, Debussy, and the melodies of Stephen Foster, including "Old Black Joe," which stirred my interest in the plight of black people. She would talk as she played and taught me about people. "Famous people love the attention, too," she said. Her words set up a lifetime of meeting people from all walks of life.

Write Something Every Day

Carl Sandburg

I met the Midwestern poet, Carl Sandburg, at the Waldorf Astoria hotel in New York City in April 1945. I was eight years old, and this was my reward for writing poetry and an excellent report card. My mother took me to New York to meet him when he was receiving the National Book Award. We had a private conversation in which he urged me, "Write something every day, no matter how much, but each day write some poetry or a short story, even if it's just the start of something you come back to later. Always keep your creative mind working. One day you will be recognized and given awards as a great writer like me." He smiled at his own mock hubris and humility and his sardonic sense of the ironic all mixed together.

I never forgot his words or his kindness in talking to me. He had a soft voice, a sense of reserve, bordering on being shy. He told me he grew up in Galesburg, Illinois. He had a paper route and other odd jobs, which is how he came to learn the urban scene of cities and write his poems about Chicago and different landscapes.

He had a shock of white hair that he brushed back nervously with his right hand from time to time. He also had a bright red bow tie, homemade style, not the clip-on type. "This tie is a gift from an Indian Tribe. I wear it to honor them." He turned to my mom and said, "This boy has great promise. Make sure he writes and reads and grows his vocabulary. I read one poem that he gave me. Morris has a talent and a sense of lyric in life; Words will be his business one day. I can sense that he loves to sing, as well. I do too, and I play the banjo."

My mother wrote Sandburg quotes down in her diary on the train ride back to Philadelphia. I have kept her journal with the quotes all these years, almost 76 years as of now. "Mr. Sandburg feels you have promise. I do too. I have high expectations for you. I will be your teacher of poetry as you grow. This will let me get back to teaching; I miss it so much. We will be teacher and student together if you let me."

"Oh, mother," I replied. "You are always my teacher, my guide in life, and my guiding light. You are my shelter from the storm. I model my life after you. We will be poets together." I also told her, "I love this special day of the two of us being together, going by train to New York, seeing all the tall buildings, and the elegance of the Waldorf. I will work hard and learn words and write poetry." The words tumbled out as she held my hand. I looked up to her as the train jolted back and forth at high speed, and we smiled together. We became very connected. I was safe and at home whenever she was with me.

Just remember his words, "Something every day; a short story, a poem, or even a few stanzas of an unfinished poem, whatever comes to your mind, and keep a journal."

Sandburg was very personable, down to earth, not an elitist but more like a caring grandfather or coach, interested in guiding young people towards writing. He told me details about his milk delivery route and how milk was delivered in glass bottles in those days. He told me about his good friends as a young boy and growing up in Galesburg, Illinois.

Sixty years later, in 2015, I visited his home in North Carolina and thought back to that date when we met. This was my first "Lucky Conversation." I have come to love and treasure meeting writers and other talented people who have accomplished something good and memorable with their lives.

The year 2015 was when my first book came out. As I walked through Sandburg's summer home, I remembered the words of his encouragement to become a writer and to write something every day. I have adhered to his suggestion and request. I do love writing a little something each day at the age of 85. It keeps me young and my brain vibrant.

Being an Individual and Non-Conformist

Robert Frost, 1959

In 1961, Robert Frost was named Poet Laureate of Vermont. Frost espoused individuality and nonconformity in his poetry. His popular poem, *The Road Not Taken*, symbolizes that feeling of striking out on your own, and not worrying about what the crowd thinks. Pursue your own dreams, and create your own understanding of life. Accomplish what you set out to do, after considering all the options and do not quit. He was a maverick, who would not follow the herd of professors, or kowtow to others. And so, after just one year at Amherst, "the fairest college of them all, as the alma mater says, he was fired for intellectual insubordination. "I became a free man, free to write my poems, and march to my own drummer. I must thank conservative Congregationalist Amherst for setting me free to become the power I wanted to be," he said, with a twinkle in his eye. We met at Amherst, one on one, for a golden precious hour to discuss poetry and individualism in the spring of 1958.

In his impish and indirect way, Frost, in his seminal poem, *The Road Not Taken*, lashed out at those who took the easy way out or failed to stand tall for their ideals of academic freedom. In his meeting with me on the Amherst campus, he confided: "I wrote *The Road Not Taken* in response to the outrageous and hypocritical demands by the English department leaders at Amherst for academic conformity. Before they fired me at Amherst, they wanted me to bow down and kiss the Pope's ring and teach according to their cookie-cutter expectations. I charted my own path, my own way as a young poet and English teacher, not knowing any better way. I was creative and well-loved by the students who enjoyed my classes. Then, I was fired without any semblance of courtesy or a hearing or review with due process. It was all political, academic politics at its worst. I was told, "Pack up, you are outta here."

I was unceremoniously run out of town on a rail. Frost stood up and refilled his pipe, took a few puffs, and continued: "Now I am the king of the hill in poetry, and the English department here at Amherst wants for me to forget how I was treated back then. They want to think that I forget and forgive. I'm not built that way. I am sensitive. I want them to own up and accept the responsibility for their unprincipled actions. I want their apology on the record for the harassment and bad behavior. He got his reward by refusing back then to conform and by striding out into the less cloistered world, including London, and winning prizes for his poetry and becoming Poet Laureate of Vermont. Frost was renowned and deeply respected all over the world, particularly in England.

Robert Frost became the Poet Laureate of Vermont the same year that I read David Riesman's "Lonely Crowd." It was the year that we studied the importance of nonconformity and avoiding the practice of "following the herd." This tendency to wear the same gray flannel suits and think in terms of the cookies we cut is all the same or genuinely similar.

It was the mythical spring of 1958, my senior year. I was feverishly finishing my honors thesis in English. I wanted to hear Frost's interpretation of the poem *Out, Out*. The verse talks about a 14-year-old who loses his hand on a wood-cutting steel lathe moving 60 miles per hour. His hand is cut off by the buzz saw and gone before he knows it. The poem is about his reaction to the tragedy and the crowd's numbed inability to grieve immediately. Frost says near the end of the poem, "And those being the ones not injured turned from the scene of grief and went on about their daily mundane lives."

The faculty did not give him a classroom for fear he might become too popular and "pollute the minds of the young," a crime for which Socrates faced charges and death. It was a case of pure jealousy. After all, who was Robert Frost? Why should he receive so many awards, including the Pulitzer Prize four times? The honor could have gone to any of several members of the current Amherst College English department! Why are we passed over and overlooked?

President Charles Cole took matters into his own hands and made sure that Robert Frost, as a returning guest, received the most favored room at the nearby Lord Jeffrey Amherst Inn. They gave him the best and largest suite with an open view of the Town Commons, a green grass lawn of color at this time of year bordered by cherry blossoms and magnolia trees in bloom. Here he could invite current students to meet with him and discuss his poems and other literary works. They gave him a room where he met with me or any student willing to learn the entirety of one of his longer poems. I was an English Honors student writing a thesis on the Novel of Adolescence. I was free and easy, loose in the joints, without a care in the world — except for the deadline of one week to submit the finished, carefully proofread, and foot-noted copy of my controversial and infamous thesis. Like the young boy in *Birches*, I climbed trees of knowledge and curiosity and swooped down a "swinger of birches," a maverick and non-conformist at the same time. That was in May 1958, some 63 years ago. I was determined to meet and speak with Robert Frost, especially since he seemed to be "out of bounds"; a non-conformist and often off of the main path on his own road "less traveled by."

Frost was 84 when I met him. I was 22, loving my work in English and American literature as an honors student about to graduate. The warm invitation on the English department bulletin board said: "Amherst College offers all students a rare treat — memorize a long poem by Robert Frost. Earn a free hour with him at the Lord Jeffery Inn on Campus."

I hated memorizing things but immediately sat down and learned *Birches*, one of his longer poems. "Otherwise, I can't get in," I told myself. "It's as simple as that." I desperately wanted to meet Robert Frost for a serious and prolonged conversation about writing. Only eight students out of 250 were willing to pay the price of admission. I felt that Frost would have a lot to teach me about life and the craft of writing poetry. I wanted to become a poet myself as well as a writer and a novelist. I decided that the price of admission was actually quite reasonable.

Most of my classmates were too busy getting ready to graduate to bother. They did not care. They did not see the intangible value in this moment of heightened conversation with a great man. There was no grade attached. They focused on playing Frisbee or going over the mountain to the Notch to our neighboring sister school at Mount Holyoke College. Visiting lovely ladies and possibly finding a wife for life held more allure than an hour with an acerbic old man.

That afternoon I went back to my room at the Psi U House, took a shower, and dressed in a clean white shirt and long pants for my visit with Robert Frost. I crossed College Avenue and walked over the Town Common's green grass, where my classmates played Frisbee and drinking beer. "Hey Moe, where are you going all dressed up?" "He's going to see the old guy, the poet," was the answer.

I walked up the red brick pathway leading to the Inn, all the while repeating the free-verse lines from *Birches* to myself. How much of this long poem must I remember to gain admission? What if I freeze or get stage fright at the moment of entry? What was the actual price of admission? Recite a complete poem, and possibly be obliged without error to stand up and recite the whole thing?

I entered the Lord Jeffrey Amherst Inn and asked for his room. "Walk up to the top of the stairs and then walk down the hall. Go to your right — the only way you can go. It will be the last room on the left. It faces out onto the Town Common." I followed his instructions. The Inn had only the lobby and the first floor. After all, it was an inn, not a hotel. With trepidation, I knocked on the door.

"Mr. Frost?" I asked when he opened the door. I felt like an idiot. I did not know what else to say. I was tongue-tied at first. I became more relaxed and talkative as Robert Frost revealed the secrets of the faculty discussion. He understood the turmoil my renegade writing without "secondary sources" was causing.

"Come in, come in." I did as instructed and met a large man in tan trousers, a white shirt, red suspenders, and a friendly smile. He had a sizable uncombed mane or head of all-white hair.

"I have been expecting you, sir. Mr. Morris Wolff, is it? Professor Bill Baird has told me all about you. You're another free spirit, I understand, insisting on having your own way in writing a thesis based on the novels of adolescence. You include 15 to 20 original novels and no scholarly secondary sources." He laughed with amazement! "Why that is considered heresy!" He chuckled out loud. "Don't you realize you'll put professors out of work if you don't rely on their so-called scholarly interpretations and replace them with your own? I like you already. You're a maverick like Ralph Waldo Emerson and Henry Thoreau. You follow in a great tradition as a contrarian."

He was artificially gruff, with a twinkle in his eye, inviting me not to take him too seriously or to be intimidated by his outer manner. I knew he loved students who took an interest in his work.

I stood there, put my hands behind my back, and started to recite the poem I memorized.

Birches
When I see birches bend to left and right
Across the lines of straighter darker trees,
I like to think some boy's been swinging them.
But swinging doesn't bend them down to stay
As ice-storms do. Often you must have seen them

Loaded with ice a sunny winter morning
After a rain.

After three or four lines, he put his fingers to his lips and waved me off. "That's quite enough. I have heard it one time before. I use that device to make you memorize to separate the literary people from curiosity seekers. I like talking with students who are genuinely interested in reading my poetry, and the poetry of others, and willing to take the time to sit down and learn one of my poems. There are not too many of you in the world today."

I met with him alone for more than an hour. We read and recited his favorite poems, taking turns together and commenting on their meaning, symbolism, and choice of metaphor. We laughed at the ironies, and at the greater irony of his winning fame by not conforming. We both favored the writings of political essayist Henry David Thoreau and his fiery book called *The Theory of Civil Disobedience*.

That incendiary book lasted through dormant decades. It emerged as the most important political writing of the Civil Rights movement in the early 1960s. We were an inactive generation in matters of political activism and justice. We were dubbed the apathetic or "silent generation" in the late sedate 1950s. This sleepiness was about to be ripped open by political unrest in Mississippi with the killing of Medgar Evers, president of the Mississippi NAACP. Trouble was brewing in the whole nation and about to explode, as portrayed in the movie "Mississippi Burning." In my work with Bobby Kennedy at the Justice Department, I became part of the "We shall overcome" movement growing throughout the Deep South and the nation's capital. I loved the battle for civil rights for everyone. A war was starting, and I was about to become part of it.

The country craved conformity, to hide out from controversy and be like everyone else. It spread like a malaise, a basis or justification for sitting by and doing nothing. Sloan Wilson's "The Man in the Gray Flannel Suit" book empathizes sarcastically with this inaction and apathy and holds it up to the light for ridicule. Conformity was considered a virtue and a value. It was the last brief era to emphasize good behavior and do as you are told obedience. It was a "late Eisenhower" era soon to give way to the "early Kennedy" era. Frost and I were both holdovers of an earlier age and a period not yet born.

"How do you get away with that? Telling professors what you will do rather than what they want?" Frost asked.

I answered, "There were no secondary sources that I could find of any value. The value was in the creative original. *Books like Sons and Lovers* by D.H. Lawrence, *Portrait of the Artist as a Young Man,* by Joyce, and *Look Homeward Angel* by Thomas Wolfe. In reading these first novels by great writers, I was able to gain more insight into my own adolescent experience of growing up in a confusing world."

"Brilliant idea. Very original. I understand. Your teachers have no idea what to give you as a grade. Half the department wants to give you a summa, summa cum laude honors, and the other half doesn't even know whether to accept your work. They say your writing is brilliant, but your adamant refusal to use secondary sources borders on sacrilege." At this point in his comments, Robert Frost gave a series of whoops and hollers and finally broke into unabashed gales of laughter.

"You have created for them a wonderful intellectual dilemma and a serious academic problem."

"Tell me, what do your friends call you?"

"My friends and fraternity brothers have renamed me, Moe." I sat down in a cushioned chair. "I'm named after my grandfather. I was called Morris until I arrived at Amherst College."

"Then your nickname Moe it shall be. Come over here. Sit down over here nearer to the sunlight. I love to sit in this little nook. New England days are often sunless. At least this alcove catches the daylight. Today there is sunlight and blue skies. Dark cloudy days depress me. They affect my mood and my poems."

"I get more work done when I get more daylight. I like working during sunlit hours."

His room had plenty of sunshine at that moment. Covering his two separate twin beds were white bedspreads with little chenille white balls. The sun was out and bright when I first arrived. We engaged in two hours of animated discussion, early on his career and his travels and his nonacceptance by many places as a teacher. I stayed, unexpectedly, much longer than the appointed one hour offered. He seemed to be in no hurry to get rid of me. Quite the contrary, it was Frost himself who prolonged the meeting.

"I love meeting with students. I learn from them much more than I teach them. They forget most things quickly. It is only the experience of meeting that we remember. Years later, next to nothing is retained except the feeling. Was it a good feeling of pleasure or one of dread?"

He shifted in his chair and lit a pipe. "As you know, I was a teacher here at Amherst for a few years. I was fired. It is good to reconnect with Amherst students."

"Now you're back, I said. "And ironically by college invitation from our college president. You're at the top of the heap."

He got up and reached for a volume of his collected poems. "Do you want to know some of my favorite poems? They are short poems like 'Fire and Ice' and 'Out, Out.' That's my favorite along with 'Stopping by Woods on a Snowy Evening,' and its last lines that say, *But I have promises to keep and miles to go before I sleep.*"

"Back some forty years ago, I quit after a dispute with another professor and the college president. I was asked to leave Amherst and told to find work elsewhere. It was tough. I was a vulnerable, outspoken non-tenured powerless rookie member of the faculty. I talked too much at meetings, and at times got quite argumentative. Now I have been invited back with open arms," Frost said. "All things change. All things happen in time."

I remember those last words of his sentence — all things happen in time — quite vividly. He showed a puckish grin, a touch of anger, and a bit of sarcasm. But he was mellow and content with his success. He sat in a chair by the window, watching the sun begin to dip in the west as another spring day in New England started to come to an end. He was always inviting me to sit down as I tended to walk about while we talked.

It was a large room, the best in the Inn. The college treated him like royalty. He invited me to sit down at the desk across from the window. Some of his first editions of published poetry were open to different poems. We talked for a while about the teaching of English at Amherst. He wanted to know my favorite professors. He knew them all quite well. I expressed my admiration for Professors Armour Craig, Caesar Barber, Alfred Kazin, Ben DeMott, and Theodore Baird of the English Department. I also mentioned my work at crafting language with my English Honors mentor, Carter Revard, a Rhodes Scholar, and graduate of Oxford. I was lucky. Carter was young and energetic. He gave me tons of time and patient attention to my writing style and skills. He taught me about the use of metaphor, alliteration, and cacophony. Frost was intrigued with my honors thesis topic: "The Novel of Adolescence."'

We discussed the novelists I chose: Faulkner, D.H. Lawrence, James Joyce, Thomas Wolfe, Hemingway, Crane, and Fitzgerald. He commented on their creative abilities as writers who could put part of their own adolescent experience of growing up into a 'bildungsroman,' a novel of adolescence and self-development. "It's like the study of a chrysalis, the slow creative development of the caterpillar into a beautiful butterfly."

"Your Professor Kazin is my favorite here at Amherst," Frost said. "We go for walks at night together. We discuss American writers and poets. His knowledge is encyclopedic."

By coincidence, I saw these two great and learned men walking near Route Nine's corner, near to the Psi U house, where I lived, just the night before this special meeting with Frost. I thought as I watched them chatting together at the corner, waiting for the light to change, of some appropriate lines from a poem by Frost called "Acquainted with the Night." The first lines —
I have been one acquainted with the night.
I have walked out in rain — and back in rain.
I have outwalked the furthest city light."
 — came to my mind as I watched these two learned scholars walking and engaged with one another in conversation, trudging along together, holding on to each other's last thought.

We spent the next few minutes talking about his favorite poets. He liked W. H. Auden, and we discussed Ezra Pound, T.S. Eliot, and E.E. Cummings. "I like Cummings," he said. "The man does not take himself too seriously. The other two men seem to have great and ponderous messages to put across. Cummings does it with humor and a touch of satire. I like the lighter touch."

When he asked my favorites, I said: "W.B. Yeats, Dylan Thomas, and you."

"I'm the only live one," he replied with a smile.

 I said: "I like your 'Mending Wall,' 'Out Out,' and, of course, 'The Road Not Taken.'"
"I especially like some of the following lines in 'Birches':"

It's when I'm weary of considerations
And life is too much like a pathless wood
Where your face burns and tickles with the cobwebs
Broken across it and one eye is weeping
From a twig's having lashed across it open
I'd like to get away from earth awhile
And then come back to it and begin over.

I finished quoting those lines of his poem and paused.

"But do not forget," Frost added, "the lines that follow:"

May no fate willfully misunderstand me
And half grant what I wish and snatch me away
Not to return. Earth's the right place for love
I don't know where it's likely to go better.

He got up and walked away from his chair, and stood before the window, with the setting sun shining over his broad shoulders.

"That is the compromise of it all. We seek the perfect and the ideal. We want perfection in both life and art, and we never get it. When we come to our senses, we know that we must settle for the real, the possible, and be happy and content with how much we do receive in terms of gifts. That is how we reach contentment and avoid suffering. Earth is the right place for love, and the only place for love."

We spent a few more contemplative unpretentious moments discussing poetry together. We discussed our plans, Frost's poetry, and my career. I remember this visit with Robert Frost as one of the most important and memorable encounters of my life. I think this evening, as I write this chapter of his great lines:

Two roads diverged in a yellow wood, and I took the one less traveled by — and that has made all the difference.

I consciously chose to go and visit Mr. Frost and spend time with him alone. On that visit, I was invited to listen to the Master himself.

I experienced this outstanding and profoundly memorable afternoon in my final year at Amherst, one that imprinted itself vividly upon my life and on my memory. It was a truly lucky conversation, a sharing, and a very personal encounter of a special kind. Time stood still for just once and then moved on.

We Need Adlai, Badly!

When and where did my interest in politics first get fired up? I was not looking for involvement. It just fell in my lap as I was headed towards doing something else, like so many other things. If you happen to have a curious mind and desire, you will find a way to invade the Phillies Ballpark for the World Series without a ticket and have a great seat in the press box looking down on the green grass under the lights for the three home games. Same thing about the fun involved in working for a candidate. You come to believe in him. It becomes a mission.

I have always been attracted to quiet intelligence, courage, strength, wit, sardonic humor, and a man or woman's ability to poke fun at themselves. Adlai Stevenson and President Kennedy had those core qualities.

Stevenson was a quietly brilliant speaker. You listened intently to every word because there was always a nuance or a double meaning. He spoke with integrity. Stevenson was not a rabble-rouser or sentimental violin player; he was a plain-speaking man. He was here in Philadelphia "to tell us what we already know." That is the way he opened his first speech in downtown Philadelphia in October 1952. Campaigns were not long drawn-out affairs in those days. They started right after Labor Day and carried forward to Election Day in the first week in November. There is a terrible finality to that day, as I learned firsthand 20 years later when I ran for the State Senate of Pennsylvania. On Election Day, the race is over, torn tickets to the amusement park lie scattered on the ground. There are no more rides. Some people dance for joy, others cry. It is like the sudden closing of an amusement park, and the leftover tickets are left on the ground — hopes and dreams for another day.

In my mid-teens, I was downtown in the fall of '52 and headed to my orthodontist Mamie Blum at 20th and Chestnut. I heard music playing. A loudspeaker on top of an all-white garishly colored Buick blared: "Vote for Stevenson. He's our Man. If he can't do it, nobody can." Makes no real sense as a boast, but it sounded appealing and caught my attention. Stevenson, the former Governor of Illinois, was running for President against Dwight David Eisenhower. I did not care if he was a Democrat or a Republican. I just wanted a man who made sense, had principles, some idealism, and vision, and spoke well and directly to the people, like Abe Lincoln.

Like so much in life, this lucky conversation with candidate Stevenson seemed to happen by chance. And yet, there was my passive curiosity, directed and tugged forward by a certain willingness to venture out and project my "personae" into play. I grabbed the opportunity to serve as his "advance man" when the position was offered.

I volunteered to work for Adlai Stevenson's election campaign day and night. As a result, I got the chance to be with him during all three days of his Philadelphia campaign. On the third day, I was granted 15 minutes with him alone at our campaign headquarters at the corner of 15th and Chestnut Streets in an old Philadelphia bank building.

I liked that he was a thinker, a great speaker, a man of wit, and intelligence and vision. I thought to myself: "If a man with his background of Princeton and "the high ground" in politics as Governor of Illinois, could even run for President, then maybe one day I will be able to be an honest candidate too. Politics did not have to be corrupt or scummy. It could be distinguished public service and a worthy profession for one with creative ideas for helping others. I was only 16, but I was already President of my 10th-grade class. I liked campaigning for my own election and being able to create and implement good programs and freedoms.

I ran and won against three "lifers," two boys and one girl who had been in my Germantown Friends School since kindergarten. I had arrived in the middle of 9th grade and, within a year, was accepted as a leader. I was viewed as "fun and interesting" and as "a creative opportunist with good ideas." I tasted politics at the local level and was ready to hitch my wagon to the "Adlai star" and move on with my life and learn how to become a politician and later President of the United States with intelligence and intellect. That was my plan. High aim indeed!

On my second day as a Stevenson volunteer, I was given a "spiel" or pep talk and a batch of leaflets to hand out on 15th and Chestnut's street corner. I stood there from 8:00 a.m. to 5:30 p.m. I stopped people. I looked in their eyes and gave a Stevenson leaflet to anyone who responded with a smile. I was doing quite well when a bald-headed man in a Burberry twill overcoat and a three-piece suit, with a gold watch fob and chain, stopped suddenly, smiled at me, and said: "You are doing a great job, young man, in spreading the word. I am Adlai Stevenson, the Democratic candidate for President of the United States, and you are helping me win the campaign." He then turned to the man next to him and announced: "And this is Senator John Sparkman of Alabama. He is my running mate for Vice President."

I shook hands with both men and was speechless. "Did the cat get your tongue?" Governor Stevenson said. "Do you want to go into politics and serve your country one day?" "Oh yes, sir," I replied. "I want one day to become President like you. You are my role model. My mother told me it is rare to see a man of your intelligence and wit step forward as a candidate." He took this last comment as a compliment. It was intended to be so. Stevenson continued: "Tonight we will have a rally at Convention Hall. Many people are coming. I want you to be there with me on stage, Morris. There will be some movie stars and celebrities who are supporting my campaign. One of

Actress Mercedes McCambridge

them is Mercedes McCambridge, a great actress who just won an Academy Award."

I was speechless, taken aback by his spontaneous invitation to join him on stage that night at Convention Hall. He shook my hand and proceeded up the stairs, entering campaign headquarters. My eyes trailed after him.

I went to the Convention Hall that night. There were thousands of people cheering, "We want Adlai. We need Adlai badly." Adlai Stevenson gave a brief address in which he called on all Americans to vote and vote Democrat. He talked about the value of public service and the need for bright people to come forward to serve their country. He spoke about the obligation of the elite: "From those to whom much has been given, much is expected." I remember those words vividly. They have guided my life of public service and teaching as part of giving back.

It was October of 1952, autumn, and the leaves were falling in Philadelphia. General Dwight David Eisenhower was a national hero. He would later smash Stevenson in the general election, but that did not matter on this particular evening in September, two months prior. All that mattered was that Adlai was my new hero, and he spoke my language. Politics could be clean, and it could be the sport of gentlemen. He had stopped to talk to me personally, on the street corner, and I couldn't even vote. The crowd chanted his name over and over again: "Stevenson, Stevenson, Stevenson." They sang, "We Need Adlai, Badly." I thought the grammar was wrong, but

Dwight D. Eisenhower

the feelings were right, pure, and heartfelt. We did need Adlai badly. But we would not take him. We needed a man of wit, urbanity, unusual intelligence, and high principles to lead our nation. But it was all in the timing, and this was not the right time. This was Eisenhower's time as a returning hero. He led the military victory in Europe and engineered the schedule with great skill and courage for the bloody D Day invasion on June 6, 1944.

U.N. Ambassador Adlai Stevenson

Meanwhile, there were red, white, and blue balloons cascading from a net tied high above the Convention Hall floor at the Hall. Confetti began to rain down. Everyone was joyful and optimistic. "This man is a man of the people. We need him in Washington," said the beautiful Mercedes McCambridge. "He is our true Oscar winner."

I wrote these words down that night in my diary, and I made a precise record of meeting the first man of public service in my life. He was more than a politician. Stevenson was a statesman. He distinguished himself as the Democrat candidate for President, taking a beating with head held high in 1952 and 1956. He was later appointed by John F. Kennedy as U.S. Ambassador to the United Nations. He performed brilliantly in the debate during the Cuban Missile Crisis, asking Soviet Ambassador Zorin repeatedly, "When will Russia take back her missiles from Cuba?" As Zorin remained silent, Stevenson uttered his famous words: "Ambassador Zorin, I am prepared to wait until hell freezes over for your answer."

Stevenson won a clear diplomatic victory for the United States and shifted public opinion in Europe in our favor. He then retired graciously from public service. When asked, "What will you do in retirement?" he replied: "I want to sit in the shade of an outdoor café, sip a glass of cool lemonade, and watch young girls dance."

I still have the poster of Adlai Stevenson that once hung on my bedroom wall. As a teenager, I was searching for a living hero. Adlai E. Stevenson, the almost President and a great man, became that hero. Later, when I entered politics again as a candidate for Lieutenant Governor of the State of Florida in 1986, he remained my role model for high-level dialogs and my commitment to dealing honestly with the real issues at that time of immigration, education, pollution, and the Florida ecosystem. As the Miami Herald mentioned in an editorial: "The people of Florida may not have the wisdom to elect this man, but here is his achievement record anyway." All compliments, left-handed or otherwise, were graciously received and welcomed! It was a brutal campaign, and the developers and dirty politics prevailed. The people of Florida and the fragile ecosystem lost.

During my high school years, between 1952 and 1954, after Stevenson lost his first bid for President in 1952, I often returned to the Convention Hall. I would watch my basketball heroes Paul Arizin of Villanova, and Tom Gola of LaSalle, play exciting "Big Five" college basketball. As I sat there amid all the basketball noise, I felt I could hear once again: the loud cheers "Stevenson, Stevenson, Stevenson: Let's Elect Stevenson: We Need Adlai Badly." Once again, I could "see" the red, white, and blue balloons tumbling from the rafters, the confetti wildly thrown in bunches, and cascading down on the crowd in little pieces of red, white, and blue, and the band playing: "Happy Days Are Here Again." The Sounds were almost ghostly. They were reminders of a better day, filled with hopes, promises, and idealism in a circus-like atmosphere.

Eisenhower brought on the new age of armaments from which we have never recovered. The Pentagon fed lucrative contracts to big mega-companies. Wars are still being fought to feed the major arms makers and dealers like Boeing, General Motors, and Ford, despite Eisenhower's warning to beware of the rise of the "Military-Industrial Complex." The election of Adlai Stevenson, a Democrat, might have avoided that terrible development.

I remember how in my second and final meeting with Adlai, on the day after his speech, he confided: "That's very poor English using the words Adlai and badly together; I have asked them to take it out of the campaign. It reflects poorly on our collective intelligence, using an adverb in that fashion." He made his grammatical point to me in just a few words. He was a man devoted to good behavior, proper grammar, careful word selection, elegant manners, keen civility, and, above all else, a high level of decorum and gentlemanly politics. I doubt that we shall ever see a man of his intelligence, wisdom, stature, presence, poise, and high ideals in politics ever again.

I respect the nature of politics as it can be without lies or vitriol. We can return to the important battle of getting good policies into law and good men and women willing to run and be elected. We must remain involved. "All that is necessary for the forces of evil to prevail is for good men and women to stand by and do nothing." Sitting on our hands does not profit anyone. Since those early days with Adlai Stevenson, I have stayed involved in politics and governing. In college at Amherst, I worked for a candidate for the State House in 1957. Then, in 1962, I went to work in Washington for John F. Kennedy and his brother Attorney General Robert F. Kennedy. In 1970, I ran for state senator in my home state of Pennsylvania.

In 1985, I was selected by Mark Goldstein, candidate for Governor of the State of Florida, to run as his Lieutenant Governor running mate in the Democratic Primary. We did well and enjoyed touring Florida and speaking out and having fabulous lunches and dinners from the posh Breakers Hotel in Palm Beach to the Everglades and back to Boca Raton, Orlando, Tallahassee, and Jacksonville. We did not win, but we had many "lucky conversations" all over the state. We spoke our minds on the vital issue of climate change, preserving the water reserves, and the fragile condition of the ecosystem from pollution and overuse.

Fortunately, we were realists and not mere idealists. We knew we had little real chance of winning. Mark and I got his positive message across: climate change, stewardship of resources, and careful management of the natural world around us and how precious it is for those of us who choose to live in Florida to protect our precious assets of clean water and clean air. We received friendly and positive support at churches, country clubs, and synagogues where we spoke. We even received endorsements from the Miami Herald, the Orlando Sentinel, and every newspaper in every major city of Florida. But endorsements do not win elections in Florida, at least not yet. Money still skins and win elections here.

Ten Dollars for a Tank of Gas

In 10th grade, in 1952, I began making life plans for what I hoped would be my future career. I could not foresee any bumps in the road. I set my sights on attending Amherst College, where my two older brothers were already going, and Harvard Law School. I would become a courtroom trial lawyer fighting for justice. Edward Gordon, a gifted teacher at Germantown Friends in Philadelphia, taught me about the individualists Ralph Waldo Emerson, and Henry David Thoreau and his book *Civil Disobedience*. Gordon and David Mallery stoked my fire of outspokenness and created a desire to make a significant difference in the world. Mallery gave me Henry Commager's brave book "Freedom, Loyalty, and Dissent," which became a handbook for courageous speech. Ed Gordon, at graduation, sat me down and said, "I trust that you will become a crusader for good within the law, speaking out, and fighting for human rights and justice. You have the power to create social change, especially for the poor people of Philadelphia's inner city. Go forth and do it."

I perceived the law as a potentially powerful instrument for social justice. I wanted to be a change agent and reformer and create a deeper reason for being within my own life. These two great teachers inspired, motivated, and helped me. Later, I followed Ed Gordon's admonition to help poor people by accepting an appointment as Deputy Solicitor for Housing and Community Development for the City of Philadelphia. I worked with the Mayor to bring millions of "Section 8 federal dollars" to Philadelphia to help build homes for the poor. It made a difference in many lives. Before that, I served the poor as Public Defender in Washington, D.C.

I chose from the very beginning to work for civil rights and social change. I needed a law degree to support my effort and my dreams. But then in my final year at Amherst College, reality came knocking at the door. I received an explosive and apologetic letter of rejection from Harvard Law School. They commended me for my work in the community and my academic record but still said no. I drove to Harvard, met with Dean Toepfer, and pleaded, but he quite coldly said no.

Earl Latham bailed me out. He was my favorite professor at Amherst and proved to be my best friend. He rescued me from the storm and saved my life. He reminded me, "there is a God." I decided God must be a trickster, one with a dry and wicked sense of humor, just like Earl Latham. Earl was a cynic, with a dry, ironic, and witty sense of humor and a feeling of forbearance in life. He said, "People get thrown for a loop. What counts is not what happened but how you get up off the mat and fight forward."

Earl Latham believed in saving lives and rescuing others. He instilled confidence and a sense of rescue inside of me. I went inward to that resource in 1985 when I tried to rescue Raoul Wallenberg after his 39 years of solitary confinement in the Soviet Gulag Archipelago. I dedicated my book about Wallenberg to Earl Latham. I felt his positivity surrounding me when I appeared before Judge Barrington Parker and argued for Wallenberg's rescue from the Soviet Gulag. It was a long shot. We won a $39 million verdict against the Soviets.

Professor Earl Latham lived quietly for 70 years, from 1907 through 1977, and was a prolific writer and a great teacher. His life covered most of the 20th century. He loved to smoke cigarettes. He would carefully flick the ashes into a tin cup when we met together after class in his office in the gothic Walker Hall to discuss his thoughts on "the true meaning of Democracy, Due Process, and the Separation of Powers." He loved the French philosopher Montesquieu and his treatise on the importance of having a balance in government between an independent Supreme Court, a strong but compassionate fair-minded President, and an active bicameral and bipartisan Congress. I tried to get him to stop smoking but with no success. He was addicted to unfiltered Chesterfields and Lucky Strikes. I grew to love this warm, quiet man of good deeds. I went to see him with my letter of rejection. The following conversation took place:

Professor Latham: "Well, Mr. Wolff. That's too bad. Harvard should have taken you, but they decided not to do so. They have a quota system for Jews. You can sit and contemplate your navel and feel sorry for yourself. That won't do you any good. Or you can attend the Penn Law School, which is eager to have you, but I understand you don't want to go home to face Dad and Mom as yet."

Morris: "That's right. I had my heart set on Harvard Law even before going to Amherst College as an undergrad. Now, what do I do?" I sat there silently as he stared out the window and then turned back to me; I was silent, listening and looking at the little man with the round Friar Tuck monk-like face and the enigmatic smile.

Professor Latham: "Well, tough luck. Life sometimes gives you lemons. Make lemonade. Get up off your duff and do something!"

Morris: "Do what? What do you suggest?"

Professor Latham: "Do you have ten dollars"?

Morris: "What for?"

Professor Latham: "You might consider a visit with my friend Dean John B. Tate in New Haven at the Yale Law School."

Morris: "What good would that do? Harvard turned me down. They take 300, and Yale takes only 110. If I can't get into Harvard, how do I get into Yale?"

Professor Latham: "Do you have ten dollars for a tank of gas?"

Morris: "Well, yes. I believe I do."

Professor Latham: "Then get your little car ready for a trip later in the week."

That brief conversation resulted in my driving to Yale Law School and gave me a new opportunity in my life. Two days later, I got a call back from Earl Latham. "I have arranged an interview for you at the esteemed Yale Law School for tomorrow morning. Here are the details: Be on time. Wear your blue blazer and gray trousers and clean white bucks, the same outfit you have for the Amherst Glee Club." And he gave me a Rand McNally map with a yellow liner marking the trail.

I drove to New Haven bright and early the next day, May 15, 1958, and toured the campus before my interview. Dean Tate received me with a cordial smile and a warm voice, and a southern accent. He was Legal Counsel to the Secretary of State in the early 1950s under Eisenhower. Tate was the author of the famous "Tate Letter," dealing with the protection of diplomats, which I later used in my brief in the Raoul Wallenberg case. He was humble and understated and loved William Faulkner, who was a Nobel Prize winner for literature. We discussed Faulkner's "The Bear," a story of a young man with courage coming of age, confronting a ferocious bear on his first hunting trip. We talked for close to 40 minutes about the parallels of Dean Tate's life and Faulkner's life growing up and coming of age in Mississippi. Our conversation focused on William Faulkner, courage, and civil rights. It was more on literature than on the law, and finally on why I wanted to become a lawyer. I answered, "To serve justice and the needs of those who are in poverty and who cannot afford to pay a lawyer."

Finally, our time was up, and the Dean asked me the 64-dollar question:

"Marse, (he collapsed my name and pronounced my first name with his southern twist). I want you to know that I have enjoyed our conversation. I have for you just one final question before we wrap things up. Why are we having this conversation today? The date is May 15. Our application deadline is on May 1st. Why have you not applied to the Yale Law School before the deadline?" (Long pause, tough question.) How can I answer honestly and still get accepted?

Morris: "Well, Dean Tate, to be perfectly honest, I had my heart set on going to the Harvard Law School since the 10th grade in Philadelphia. They turned me down. So, I went to see Professor Latham. He called you, and here I am. Professor Latham asked me if I had ten dollars for a tank of gas, and I said yes, sir, I sure do."

The Dean fell off his chair, taken aback apparently by the energy in my frank and honest answer. He got up quickly and rearranged his jacket and chair and said: "My oh my what candor. We don't hear that kind of straight and honest answer very often from young lawyers or would-be lawyers every day. That comment is in your favor. I will get back to you in a day or two."

The Dean did not leave me hanging. By some miracle, I received his message of acceptance three days later. I loved my three years at the Yale Law School and its close and warm feelings of friendship and cooperation, and the deemphasis on competition and class rankings that existed at Harvard. It was a friendly place with great students who helped each other, professors who were accessible and helpful, and a fantastic library with great librarians.

In a moment of despair, rejection, and crisis, I discovered a better locale. And from this grew my chance to become the International President and leader of AIESEC in 1960, a global student exchange program for peace, and then the invitation to work on civil rights and the end of public accommodations discrimination with Attorney General Robert F. Kennedy and U.S. Senator John Sherman Cooper of Kentucky. Dean Jack B. Tate and Professor Myres McDougal contacted Robert Kennedy in the Attorney General's office of the United States of America for me with a strong recommendation. McDougal wrote: "He hits the ball back hard." None of this exciting life could have happened without Earl Latham, Dean Tate, and Myres McDougal.

Sometimes temporary setbacks in life become a test for getting up and going forward with "new plans." As basketball Coach Jim Valvano once said: "Never Give Up. Never Ever Give Up. Live your life to the fullest. Go forward one day at a time." The opportunities to serve the cause of justice and due process will find you. Just be ready to help with your heart and your soul. Do the right thing, and go forward.

My mentor, Earl Latham, died at age 70 from smoking too many cigarettes, things he put in his mouth incessantly, despite my encouragement that unfiltered Lucky Strikes and Chesterfield's harsh tobacco might limit his years on mother earth. The habit cost him at least a decade of life. He was a shy and friendly man who loved his students and especially loved being the faculty advisor for our Psi Upsilon fraternity. He took that role seriously and often came to the house to talk with students, and even came occasionally on Saturday nights to enjoy the music of the 50s and the jukebox playing Elvis Presley, the Drifters, Ray Charles, and Little Richard. He enjoyed coming over and having a beer.

Eleanor Roosevelt

Eleanor Roosevelt, 1949

Franklin Delano Roosevelt was a hero in our family. My father sincerely believed that FDR saved our country during the Great Depression and helped us survive as a nation by leading us to victory in World War II. My father had a big picture of FDR. I remember the day he took a hammer and nails and hung it in a revered corner of our living room for all to see. Roosevelt created trust and loyalty, especially among immigrants. When he died in spring 1945, we were outside raking leaves when the news came over the radio. We all went inside to the living room near the portrait to hear the sad news.

FDR should be here right now on April 1, 2020, to lead us through the dark nights and days of Covid-19. We are engaged today in a third world war with no defense to keep the enemy out. We have no idea what will happen. We have no real plan of defense of America and success.

FDR's intelligent and steadfast wife, Eleanor, was a role model for my mother as a humble and effective quiet woman of accomplishment. She was a great example of a woman willing to adopt important causes like racial injustice when such endorsements were not politically popular. I would read her daily news column "My Day" in our daily *Philadelphia Inquirer* and found myself in agreement with her liberal and progressive themes. She had guts and courage, a role model I came to emulate for speaking out with candor on matters of importance.

I never imagined I would ever meet and speak with her, much less on an individual one-on-one basis. Fortunately, this occurred one afternoon in my senior year, spring of 1958, at Amherst College. I was getting ready to graduate and enroll that fall at the Yale Law School. But I am getting ahead of my story.

As children in the 1940s, we gathered around the radio after dinner to listen to her broadcasts. I remember her unusually high-pitched voice and her deep and unswerving commitment to human rights. My mother read to us about Eleanor Roosevelt's civil rights accomplishments in the south, working with Mary Bethune in chipping away at the Jim Crow laws of strict segregation "of the races." Eleanor was deeply offended by black men's injustice like the Tuskegee airmen fighting to save our country and then treated like shit once they came home. She would say, "It is better to light a candle than to curse the darkness." She worked patiently and incrementally to create change and not as a revolutionist.

Quietly, she gathered support from among her influential and wealthy friends and then worked hand in glove with Mary Bethune in financing the building of a black woman's University in Daytona Beach, Florida. That was 1945. Now, 70 years later, in 2015, as if by 'spiritual coincidence' I found myself on campus as one of the first and very few white professors at Bethune Cookman University heading up the freshman writing program dubbed "Wildcats Write!" What goes around, I guess, comes around! Again, I am ahead of my story.

In the spring of 1958, as I was about to graduate from Amherst, I learned that Mrs. Roosevelt would be coming to Amherst from New York to attend a tea party in her honor at our Psi Upsilon fraternity house and to speak to "the brothers." I would get to meet her in a small group and talk with her. I was delighted, jumping with anticipation and joy. She is one of my true heroes. Her grandson, John Boettiger, scheduled a tea party at our Psi Upsilon fraternity and asked me to introduce her to the brothers. I was curious; what would she be like?

Psi U brother John Boettiger, one of Eleanor's many grandchildren, came up with the idea of inviting her to an exclusive at our fraternity. He organized the English tea party in our house's living room, replete with matching little plates and teacups, a large silver urn for tea, surrounded by English crumpets and cookies.

John and I set up the living room for the old-fashioned English tea party. I then fetched her at the Bradley Field Airport, near Hartford, Connecticut, and bring her to the Lord Jeffrey Amherst Inn. She was seated in the small airport's lobby, and upon my arrival, she stood up and greeted me with a big smile and a squeaky warm voice. She dispensed with formalities; she was very down to earth with no airs. I offered to help her to the car. She resisted my effort. "I can do this on my own," she said politely. "But thank you for your kind offer of assistance."

She arrived on a Thursday afternoon in May without fanfare. She was taller than I imagined and noticeably quiet and refined. She was patient and an excellent listener. FDR had been a lucky man. This woman made each one of us feel special. She took an interest in what we were doing for our Amherst community, especially as tutors for less fortunate kids in the local schools.

"John is my favorite grandson," she confided, with a broad and friendly beaming smile, showing a bright line of perfect white teeth. "I want to see and meet his friends and look at his school environment. I want to make sure he is taking his studies seriously and not wasting his time playing games at the fraternity house."

Franklin and Eleanor Roosevelt seated on the south lawn at Hyde Park. 1932

"That is one reason why I made this long trip." She

told us anecdotal stories of her years in the White House and visiting the troops in the hospitals in England and the USA during World War II. She also spoke about the hours and days of constant nursing and personal management of FDR and how he suffered constant pain from polio.

"He never recovered, but he never quit. He went down fighting. He had the Secret Service detail carry him from his bed to the breakfast table. And after breakfast, into the White House Oval Office and then seat him gently behind his desk. He never wanted the public or the Nazis to see this helpless condition or make propaganda from it. He feared the Japanese would take it as a sign of weakness or self-pity and try to make points of this condition during World War II. From September 1, 1939, when Hitler first invaded Poland until his death in April 1945, he would not permit any photos to be taken inside the Oval Office."

"Franklin conveyed a picture of steady and permanent strength and conviction. He was actually quite strong from the waist up. He never faltered, always presenting that wry strong, self-confident Roosevelt 'I do not have time to worry' attitude. He would force a smile and put forth his 'this is a piece of cake' attitude."

"FDR never recovered: he just learned to live with the pain of polio. He avidly supported the March of Dimes charities and gave for the recovery of others, especially children. He was obsessed with wiping out polio and favored strong research efforts and funding. Whenever possible, I would hide his metal braces and crutches. He wanted the world to see him as robust, an active man, and a vigorous leader of the free world." As we arrived at the front door of our fraternity house, she continued talking non-stop, with interesting anecdotes and insights on FDR's courage and will.

"He prohibited the taking of photographs that showed him as an invalid or injured person. He would order them trashed and destroyed. Amazingly they were never published. The press cooperated and agreed with that. He made no enemies among members of the press. He cultivated them, massaged their egos, and made them feel important and part of his mission to end the war. The press gave him a honeymoon. In those days, the press was not an adversary. The press was a vehicle for getting the good news out to the public on the New Deal programs, and the fighting and winning of the war during all those long years of endurance after the Japanese attacked Pearl Harbor on December 7, 1941."

Eleanor Roosevelt was a warm and kind human being. She did not talk down to anyone, including "the brothers," but instead simply gushed out stories with spontaneous informality. Mrs. Roosevelt stayed on her feet in the receiving line for an hour. She was open to and answered all of our questions.

On the way back to the airport, she asked me, "Well Morris, what are your post-Amherst plans? What do you plan to do with your life?" I told her, "I will attend Yale Law School and study international law and human rights. I want to work on some of your favorite issues, like social justice and the American Dream's fulfillment for everyone. I want to use the law as an instrument for achieving social justice and create a more even playing field for everyone."

"Yale law is a good school, actually a great school," she said. "Great teachers and professors." She continued: "They focus on social justice and what the law ought to be. You will fit in there quite nicely. Harvard has become a stuffy place with its quota system against minorities. It has a discriminatory policy for limiting the number of Jews in each law class. You would be uncomfortable there. Yale is a much better choice."

I was surprised by her openness, bluntness, candor, and awareness. She let the chips fall where they may. Her honest and candid attack on Harvard, FDR's alma mater, caught me by surprise. FDR had gone to Groton Prep and then to Harvard University.

We walked out earlier to see the rose garden behind the Psi U House. She stopped to look back at the imposing structure of our misplaced southern mansion with its tall white Doric columns that supported our elegant large, and majestic home away from home. She walked back inside through the large hallway into the living room and laughed. "All of your brothers are still standing at attention as if I were an army general from the military. At ease, gentlemen." Everyone laughed. Eleanor had broken the ice. She felt at home, a skill she had used on many occasions when Winston Churchill and other dignitaries visited the White House. She once again proceeded down an informal receiving line shaking the hand of every Psi U brother, who remained standing there patiently out of respect. Each one of the 26 brothers was treated to a few private and personalized words.

After the second "receiving line" disbanded, she came over and sat next to me on the sofa. She tugged my arm and commented, "There is so much you can do with your law education at Yale. It is a small school. I am fond of Professor Fred Rodell. He teaches there, is a brilliant writer, and the number one critic and scholar on the Supreme Court today. He is a genius studying the Supreme Court and the quirks and personalities of all the different Justices. I will write to him and let him know you are coming there in the fall."

"Thank you for your kindness. I will certainly stop by and pay my respects."

"You and he already have a lot in common. He is a maverick and an agitator. My nephew John has told me all about you, your true nature, and your civil rights interest. Fred Rodell started out as Fred Rodellheimer, but he cut his name short during the war, thinking it might be better not to be identified as a Jew. Tell him from me that Eleanor says keep on writing but stop your smoking, or it will kill you."

Her warning was prescient. On my arrival at Yale, I did stop by, meet, and begin to work as a personal assistant and researcher for Professor Fred Rodell as the direct result of Eleanor's introduction. I became his research assistant on Supreme Court matters. During my senior year in the fall of 1962, Rodell took me to meet each of the justices, including Chief Justice Warren and judicial activists

Justices Black and Douglas. Under Fred's guidance, I wrote an article on Justices Hugo Black and William O. Douglas called "Justice Felix Frankfurter and the Myth of Sisyphus." Fred contacted his friends and got my article published in the New Jersey Bar Journal (Winter 1963). Fred gratuitously wrote a banner at the top of the published article that read, "This is the finest piece of law student writing I have seen in my 36 years of teaching."

Eleanor Roosevelt was invaluable and helpful in her conversation with me. "You can achieve so much. Just as you have been fighting to open the doors of fraternities here at Amherst to your fellow deserving black students, you can take the same fight with you to the Yale Law School. One day you will be able to fight for civil rights for the Negro in America. You can also fight for equality and fair opportunity for the deserving poor to receive a good education."

"You are privileged to be attending Amherst and now going to Yale Law. You will rub minds with the brightest men in America. It is now time for the women to attend Yale and become lawyers too. The statistics are terrible. Right now, Yale takes 10% women and 90% men. At least Yale Law is unpacking its past anti-Semitism and becoming a bit fairer by admitting super qualified Jews. Not every law school plays fair with admissions. Close-minded anti-Semites like Erwin Griswold and Dean Toepfer still lead Harvard Law, persons insensitive to Jews. It's true, I did my research, and I wrote about it openly in my news column, "My Day." Harvard has quotas limiting Jews admitted to 3% to no more than 5%. Yale has done away with that. At least Jews there have a fair chance to be accepted, get a great education, and then graduate. There are simply no dropouts among the Jews. Their parents would kill them."

I listened carefully and remembered what she said. I was shocked, taken aback by her passion and her honesty. She had the facts in hand before she spoke. This made her an authority. Her outspokenness and concise insights were impressive.

There is and was a positive side to fraternities. Phi Psi and Psi U at Amherst were brave examples of fraternities fighting for civil rights on campus. We fought for full integration of all fraternities and the removal of all racial and religious discrimination.

I reflect on this conversation, especially today, with the current reports on December 15, 2019, of fraternity abuse and the killing of a pledge seeking admission. I suggest an end to hazing, a terrible anachronism unworthy of any discussion as to its prurient value. Also, we need a cleanup of the under-the-table bribes paid to a few top college admission programs, as revealed in the New York Times and the Wall Street Journal on March 12, 2019.

Eleanor finished her chat with me and asked for a second cup of tea. "Lovely tea party, this is," she said. "All you young men are apparently on best behavior. I know about nighttime parties from the stories John has shared. I bet it's not this calm on Saturday nights. My grandson tells me things get a bit rowdy, but today you are behaving like little gentlemen." I got more tea and did not answer her perceptive comment.

I can still see today that vivid picture of the gray-haired Eleanor Roosevelt standing tall and patiently with grace in a receiving line saying hello, with a few words to every member of the Psi U fraternity. "John Boettiger, the son of my daughter, is my favorite grandson. He is the one on whom I dote the most," she told me in an aside. "No one else could get me to stand in a receiving line like this and chit chat with young men for an hour."

She was brave and honest, a trooper and a pro in politics, a woman leader, and a quiet feminist well before her time. Mrs. Roosevelt argued for the rights of women and civil rights for blacks. She became remarkably close to Mary Bethune Cookman, the dynamic founder of Bethune Cookman University, and a leading black female educator. Eleanor raised millions for that one school, which still thrives today. I was privileged to teach freshman English there to all-black classes in 2017. Eleanor counseled Mary Bethune Cookman on building her all-black university and advised Benjamin May as he built up Morehouse and Spelman College in Atlanta.

She stood there patiently, teacup in hand, in an ankle-length gray dress with a scarf fastened by an orange and white cameo pin, right out of the Victorian Age. She wore a broad black hat with roses on the edges that she never took off during the 45-minute reception line. She stood tall; she graciously and stoically endured. She seemed to genuinely enjoy talking with each student as they came through the line.

Each person felt important; none more and none less. She practiced equality, graciousness, and courtesy. As she left, she came over to me: "You have a great opportunity. Use your law education well. Care for and represent the poor and defend the unjustly accused. Don't just go to Wall Street and make millions. Become an instrument of peace and a voice for human rights."

I do remember her words. I treasure her message. I still have a clear memory of her warm smiling face and her special visit.

On May 30, 2018, I returned to the Psi U House at Amherst for my 60th college reunion. I entered the Psi U house and drifted towards the living room. I stood in the exact spot where I once talked with First Lady Eleanor Roosevelt. I remembered the moment and her "glad grace" all over again. I recalled our warm and cordial conversation, and her words of encouragement, guidance, and direction.

Her introduction and her letter to Fred Rodell made all the difference in the world of my law school education. The fact that I became a published young law scholar upon graduation gave me a boost upward and my chance to work with President and Bobby Kennedy.

There are few moments in our lives that seem like 'chance meetings' when they happen. They are not by chance at all. The hand of God is present, nudging us forward in one direction and not the other. They are a mixture of good luck and God's gentle hand on our shoulder. He is telling us to be kind and patient with other sentient beings. I learned that lesson from Eleanor. They do not make fabulous in-depth First Ladies like Eleanor Roosevelt anymore; she was the greatest! She had a vital and significant impact on U.S. policy during the gritty years of war from 1939 through 1945. She reminded me of Voltaire's elegiac calming comment: "All is Well."

Expanding the Vision in Africa

"Mr. President, I bring you greetings from Philadelphia!"

In the summer of 1959, I took a flier and went abroad on an adventure. I was an exchange student working in the Chamber of Commerce in Cologne, Germany. The AIESEC program had given me one of the plum traineeships in Europe. I enjoyed working and living there and learning fluent German in two months, with evenings on or by the river Rhine.

In October of 1959, after returning to Yale after two months in Germany, the AIESEC international student exchange program elected me as their full-time International President. We built a new headquarters in Geneva, Switzerland, and expanded the program from Europe to new nations in Africa. We moved the world towards a permanent peace and an end to war. John F. Kennedy was about to become our President. In 1963, I met with him in the White House Oval office to discuss these possibilities and received his strong endorsement and support. He said: "I believe ending wars can be done by dedicated young leaders building international friendships and ties for a lifetime with no political agenda other than peace."

World peace was our goal. The AIESEC team developed a comprehensive plan to turn our European and American student exchange program into a truly global one. We wrote down together our carefully established purpose and mission. As the President of AIESEC, I decided it was my task to sustain momentum, boost growth, and integrate our international student exchange program into a global reality. I needed to change our regional European all-male and all-white privileged student exchange program. We needed fresh blood, dynamism and humor, and new perspectives. We needed to go and get men and women from the developing nations of Africa to join our inclusive, non-political, and non-discriminatory program. All this came to me in a dream one night. God beckoned me to expand the program. I brought into consensus the support of the 33 national committee Presidents from Italy, Spain, USA,

France, Belgium, the Netherlands, Denmark, Norway, Finland, England, Malta, Greece, Portugal, and elsewhere with me.

I had no idea at that time how much help I would receive from God. I prayed each night for success, and I remembered my mother's admonition: "The Lord helps those who help themselves." I do know that my timing and scheduled arrival was a miracle from God. He had the right time for my entry: August 7, 1960, at 7:15 a.m. at the Ghana International Airfield.

I felt as if God's hand had placed itself gently on my shoulder during the entire time as I prepared for my first trip to Africa. Working on expansion to Africa with diplomats from Ghana, Nigeria, and Sierra Leone stationed in Geneva worked out to the benefit of all concerned. The International Labor Office (ILO) was headquartered there just up the street. I took the ten-minute tram, and free of charge, and attended their meetings as President of AIESEC, the head of an accredited NGO. I cultivated excellent working relationships and trust through new and vibrant friendships with the Prime Ministers and Labor Secretaries of three West African countries — Ghana, Nigeria, and Sierra Leone.

The International Labor Office (ILO) headquarters in Geneva provided a meeting place for negotiations and sowing deep seeds of interest during the 102 member nations' annual meeting for two weeks in early March 1960. I was only elected President of AIESEC in February in Barcelona at the yearly AIESEC international conference of our program.

I also tried to extend the program to Russia. But they refused to let their students travel alone without "the benefit of" an adult monitor. That was against our principles of trust, freedom, and personal autonomy. So, I drank their vodka, said a polite thank you at the first meeting, and went on my way to focus on Africa as the place for AIESEC expansion.

I took the trolley. I then hobnobbed at age 24 with Secretaries of Labor from each of the three selected nations. By August 7, 1960, I was underway from Zurich to Accra, Ghana, with a generous donation from the President of Swissair to pay airfare and grow and prosper the program. He had no children of his own. "You have become my AIESEC children." We were happy to become his children. I reported on our African development with regularity. Swissair paid my international travel expenses and gave me a free pass for anywhere in the world.

I felt God's hand resting on my shoulder and guiding me forward as I set out on my peace mission, African safari/journey. As my plane circled the airfield, I looked down on Africa's green fields and the jungle and animals, water buffalo, and hippopotami surrounding Accra. I was taking this mission at considerable political risk. I did not have the full support of my 33-nation program. Some wanted to cashier me on the spot for even thinking about expansion. The Italians, French, Germans, and Americans strongly supported our destiny to grow and become truly international and serve "all God's children." As children of ex-colonialists, the conservative Dutch, English, and Belgians were dead set against an American leader creating this growth. Their reservations were ingrown and unconscious. Even young leaders, on occasion, fail to outgrow the prejudices of their parents.

I called a special meeting of all 33 of the AIESEC member nations at our International Secretariat in Geneva to reduce fears and tensions and discuss the issues. I introduced my plans to accept the invitation of Ministers in Nigeria, Ghana, and Sierra Leone to visit and establish the program in West Africa. I said to my national committee presidents, "I feel that I must go and develop our program in Africa now. There is no legitimate reason to wait. We must have the courage to open our doors of opportunity to all business and law students everywhere, regardless of race, color, or national origin. Otherwise, we will stagnate and die as a provincial program without a global purpose. Either we grow and become fully international, or we will stagnate and have other programs surpass us. We presently have a monopoly of opportunity for traineeships with business firms and government ministries for all the students of the world, and that includes Africa and Asia."

I packed my bags and flew off to Africa, expecting to be met by small committees of eager and welcoming students. Little did I know that God had even larger plans, other, more extensive methods. My plane landed in the hot heat of an African summer morning. I stepped down from the airplane in Accra, the capital of Ghana. In those days, you walked on the hot tarmac to the reception hall to pick up your stored luggage. At that time, I thank God the powers that be did not invent or deploy new accordion passageways connecting planes directly to the terminal. Otherwise, the miracle would not have happened. I needed the tarmac for the miracle to happen.

I walked gingerly down the steel gangway steps to the ground. A blast of African humidity and heat greeted me. Even at that time in the morning, the temperature of the tropics was oppressive. There was a stadium filled with people surrounding the airport who cheered the landing of each airplane. The people sang beautifully rhythmic African tribal songs in eight-part harmony. What a cheerful greeting for visitors! There was a marching band, making its way onto the steaming black tarmac. The ensemble was well fortified and balanced, replete with loud trumpets, tubas, trombones, clarinets, and drums. The golden trumpets and trombones and french horns were shining in the hot sun. A celebration was taking place, but I had no idea about the occasion. "Are they turning out for you?" someone behind me jokingly inquired. "After all, you are on a mission to Africa for an international program?" They saw me stop still to observe the passing surge of musicians. "I think not," I replied, "But I do want to know what this is all about."

President Kwame Nkumrah

Suddenly I saw the reason. As I stood stock still, there walking towards me, was Kwame Nkrumah, the President of Ghana, the very man I had hoped for and prayed to meet. I had read his biography and how we had Philadelphia as a common meeting place. I was born and grew up in Philadelphia. He had gone to school there at the University of Pennsylvania as an international exchange student of all things. He had washed dishes at the student common to put himself through school. He knew the value of self-help and student exchange. I said to myself, "Morris, this is the man you want to meet. Say something, or he will walk right past you. He is taking President Lumumba to the United Nations plane parked over there, and he will be gone. Opportunity lost!"

A light bulb in my head went off. "Say something smart and catchy quickly about Philadelphia. You both went to school there, and he washed dishes sometimes at the University of Pennsylvania," the inner voice said. "That is your spiritual and real connection." And so, I blurted out as loud as possible. "Mr. President, I bring you greetings from Philadelphia!" And believe it or not, it worked. Everyone stopped in their tracks. The band stopped playing as if on cue. In the sudden silence, everyone was looking for where the voice came from." Who is bringing me greetings from Philadelphia?" bellowed the President. "Let the man pass. Let him come forward."

I could see through the phalanx of guards that Nkrumah was looking for me too. He was dressed in a long white robe, with gold embossed lapels, brown sandals, and gold chains around his neck, standing behind his security force. His head was bare and bobbing back and forth, trying to see just who was bringing him "greetings from Philadelphia." Why gold chains? Because he was dressed and decked out like a king. After all, Ghana was once called the Gold Coast before he changed the name to the Republic of Ghana in 1957 when he was first elected President. He was called "Osagyfu" or the Redeemer. His closely cropped wooly black hair was under a cap made of gold and green kente cloth. His short 5'6" frame bobbed back and forth behind a phalanx of guards, with their right hand on their rifles ready to load and shoot. "Let the man pass, let the man pass." Nkrumah entreated and then ordered his men, "I want to speak to this man."

The guards parted, and I walked up to Nkrumah. He smiled, "Ah, Philadelphia," he said. "Chestnut Street, Walnut Street, Pine Street, Spruce Street," naming the major tree streets of downtown Philadelphia, as if to impress me. He stopped and looked up to Lumumba. "And young man, what brings you to Ghana with these greetings from Philadelphia, my second hometown in the world?"

I took a deep breath, "Mr. President, I have come to Ghana to recruit 12 of your best honors students of economics and business. I will take them to Europe and America for executive training and work for six months with major international companies. Then, Mr. President, I will bring them back home to you to help you lead your great nation." These were my exact words. I do not know where they came from; they just flooded out of my body and hit him right between the eyes. Nkrumah was keyed in and listening. He paused for a moment. "The last part is the most important," he replied. "Bringing them back home to help me lead my great nation. We do not want a brain drain. We do not want our young people going to Europe and America and getting comfortable and not coming back."

"I give you my word," I said. For a moment, all was silent. Then in a moment of courtesy: "Mr. Wolff, this is indeed a fascinating possibility. But I must see Mr. Lumumba on his plane. Will you please stop by the government house this afternoon? We will have a chat. Right now, I must be polite and take leave of you until this afternoon. Mr. Lumumba is returning to important business in the Congo after our meetings on African Unity during these past few days. Please come by Government House at 2:00 p.m., and I will see you then."

Prime Minister
Patrice Emery Lumumba

He then asked, out of the blue, like a total non sequitur, "Do you know Mr. Lumumba? Please shake hands with the Prime Minister of the Congo. You now get two African leaders for the price of one." He laughed, and we all laughed at his sense of humor, quick mind, and down to earth courtesy, which broke the ice on what could have been a stiff and tense moment. I shook hands with both President Nkrumah and Prime Minister Lumumba. I was delighted. Mission accomplished before even reaching the terminal and the delegation of students from the University of Ghana's economics faculty waiting there to meet me as planned. They watched and were amazed that I had stopped Nkrumah and Lumumba and pitched AIESEC to them right there on the hot tarmac airfield. I got what I came to do. Negotiations were starting at the highest level. My first morning turned out even better than expected. Nkrumah and I were on the same wavelength.

At 2:00, I appeared as requested at the Government House and waited two minutes. He was prompt, courteous, and on time. I could sense his eagerness to have his University of Ghana recognized by an international organization of students. He had a quick mind and acted in the interest of his nation. Yet his first question: "How much money will your organization give us?"

I answered politely but firmly, "We don't give money. We provide experience. We offer an opportunity for students to have a traineeship working abroad with good companies. It is a cultural experience because there will be at least ten other students in the program in that city from other countries. The students reside in the same city during their six-month or one-year training program. It is a profound cultural and executive business experience for ambitious men and women seeking to make something of themselves, and to lead their countries towards greater economic development."

"That part is important," Nkrumah replied. "AIESEC is a program for legitimate opportunists and go-getters. Young men and women with a positive attitude and initiative."

I added, "If your government commits to invest and pay the freight, you will observe and monitor the outcomes of what we achieve in training your first 12 students. They will get a practical education in leadership and business. You will follow up and see that you get your money's worth. This program is not a throwaway money situation. It is a genuine investment."

Of the first 12 AIESEC students from Ghana, one became Minister of Transportation at age 27 after a summer of executive training with Swissair studying international travel systems. The program paid off for the other 11 as well. AIESEC educated an elite group of business and government leaders for Ghana for the next ten to twenty years.

Nkrumah called in his finance minister K.A. Gbedemah from the next room and had him write out a check on the spot for $30,000. Both men trusted our program and my word. We had been in business since 1948. I kept my word of commitment to West Africa even though it almost cost me my job. AIESEC in West Africa was now underway. I went to the University of Ghana to find her leaders and selected Charles Doku and his team. Doku became a significant figure in the development of the nation. He began his career as an AIESEC leader of the national committee with a group of eight hand-picked assistants, all volunteering their time for the greater good of the nation.

Chief Festus Okotie-Eboh

I employed the Nkrumah success example as I traveled to Nigeria and met with Chief Festus Okotie-Eboh. The colorful and loquacious Finance Minister appeared in a white robe and an American cowboy hat with a white feather. At 240 pounds, he looked more like a linebacker for the Chicago Bears. The chief was cunning, smart, and well-respected as a finance wizard for all of Africa. "I heard already about your good work in Ghana," he said as he took and squashed my hand in his beefy grip. "You made quite an impression on President Nkrumah." Fascinating how the news spreads along the west coast of Africa as if by drums beating out a rhythm in a relay of positive information. "The white man is coming, but this one can be trusted."

The Nigerians also wanted and needed the program. The chief was especially supportive. "Just a matter of practicality. The British colonials have left and taken an entire layer of administrative executives. We must train our own. This experience abroad for future business leaders will be invaluable. He wanted the AIESEC program and was into "one-upmanship" in competing with Kwame Nkrumah. "We will double whatever you got in Ghana," he exclaimed. He sat laughing in his large throne with the white feather in his straw-hat quivering. "We will double Nkrumah." He wrote out a check for $60,000 for the first Nigerians in the program. We saw the same positive results. In Nigeria, 80% of the business leaders from 1960-80 were AIESEC graduates who had experienced traineeships abroad with leading multinational companies.

The AIESEC program paid significant dividends in both nations. The program educated an elite, dedicated, honest, and patriotic group of young leaders who kept the country healthy for the next two decades.

Things turned turbulent in the Congo. I never got to see Lumumba again, nor was AIESEC ever started in the Congo. In my mind's eye, I can still see him standing there quietly and patiently while Nkrumah spoke with me. He waited for Nkrumah to finish, and then they walked together up those last few steps to the United Nations plane. Lumumba was wearing a custom-tailored dark blue business suit, light brown shoes, a white shirt, and a tastefully colored red and blue striped tie, ironically the colors of the University of Pennsylvania.

He was very tall, a member of the Watusi tribe. In his rimless glasses and quiet smile, he stood there quietly and patiently offered a few words of encouragement. Lumumba gave me an invitation to bring AIESEC students and our exchange program to visit the Congo. That was his last official state ceremonial and business visit with another African leader. He was assassinated a few months later. I still wonder, "Blue suit and brown shoes?"

Nkrumah was not just "another African leader." He was the President of the OAU, the Organization of African States, elected by its 24-member nations. Lumumba was a charismatic revolutionary, moving things fast, extremely fast, in what had been a quiet, Belgian-dominated colony. The United Nations plane, waiting patiently for him on the runway, would carry him home. Little did anyone know that Lumumba had only two months to live. On January 17, 1961, he was assassinated by political opponents in the Congo, financed by Belgian diamond business interests and the CIA.

In the early 21st century, declassified documents revealed that the CIA had plotted to assassinate Lumumba. These documents indicate that the Congolese leaders who helped to kill Lumumba, including Mobutu Sese Seko and Joseph Kasa-Vubu, received money and weapons directly from the CIA.

The country split apart in a civil war. The Congo and the diamond-rich province of Katanga split up. Turmoil ensued as Belgian mining interests fomented disintegration. Greed and power politics and ego battles over who gets the most split the young nation asunder, sending the young country back into the colonial domination and anarchy of the 19th century. The students never had a chance to form international friendships through AIESEC or to attend stable universities.

But fortunately, AIESEC did take hold in the West African nations of Ghana, Nigeria, and Sierra Leone. Later, with the help of new pioneer leaders with vision, we added programs successfully throughout all of Africa, Japan, China, and Latin America to its present-day world-wide strength of 102 nations. All of that growth can be traced back to that day on the open airfield in Ghana when a young student leader greeted a head of state by blurting out, "Greetings from Philadelphia!"

Securing Water Rights with Moshe Dayan

The recent 2021 11-day war in Israel between the Hamas and Jewish state reminds me of my tow happy months in Israel in the summer of 1962. My first visit to Israel was during the summer of 1962. I had already served from 1960 through 1961 as the first full-time President of the AIESEC international student exchange program in Geneva, Switzerland. I had one summer of total freedom left before my scheduled graduation from Yale Law School in January of 1963.

I always wanted to go to Israel, ever since reading "Exodus," by Leon Uris. I obtained a grant and scholarship to work as associate legal counsel to General Moshe Dayan, in the Israel Ministry of Agriculture ("Misrad Ha'hacla-ut") in Tel Aviv.

Dayan was the military hero of the 1957 Suez War against Egypt. He was strategically and conveniently "parked" as the Ministry of Agriculture's leader, a safe place to house him between the 1957 and 1967 wars. Dayan was a world-famous war hero. He saved Israel from permanent annihilation by the war forces of Egypt, Jordan, and Syria.

Israel was still a dangerous place to be working in Tel Aviv in 1963. The battle of the Sinai in 1957 was only six years old. The Egyptian air attacks in 1967, the "Yom Kippur War" was only four years away. I went knowing that there is a danger. A war could break out at any time, and surprise attacks could not be ruled out. But I went anyway. I had a mission to create peace, and I had no choice. Something drew me there.

I was a returning Jew coming home to "Eretz, Israel." My two-month assignment in Tel Aviv was to work with Israel's government as a Deputy Legal Advisor to the Ministry of Agriculture, specializing in Water Law. I wrote a brief for argument in the World

Moshe Dayan, 1978

Court to support Israel's position on sharing the Jordan River's upper riparian[1] water rights and its tributary, the Yarkon River.

The challenge to find and develop new water resources in Israel, necessitated by the massive Jewish immigration, was handed to General Moshe Dayan, a courageous and brilliant military tactician. He turned back Egypt's 1957 surprise attack. No one knew at the time, but he was on a peace assignment between wars.

The next war would not come until 1967. Between '57 and '67, Dayan was conveniently parked at the ministry of agriculture, intimately connected with water rights issues. Dayan had first been a farmer with his father. He grew up on a farm in what was then a pocket of Judaism in the Ottoman Empire in today's Syria. His parents emigrated from Russia to the Jewish agricultural community of Degania, a kibbutz.

Moshe Dayan was named after Moshe Baretsky, a brave farmer, refugee, and pioneer ("halutzim") who defeated an Arab attack and gave his life for his family and the Degania Kibbutz's protection.

In our first meeting, Moshe Dayan laughed when he learned my first name. "We are both Moshe," he said. "Drawn from the water and placed there by our intelligent sister Miriam to save our lives." We chatted about this wonderful coincidence and honor to have the legacy name of Moses, a leader of the Jewish people who brought the enslaved Jewish people out of years of horrible bondage in Egypt and to freedom in the promised land.

---

[1] A system for allocating water rights between those who possess land along water paths, such as rivers.

Dayan continued: "It is no coincidence that we three are named after Moses. We have a common name and a common responsibility to preserve and protect Jews and Jewish life, and to bring more water desperately needed by the Jewish people here in Israel today."

I was ushered into Moshe Dayan's office on my first day of work in late June 1962.

"I'm glad you are here," he said. "We need all the help we can get." He had a great smile and an abundance of self-confidence. A black eye patch covered his right eye, which was lost when a bullet hit the binoculars he was using to study a war position during the Israeli war of independence, in 1947.

"I intend to make water available in abundance in the Negev desert and make it a place of flourishing peace," he said. "We will turn the desert into a garden of blooming flowers and vegetables. We will siphon some of the Jordan and Yarkon rivers' waters to build new communities, schools, and kibbutzim."

"We will build our nation and its defense system by scattering villages throughout the country. We will share our technology with our neighbors and live in peace. You are here to help me make this vision come true," he told me. "We need you as our lawyer-in-residence to prepare and present the contract and compact for shared state ownership of the international rivers. No nation that finds itself twenty or thirty miles upstream should divert water away from downstream nations. But that is what the Jordanians are trying to do, and we cannot permit this. It seems that each of our neighboring nations wants to extinguish Israel, but I will not let this happen."

I discussed the theory of '*sic utero laedes*' — that each water user, whether rancher, farmer, or even a nation, could only use water with due regard for its downstream neighbor's needs. I told Moshe that this gives us a chance to sow seeds of peace through unselfish cooperation and resource sharing.

"Formulate that for me," he said. "We will be meeting with the Jordanians in just two weeks. I want them to agree to share the vision that they get back more by sharing than taking. We will give them our technology in exchange for a fair share of the precious water. Thus, we can all live together peacefully.

A few days later, I walked into Dayan's office with a ten-page memorandum. Sitting with him was General Chaim Herzog[2], who was a hero of the Israeli people. This shrewd man planned the strategy of the 1948 war and the one in 1957. I was introduced to General Herzog, whose peacetime position was chief of Israeli military intelligence. Herzog was a big man, with a full head of hair graying at the temples, and bushy eyebrows. I could feel his bone-crushing strength as he shook my hand.

Born a Jew in Belfast, Ireland, in 1918, Herzog, as a thirty-year-old, was placed in charge of Israel's Seventh Brigade s Operations Officer. He and Dayan loved to recount their adventures as soldiers. So, at their invitation, I put aside my briefing materials for the moment and sat down and listened to their war stories. They all ended in victories.

Herzog was a great storyteller. He had already risked his life three different times for his country. He would be mentally prepared to lead his troops into a defensive war in 1967 before becoming the first military governor of the occupied West Bank in 1967.

I shared my ideas and research on water law with Herzog and Dayan. They both had many questions, and each had a quite different approach. Herzog wanted to have the whole picture and decided for himself the best strategy. Dayan, on the other hand, wanted me to present the bottom line. He was like a civil engineer with a blueprint. Dayan thought linear and wanted to know how to get from point-to-point-to-point with the least effort and abrasion.

---

[2] For more about General Herzog, see the Britannica article at https://www.britannica.com/biography/Chaim-Herzog.

He saw the goal: get the water Israel needs and have Jordan feel they got a good deal.

We met with the Jordanian water experts as planned and hammered out an agreement for sharing the Yarkon River water resources. "There is enough there for everyone," Dayan said as the peaceful sharing international water agreement was signed. I wrote the deal over three weeks, researching ancient laws and experiences of sharing resources. Minister Moshe Dayan accepted my version of the international compact as written.

Today as Israel moves away from fighting and again moves towards sharing technology in new alliances with Bahrain and the United Arab Emirates, I am reminded of the summer negotiations of 1962. I smile at remembering the special moment sitting with others at the treaty signing table, the jovial air of rekindled friendships, and the healthy ability to compromise and agree. During those peaceful days of give and take in the unceasing heat of June and July of 1962, we brought warring nations to the peace table. We had an open and candid series of "lucky conversations." We then solemnly agreed to sign and enter an international water-sharing agreement, which benefits Jordan and Israel and is respected. The treaty is still in force today.

Working with John F. Kennedy

John F. Kennedy, 1961

One of my luckiest conversations was a one-on-one meeting alone with President John F. Kennedy in the Oval Office on April 12, 1963, at 8:00 a.m.

In our private conversation, I learned how frightened the President was when the Cuban Missile Crisis in 1961 almost resulted in a nuclear confrontation and a global war of mass destruction. He averted a global atomic war by just a few hours. He told me, "I knew that Premier Khrushchev considered Castro a madman, willing to reduce his island of Cuba to powder. Castro was out of his mind, obsessed with the idea of shelling South Florida and the Cubans in Miami to death."

The President sat in his famous simple rocking chair, seated uncomfortably on a pale blue cushion. I sat a foot away and could see lines of pain on his young face; he grimaced and smiled rather than cried. He was in severe pain, suffering still from a severely damaged back, injured when his PT-109 ocean craft was attacked by the Japanese in the South Pacific during World War II.

He continued telling me about the near Russian attacks and nuclear disaster that almost ended the world. "The Russians were prepared to launch a shelling of South Florida from missiles stationed in Cuba, ninety miles away. Fidel wanted to kill all the ex-Cubans in

Miami. The CIA knew Castro had been given a Russian Intercontinental Ballistic Missile (ICBM). Khrushchev was prepared to fire another one from a home base in Russia. That is how serious the situation was before we persuaded the Russians to pull their missiles from Cuba and to stand down on their plans to fire a second missile from Russia."

I was surprised that the President chose to share this information with me. He had his reasons. He continued, "I share this information now because we must take concrete steps towards a genuine peace that the world can feel and see: no more guns, no more armaments. We have enough to blast each other into a full world annihilation. We need peace."

He stood up for a moment, putting both hands behind his back and grimacing from the constant pain. "We must work towards a lessening of tensions and world peace. That is where your AIESEC peace program might, with your permission, come into play. Your business and law student exchange program in 33 nations is a working showcase of positive peacebuilding activity and goodwill. You and your idealistic students are already active in all the countries of Europe, including France, Germany, Sweden, Finland, Italy, Yugoslavia, Poland, Denmark, Norway — all of the strategic NATO nations that form a western front on Russia." I could see where he was going, but I did not want to see our program politicized. I simply listened without saying a word.

"I know from your brother Robert Kennedy, with whom I work at Justice, that you are planning a major speech on strategies for achieving world peace and nuclear freeze among all nations. This will take place in just a few months with an address in September at American University here in Washington."

"Bobby talks too much, but I am glad you know about my peace initiative plans."

The President was actively putting together a comprehensive agenda and plan for implementing strategies for achieving détente and achieving genuine and lasting peace. He saw the value of student exchange as a strategic part of the picture. Kennedy was investing millions in the active growth of the Peace Corps. Now he wanted to finance an enlarged AIESEC as well.

"This will give a boost to the AIESEC program. Your NATO nation graduate business school students working on their graduate degrees will become an essential part of the peace strategy during my presidency."

He moved to change the subject, noticing that I was not engaging in the idea. AIESEC was always non-political and was not under any one nation's political system. We could not be bought. We kept our commitment to creating friendships and providing business internships. In this way, we held our integrity and independence.

"Tell me how did you come across or discover AIESEC? And how did you rise in three months from being a lowly summer exchange student to Cologne, Germany in 1959 to become the President, chief honcho of the organization in 1960? That's a rather rapid rise!"

I replied, "My rise within the program was fast because of my deep interest in world peace. In February 1959, I saw a little homemade sign on a 2x4-inch blue card on the bulletin board at Yale Law School. It said: "work abroad this summer, all expenses paid." That idea hit me like a ton of bricks between the eyes. In the summer of '59 I went to Cologne, Germany, for two months working and learning at the International Chamber of Commerce of Cologne. I learned some basic German, drank German beer, sang for extra money in a Biergarten night club on Wednesday evenings, and studied international trade. Three months later, after resuming my law studies back at Yale, I was asked to stand, and I was, to my great surprise, elected in absentia President of the whole international program. Other people, such as Norman Barnett, Steve Keiley, and John Tuschman of Columbia Business School, boosted my candidacy at Rotterdam's international meeting, and I was elected global leader of the program. I was chosen based on my resume and the fact that I now spoke German and French. The positive and healthy energy of those three men collaring people at the international meeting and lining up votes for me was awesome."

"I wasn't even there. So then, in December 1959, just three months after I was a lowly exchange student — one of 5,000 — I was elected President and international leader of AIESEC. With my father's permission, I took time out from my studies at Yale Law to go to Europe and serve as the Secretary-General and President of the International Association of Economic Students (AIESEC) in Geneva."

I explained to President Kennedy how the program, during my two years in Geneva at the International Secretariat, grew and flourished in 31 European nations and the United States with an annual exchange of 2,130 students. "I helped to expand the program with a 50% increase in exchanges and extended the program as you know, Mr. President, to Ghana, Nigeria, and Sierra Leone." I shared my meetings with President Nkrumah of Ghana and Prime Minister Patrice Lumumba of the Congo on the tarmac in Accra, Ghana. He asked my assessment of both men, which I gave.

In my meeting with President Kennedy, he indicated his commitment and support of the AIESEC exchange program. I expressed my belief that the AIESEC program in developing future business and government leaders of the world was an ideal instrument for achieving peace. I emphasized my belief that better communication and friendships among future world leaders would help move us towards global peace. Kennedy was excited. He wanted to see a massive increase in the number of AIESEC exchanges on a worldwide basis. He also wanted to use the program to advance the possibilities of peace with Russia and Africa's business infrastructure as a world economic power. President Kennedy wanted to see Africa vitally involved in free enterprise programs. The Soviets and the United States were in a cold war ideological battle over Africa's economic future as a third world power.

The President seemed quite able in 1963 to peer into the future. That was part of his greatness. He could see into the future and probable outcomes. AIESEC, between 1948 and 1963, had already been a power for peace. It was a significant force in avoiding World War III between France and Germany, through a massive student exchange of over 50,000 trainees between those two countries in that period. One was Giscard d'Estaing, who became Prime Minister of France. There were many presidents of major companies, including a Nobel Prize winner from Finland. Most important is that peace has prevailed.

Consistent with the President's vision, the AIESEC exchange program still thrives today. The self-help program is active on all continents. There are 95 member nations, 700 universities, and over 9,000 exchanges annually. AIESEC is still non-political and runs exclusively by students! It is devoted to nurturing "close and friendly relations among students of the whole wide world," as its fundamental charter still provides. It remains non-political, after 50 good years, and remains open to anyone who qualifies without regard to race, religion, or national origin. President Kennedy immediately saw the value of the program.

During my hour of thoughtful conversation with the President, we discussed the possibility of gaining world peace through a massive positive movement of university students and other young people. They would get to know each other and to respect each other through global exchange programs and homestays. By joining mutual economic and personal interests, the "new generation" of leaders trained in the AIESEC spirit and managerial experience would compete for business in a peaceful environment rather than fight wasteful wars.

In the privacy of the Oval Office, this meeting with President Kennedy, sitting next to him as he rocked back and forth gently in his rocking chair, became one of the highlights of my public service days in Washington D.C. Working with his brother Attorney General Robert Kennedy, in the Office of Legal Counsel (OLC), became a postgraduate legal and political education, a working seminar with eight of the nation's brightest lawyers. The OLC was a pinnacle appointment, sought by many young lawyers but offered to only a few.

Shifting from the Office of Legal Counsel at Justice to an even higher level of public service, I soon began working on the floor of the U.S. Senate as a trusted legislative counsel to Senator John Sherman Cooper on the passage of the historic Civil Rights Act of 1964.

After three exciting years in Washington, I returned home to Philadelphia. Washington was exciting and vital to my life. But I wanted to run for elected office and become an architect for social change in America and world peace. I fought poverty and discrimination and helped to reduce juvenile crime and delinquency. Philadelphia was my home base, where I had my roots. I went back home, got married, started a family, and began working as Chief Assistant District Attorney of Philadelphia, a stepping-stone towards a political office. I worked with District Attorney Arlen Specter, a fellow Yale Law graduate who later became a United States Senator.

I made some mistakes along the way. I ran for public office too soon and in the wrong district. Timing is everything. I was simply too eager. My driving passion was to get elected and to become one day a U.S. Senator and then possibly the President of the United States. These were big dreams, but as my father said, there is nothing wrong with that. "The only sin in life is a low aim," and just tell yourself, "It can be done." He was my motivational coach, always in my corner. My mother supported me too. So, I went for the battle for state senator in Pennsylvania in 1972. (Wrong place, wrong time, wrong everything.) It was to be my first stepping-stone towards the top. When elected, I would be able to converse with foreign leaders in Spanish, French, and German. Where President Kennedy had said in one of his famous speeches, "Ich bin eine Berliner," I would one day be able to give the full address in German, French, or Spanish. I would have been a literate President in four languages. God had other plans for me. I have had a vibrant and productive life of public service and doing good things for Raoul Wallenberg and Henry Rota and other good people.

Now, as I approach age 84, I have lived twice as long as JFK, who died at the young age of 42 as the result of two assassin's bullets; one fired from the "grassy knoll" that was in front. That bullet landed in his throat, and one fired from the back, blowing off part of his head. Kennedy was a young 42 with lots of life left in him. The mystery of who caused his death lingers on unresolved. There was another man involved. The name of the other killer will eventually be revealed. I learned all about the assassination's truth from a member of the Warren Commission, Senator John Sherman Cooper. He was a man of integrity and one of two senators on the Commission. He was my boss. I was hired to be his legislative counsel for Civil Rights, but I was also his bodyguard and driver. I drove him over and back to Chief Justice Warren's JFK assassination commission every day. "It's a coverup," he confided to me one day, on our way back to the office. "They are refusing to admit that there were at least two gunmen just because they never found the other assassin."

My lucky conversations with Senator John Sherman Cooper, the architect of the Civil Rights Act and the lone dissenter on the Warren Commission, and a man of deep honesty and integrity form the guts of the next chapter.

There Will Never Be Another Camelot

After that special day of April 12, 1963, when I first met with President Kennedy in the Oval Office, a feeling of trust with the Kennedys began to slowly develop. We had good chemistry and with a level of respect and trust evolving. We were ambitious, opportunistic, and eager to create a better world. We focused on the positive, not the negative, as a basis for action. We wanted peace with a passion and looked at life as an opportunity to do great things. We felt we could attack poverty and either change the world or at least move it forward to a new frontier.

We were young and "idealistic-realists," as Ted Sorensen, Jack's speechwriter, called our mutual condition. Bobby was 33, Jack was 42, and I was 27. "What the hell, I survived the PT-109 destruction for some decent reason," Jack said one late afternoon. "I must have been saved by God or by weird luck to do something great." We had the same core values and the rigors of a good education at Harvard and Yale. "From those to whom much has been given, much is expected." We were prepared to serve.

After graduating from Yale Law School in January 1963, I went straight to Washington to work with Attorney General Robert Kennedy on civil rights. My place was in "the cockpit," known as the Office of Legal Counsel of the Department of Justice on the 5th floor, actually right next to RFK's office. I was given the assignment of writing and crafting the first draft of Title II of the Civil Rights Act of 1964 to end the hurtful and unjustified racial discrimination blacks experienced in America. These individuals could not sit at Woolworth lunch counters, Howard Johnson ice cream parlors, book a room at Marriott Hotels, or use publicly available tennis courts.

There were "whites only" children's playgrounds, "exclusive" swimming pools, and movie theaters where blacks were forced to sit in the balcony. In 1963, these restrictions also included public water fountains "for whites only" and other forms of humiliation and exclusion. "Places of public accommodation" was a joke. You could get arrested if you were even a little bit black for sitting down or sleeping in "the wrong hotel." These places were allegedly open to the public, but not for African American people. It was the same in churches. "Sunday at 11:00 a.m. was the most segregated hour in America," said Billy Graham. I was 26 years old in 1963, and I am now 84 and still angry as hell about it. But I decided to act and do something about it way back then and am still fighting for civil rights for all people.

Blacks could not eat in all-white restaurants or tennis courts where whites claimed they were the only ones allowed to play. These were power plays by big racist white bullies who beat up other people. This snubbing, shunning, assault, and battery of the heart were hurtful and painful.

On my first day at work, Bobby Kennedy called me into his office. "Morris, as you know, most people do not like being snubbed, humiliated, and turned away from public places freely open to others because they're black. I want you to start a one-person army like Spartacus to begin the revolution of changing this tangible and intangible experience of human pain and discrimination that affects millions of black people here in America. Are you up to it?"

"Yes, sir. This is what I came to Washington to do. I accepted your offer for this very reason of achieving civil rights through a change in the law. I want to be part of something real and to continue to work side by side with you, and the NAACP, and others in a program of reform."

"Go to it. Keep me informed daily."

At first, I talked to a whole bunch of black people to learn more about their painful experiences in being turned away. I traveled throughout the south and part of the north by bus to see what it was like to live in a segregated society, attend segregated schools and play on segregated playgrounds and tennis courts. Exhilarated by what I learned from people on my travels, I returned to Washington. I began to craft Title II, which applies to free access for all to places of public accommodation, like tennis courts. I turned my mind towards the essential research on where to place the Civil Rights Act. There were two possibilities; we could use the 14th Amendment or The Commerce Clause as a "hook" since black people traveled on highways only to be humiliated at the entrance of either the Waldorf Astoria, Sardi's restaurant, or the nationwide chain of Marriott hotels.

In my spare time, I also became close to Bobby Kennedy. I would spend part of every day in his office, and especially on Saturdays when he brought his kids and Boomer, his big brown and white Saint Bernard, to the office to play. Sunday was spent at his home in Virginia at Hickory Hill.

In a few weeks, I knew Ethel and the whole family. I became a liaison, a trusted messenger between Robert and John Kennedy, for the remaining five months of the President's life. I was trusted. We had good chemistry and the same core values.

One day, I was called unexpectedly to the White House. I walked over from my office in the Attorney General's inner sanctum. President Kennedy told me, "Morris, Bobby, and I have decided we want you to serve as our personal courier, as long as I'm alive. You will, from time to time, be tapped to hand-deliver important messages from the Attorney General into my hands here in the Oval Office."

"Fine, Mr. President. If I can serve you in any way, I am glad to do so. I have never been a private courier, but I will learn."

"This will provide you with some needed fresh air and exercise during daylight hours. You will need that from what I have heard," the President chuckled.

"You will be called upon to deliver classified information. Since you received a top-level security clearance, there will be no further approvals today. You will receive a bike and a pair of running shoes. At any time between 8:00 a.m. and 5:00 p.m., Bobby may have something too precious or sensitive for 'J. Edgar' to know about or overhear on our tapped phones. Hoover, as head of the FBI, sticks his nose into everything. He is silently intercepting Bobby's phone calls. His office is on the floor above yours at Justice."

The President commenced rocking in the baby blue rocking chair next to his desk. He shifted his rear end quarters in obvious pain. "This is where you come in, Morris. You replace the telephone. And we will not communicate in writing except with you as our go-between messenger."

His ominous words, "as long as the President was alive," struck home as a dark note. The President had premonitions of early death. His back ached with pain from injuries suffered 20 years earlier in 1943 in the South Pacific when his PT-109 capsized under enemy fire, and he swam ashore. Kennedy also had severe Addison's Disease. This information was kept from the public by sensitive journalists and news mongers. He had a dark and fatalistic view of his chosen fairy tale location. He believed he was part of "one brief shining moment known as Camelot."

Camelot, for JFK, was a transient and temporary thing. He could laugh at himself as "C'est Moi, C'est Moi, I am the King, and Jackie is Queen." He was light-hearted and pleasant, rarely taking himself seriously, except when crises arose. Then everything changed. He became visibly upset, cryptic, highly impatient, a short fuse for others, demanding the facts in short form and stern. He could change from happiness to dead serious in a few seconds, but he had a razor-sharp mind and an excellent impromptu gift of speech. His words elevated and inspired all of us, including his staff. When Bobby had a confidential document or memo, I was tapped to leave my desk at Justice and serve as a secret messenger. This method of communication was before computers and the internet. I would run with messages from 10th and Constitution to the White House at 1600 Pennsylvania Avenue in 15 minutes.

They used my "fast walking foot power" to deliver and receive sensitive information. And I thereby stayed in shape. We were still in the scary trenches of the Cold War in 1963, and spies were everywhere in Washington. The red phone connecting the President with the Soviet Premier and his underground shelters in Maryland was still in use.

Jim Douglass, in his book, *JFK and the Unspeakable*, deals with Kennedy's passionate drive for peace and the efforts by the military, industrial complex, and the CIA to spy on him, slow him down, and to oppose his efforts to achieve lasting peace. This resistance may have led to President Kennedy's death in November 1963 at Dealey Plaza. The author offers proof that the single bullet theory is not accurate. In the still-secret autopsy report, it is clear that at least one bullet was fired from in front of the motorcade, possibly from the grassy knoll. I read the private notes of Senator Cooper, taken down in pencil by Cooper as a member of the Warren Commission. He agrees with Jim Douglass.

The beyond gross negligence of the Secret Service that failed to keep up with the motorcade and protect the President in Dallas is evident from the notes of Senator Cooper, the President's best friend in the U.S. Senate. Cooper nurtured and trained JFK in the art of politics and statesmanship as a young, new Senator, a little-known fact. Young Kennedy idolized and looked up to Senator Cooper for his integrity and his Lincolnesque stature. Cooper was a man of honesty and wisdom and committed to the poor people and brave coal miners and other people in "Butcher's Hollow" back home in Kentucky. John Sherman Cooper, a rugged man of independent thought, was loved by the President.

I worked from January 1964 through July of 1965 as a chief legislative assistant and legal counsel to Senator Cooper during his days of service on the Warren Commission. He was one of only two Senators appointed to the commission — the other was Democrat Richard Russell. I drove Senator Cooper to and from the hearings in my little yellow and black Fiat car. This was during the bleak days after Kennedy's assassination. I loved, idolized, and protected

Cooper during those dangerous days when we wondered what will happen next. These were dark days in our nation's history, where we looked for new leadership and never found it.

I have read with my own eyes the Warren Commission Report, and all the testimony. I was allowed by Cooper to read these reports in 1964 when I was Cooper's aide and sworn to secrecy. Now, in 2021, I am free to speak. "Jack Kennedy was a goner as soon as he stepped off the plane in Dallas," according to Senator Cooper, and confirmed by a candid recent FBI report. Cooper shared this security secret information with me in February of 1964, just three months after the November 22, 1963 murder, how the Secret Service knew Kennedy was a dead duck as soon as he descended the steps of the plane. Lyndon Baines Johnson was involved in Kennedy's death. The Secret Service stepped back and let it happen. Cooper's private handwritten notes from the Warren Commission were shared with me briefly at that time. The real report is still under lock and key. It may never come to light or be read and discussed by the press and the public. There was big Texas oil money behind the killing of President Kennedy.

One afternoon, after I picked Cooper up, he burst out in anger: "It wasn't fair. President Kennedy was a dead duck, and it was a setup. There was no real security provided in Dallas. Security stepped aside and let the tragedy happen. The difficult route around Dealey Plaza was a death trap."

Senator Cooper knew the real hardcore evidence. According to Cooper, "a group of zealous Cubans, hand-picked by Castro, landed in the USA in November of '63 and headed for Dallas. They were apparently joined there by other sharpshooters from the Mafia, angry with Bobby's crackdowns. It was a combination of Cubans, Texas oil money, and the Mafia," Cooper said. "Oswald was a fall guy, a naïve American duped into taking a major role. He became a victim. Jack Ruby was sent by the Mob to kill Oswald. Others were deeply involved. They wanted to get Kennedy before he took out Castro."

They learned a few days before Dallas that JFK had approved plans to have Fidel Castro, the President of Cuba, murdered. Castro, ever alert to U.S. activities, beat Kennedy to the punch. Castro took steps to act first. Lee Harvey Oswald was only one of three gunmen. Secret Service negligence — men drinking and partying with prostitutes in Dallas — just before Kennedy's visit was a Presidential cause for profound concern. Partying and unprofessional preparation and loose behavior occurred in Dallas the night before Kennedy's presidential visit.

History, unfortunately, repeats itself. Little in governmental behavior seems to change. Author Douglass conclusively proves that President Kennedy wanted desperately to achieve a genuine long-term peace with the USSR. Kennedy also wanted to bring an end to the dangerous Cold War in which nuclear annihilation was at the fingertips of both powers. The Defense Department thwarted his efforts to pry open the door to peace in combination with Boeing, McDonnell Douglas, Ford Motor Company, and other industrial complex giants. The ending of the Cold War met resistance from the military-industrial complex. Also, the CIA fought against peace efforts and perversely wanted to see a continuity of tensions.

Ironically, Nikita Khrushchev was open to the peace option to end the Cold War. The cost of maintaining expensive armaments was driving the Soviets into bankruptcy. During a short window of time, from March through June of 1963, there were serious, productive, and secret negotiations. Kennedy was the initiator. Kennedy's private notes and publicly telegraphed letters to the Soviet leader promoted his desire and strategy to achieve genuine, lasting peace. This message was openly communicated — with a briefing in advance to Premier Khrushchev — in a speech given by President Kennedy at American University in Washington in early September of 1963, two months before his death.

The President asked me in July 1963 to assist his speechwriter, Theodore Sorensen from Nebraska, in writing that famous September speech. Ted said, "Your experience with AIESEC has given you, and through you, the vision we need for lasting peace.

Your work with 33 nation members and 512 universities gives you a unique perspective. It will be the duty of the next generation, you and the other young people, the student activists and idealists who will now begin to make a better world."

All of this began when I first met President Kennedy on April 12, 1963, in his Oval Office. We had a candid conversation about peace. Some of my words during his April interview with me about "achieving a lasting peace" through "building a shared and interdependent world economy where nations are busy building the structure of lasting prosperity to have time for destruction and war," went DIRECTLY into his speech at American University.

That time with the Kennedy men in the harmonious and productive years before Dallas was the most exciting of my life. We wrote a new immigration law that made countries' quotas more even and balanced between all nations and not just the "white privilege nations" of Sweden, Norway, Denmark, Ireland, and the United Kingdom. We took the racist sting out of the immigration law and moved a little bit forward.[3]

I did not have time to think about the history I was walking in every day. I just did the "next thing," loving my work and my new drafting and research assignments. I loved being invited to attend the exciting private meetings of the eight Senate leaders for breakfast. Cooper was one of them, and I sat behind him listening, two ears open and my mouth shut. I learned and watched the maneuvers and strategies used to get a 66-member vote in favor of the Civil Rights Act of 1964, which the southern senators hated but realized the time had come for change.

---

[3] See John F. Kennedy's book *A Nation of Immigrants*, © Pickle Partners Publishing 2016, all rights reserved. Available on Amazon Kindle, hardcover, and paperback. It provides an insightful history of immigration from the original settlers through 1959. It also details how attitudes towards immigration changed over the centuries.

The men I met during the historic Civil Rights debates on the floor of the Senate, in the Halls of Congress gave me a valuable and matchless education. I had floor privileges and got to talk to all the senators. These include Everett Dirksen of Illinois; Clifford Case of New Jersey; Richard Lugar of Indiana; George Hart of Michigan; Margaret Chase Smith of Maine; Norris Cotton of New Hampshire; Joe Clark and Hugh Scott, Senators of my home state of Pennsylvania; Daniel Inouye of Hawaii; J. William Fulbright of Arkansas; Hubert Humphrey of Minnesota; and John Stennis of Mississippi. History remembers these men and women in various ways:

- George Hart has the Hart Senate Office Building.
- Senator Cooper has a major bridge in Kentucky.
- President Kennedy is a space center, the Kennedy Library in Boston, and a memorial in Arlington National Cemetery.

I was privileged to meet with them daily.

Waking up on spring mornings in the magic of colonial Georgetown, I would steal an hour to play tennis at the green hard court near my 33rd Street apartment. Earl "the Pearl" Silbert, the U.S. Attorney for D.C., would join me. We played for 45 minutes. We watched as the luminaries walked by, Dean Rusk, Secretary of State, and Allen Dulles, head of the CIA.

Afterward, we would take a quick shower, eat toast and eggs, and coffee for breakfast prepared by his wife, Patricia. And then Earl and I would drive to town together and go to our separate positions of responsibility, challenge, and fun. A few years later, Earl Silbert became the Chief Investigator of the Watergate scandal, the Robert Mueller of his day.

Life moves forward as I near my 85th birthday. It is time to wrap up this chapter on my life devoted to lucky conversations in the hallowed halls of the Department of Justice Office of Legal Counsel and the White House. I acted as a lawyer and as a messenger boy for the Kennedy's, fast walking, jogging, running, or biking between the Justice Department and the White House delivering classified information and intel on the "Baya del Cochino," Bay of Pigs trapped marines rescue operation. At times, I was invited to be privy to the message's content, especially as we went to rescue those brave men who tried to invade and take over Cuba for America. That made Castro mad and led directly to the JFK assassination. But when Castro received an unexpected "gift" of medicines, he was happy and grateful.

My work with the Honorable Louis Oberdorfer, head of the U.S. Department of Justice Tax Department, is still a secret. It will have to wait for another day. Louis Oberdorfer and I worked on a plan to rescue our U.S. Marines from the ill-advised Bay of Pigs secret invasion of Cuba.

Our brave U.S. Marines ("semper fi") were led into that swamp, captured, and abandoned. Lou and I quietly went around the country, urging big pharmaceutical companies to give up surplus production and get a huge tax break. Merck, Baxter Travenol, and Warner-Lambert of New Jersey complied as patriots.

The deal worked. We did the dirty work and the heavy lifting. That is why we received the United Nations Humanitarian Award at Carnegie Hall in New York in August 1993. We collected pharmaceuticals from all the big companies, gave them a huge tax break, and looked the other way. Their donation gave tons of second-generation medicines to the desperate Cubans and Castro, who desperately needed these drugs for human beings in a dire and life-saving situation. We brought our Marines home as an exchange of goods for people/prisoners.

Working for Bobby Kennedy

Soon after graduating in January 1963 from Yale Law School, I received an invitation to work with Robert F. Kennedy, Attorney General of the United States. This incredible opportunity was made possible by my International Law Professor, Myres S. McDougal, who volunteered to put my name forward. Without his help and that of my devoted parents, I would never have arrived there. McDougal was admired by Bobby Kennedy and thousands of professors throughout the world. Kennedy had called "Mac" to ask him to recommend one law graduate for his Office of Legal Counsel.

"I suggest you take Morris Wolff," Mac replied. "Morris is an intellectual competitor; a good tennis player and he hits the ball back extremely hard. He has a quick, creative mind and does not tolerate hokum even from his superiors. Morris is a good team player and is loyal and humble, and he will fit in well with your staff of lawyers in the Office of Legal Counsel. Morris is devoted to achieving human rights and establishing civil rights for our nation's black people. He is a great young man with international experience." Mac put these thoughts forward in his letter to Robert Kennedy.

Myres M. McDougal was a brilliant international lawyer, a civil rights advocate who fled deeply racist Mississippi for the safe confines of Yale Law School in Connecticut. "I had no future there; everything was racist, keep the blacks 'in their place,' whatever that meant." Once out of Mississippi, he was free to speak out and act out. And he did. Mac knew all about the horrors of segregation, black people's humiliation, and lynching in the South. He had a motive for recommending me. I would be a "young McDougal," standing in for him at Justice for civil rights, something he wished he was young enough to do himself in 1963. Time had passed him by on this opportunity. I would go in his stead.

Mac knew my track record for doing and going out into the world and achieving civil rights and inclusivity for black students. When I was 25, I traveled to Africa and integrated the AIESEC International

Student Exchange Program by hand-picking top-flight local student leaders to be the first international exchange students. I personally built the program in Ghana, Sierra Leone, and Nigeria as new full member nations. I negotiated AIESEC programs directly with Kwame Nkrumah, President of Ghana, Chief Festus Okoti-Eboh, Finance Minister of Nigeria, and Doctor Sir Milton Margai, President of Sierra Leone. Sir Milton attended high school in Philadelphia, my hometown as many Leonine had done both before and since. It is a family tradition! Small world indeed!

The previously all-white AIESEC program became diversified healthily and inclusively. I insisted that we include Asian and Black Africans as members of our program. As a result, AIESEC continues to thrive 60 years later. I care deeply about the AIESEC program's future and the opportunity for black people in America and across the globe. I continuously work to help end their humiliating second class citizenship status.

When I arrived at the Department of Justice, my job assignment was undefined. I knew I was selected by Attorney General Robert Kennedy to work in the Office of Legal Counsel on the fifth floor next to his office. I quickly learned that proximity could be a blessing and a curse. I also knew that the role of the Office of Legal Counsel, or OLC, was to be the lawyer or the advisory legal counsel to the Attorney General as he is called upon to determine and issue written opinions on the constitutionality of all legislation put forward by Congress.

At certain moments in our nation's history, the OLC drafts the law, and then sends it to Congress for review. Such would be the case with the historic and momentous Civil Rights Act of 1964. I walked into the OLC at that very moment in history (February 1963) when a wounded nation was seeking fairness and justice for a victimized and mistreated segment of our society.

We were about to write the first draft of "An Emergency Relief Civil Rights Bill," as the Attorney General called the now historic Civil Rights Act of 1964. We drafted the bill secretly and silently in the cockpit of Justice on the 5th floor overlooking 10th and Constitution Avenue in the nation's Capital.

On my first day of work, I organized my desk and said hello to new people when I got a call on the intercom from the Attorney General at 9:00 a.m.

RFK: Morris, can you pop in for a few minutes to chat with me?"

MHW: "Yes, sir, I will be right there."

I had no idea what to call him, so I rattled off all of his titles. I grabbed a yellow legal pad and a ballpoint pen and stepped next door. I entered his private inner sanctum and saw several open case books in front of him. The books all focused on historic civil rights laws in America. Three other men were present. The attorney general looked up over his horn-rimmed glasses and beckoned me to sit down.

Robert F. Kennedy in his office

"Morris, I want you to join the brain trust that is already engaged in writing the Civil Rights Act. The four of you will form a team to be known as 'the gang of four.' Your work will be completely confidential until I am ready to divulge and disclose your work, as your final product goes to the Hill for review. I expect tact, diplomacy, and confidentiality at all times."

"Morris, you are the youngest. You will work with three hand-picked colleagues: Sol Lindenbaum, Harold Reis, and Nathan Segal. These three brilliant men are experienced Justice Department lawyers. Your job, Morris, is to focus on what will become the specific language of the Public Accommodations section, which I believe will be Title II of the Civil Rights Act. This part of the Act deals with the controversial and contested right of all citizens, regardless of skin color or national origin, to access and receive service as a customer in "places of public accommodation." The Act includes hotels, restaurants, theaters, public parks, libraries, and other fun, relaxation, and recreation places.

Morris: "We all need to sleep safely at night, relax and have a chance to 'recreate' ourselves, as Mark Antony said to the crowd of unruly Romans after the assassination of Julius Caesar. It was part of Caesar's living will and legacy to give to every Roman 75 acres — 'common pleasures, to walk about and recreate yourselves.' If it was good enough for Caesar's legacy, as left to Rome's citizens, it is good enough for us. We all have a human right to have fun, relaxation, and to enjoy life."

I looked around the table at my three new colleagues. They got up to shake hands with me and sat down quickly. They were intrigued by my allusion to Julius Caeser and William Shakespeare.

RFK: "We need to write a strong law that deals without delay with opening up restaurants and hotels across the nation so that black people and other minorities have an equal chance for recreation, to go there to have a meal, to sleep comfortably at night and to do business. We will include the big boys, the Hilton, the Marriott Corporation, Howard Johnson's, Holiday Inns, and all the other major chains. Until now, the southern states have been reluctant, albeit worse than reluctant, and refused service to blacks based on their skin color and not their behavior. These chains have been totally obstructionist in refusing to allow black people to eat, sleep, or gain access to any of their superior hotels and public accommodations. What's challenging about this, Morris, is that we have to find the correct constitutional basis for this new civil rights law. We need to pin it on a specific clause in the U.S. Constitution for it to stand up in the courts and not be struck down by the segregationists. As soon as it becomes law, they will attack it as an invasion of private property rights. We will face special hell from the South's family-owned hotels and restaurants where segregated dining and living have been a way of life for over 100 years."

I listened and took notes. Attorney General Kennedy turned toward me, his hooded hawk eyes tired but blue, still penetrating. He fiddled with his yellow Ticonderoga #3 pencils, balancing one on his fingertips while looking up at the ceiling, lost in thought for a moment. "Well, Morris, you are fresh from law school with a bunch of new knowledge. Tell us your take on which part of the United States Constitution should become the basis for the new civil rights law?"

I sensed a possible trap, but there was no way out. The Attorney General asked a direct question. I had to answer; I had to create the best answer, or else I would be demoted and moved the next day from the 5th to the 2nd floor. As of a minute ago, it was my job to give my best answer — the only solution.

MHW: "I can see two possibilities, two options. First, we have the 14th Amendment, which provides for due process and equal protection of the laws. We argue that equal protection means equal right to enter and enjoy restaurants and hotels and other places of 'public accommodation.' Then there is the interstate commerce clause of Article One, Section eight, Clause three. In recent years, this flexible and seemingly elastic clause has become a platform for a few social legislation pieces."

RFK: "What do you mean by social legislation? I don't get it. There is no language in the Constitution about social legislation. Is there some provision for social legislation?"

MHW: "Well, the federal Wage and Hour Laws passed in the 1930s are considered social legislation. The law protects individuals and families from their behavior, protecting people and their families against men working too many hours and too many days per week and getting sick, having heart attacks from too many stressful hours. People, breadwinners, were dying from overwork. Congress has dealt with the problem and has placed this law in The Commerce Clause, and it has withstood constitutional attack in the courts. Same with the Fair Labor and Standards Act."

MHW: "Both federal laws were found on review by federal courts to be constitutional. I believe these are two viable possibilities. We can base the new civil rights law's legal authority on the 14th Amendment or The Commerce Clause. The Supreme Court loves to rely on past precedent as a basis for new decisions. They do not like being criticized for inventing or "making new laws." Even with all the liberal constructionists on the Court today, like Justice Hugo Black, or William O. Douglas and even Earl Warren, these men will be reaching for useful past precedents as justification for a carefully written new decision."

NATHAN SEGAL: "The Commerce Clause might seem to be an unlikely place because that particular regulatory power of Congress normally focuses on interstate truck movement, and safety standards for trains and buses moving in transit between the states. However, a few times, The Commerce Clause has been "stretched" to deal with people. In 1936, in the Hammer v. Dagenhart decision, the Supreme Court upheld a federal law outlawing child labor based on The Commerce Clause. The Court found that "unprotected children" deserve government protection, so they made up the fiction that "children were goods moving in interstate commerce." Their safety could be "regulated" by Congress based on The Commerce Clause. And The Commerce Clause is part of 'the supreme law of the land."

MHW: "So now we have "tools" for stretching The Commerce Clause once again. Will we claim that black Americans and people of any shade, when they are moving on interstate highways towards restaurants, hotels, movie theaters, or other 'places of public accommodation,' are chattels in the stream of interstate commerce? I don't think that will sit very well with Roy Wilkins and the NAACP or with Vernon Jordan, National Chief of CORE, the Congress of Racial Equality. I have discussed it in Philadelphia with the Honorable A. Leon Higginbotham, the first black federal judge, and a Yale Law School graduate. They would all resent being reduced to chattel."

"Those men find it humiliating and insulting to see themselves placed under the rubric of chattel or considered 'goods in interstate commerce.' They are offended and find the very idea an insult. I'm looking at the practical and potential political response and repercussions. There may be trouble ahead, caused by blacks' unfortunate categorization as chattel or goods in commerce. Perception is essential when we are creating new laws, and for some, perception is everything."

RFK: "What do you suggest we do?"

MHW: "I suggest we find a mooring for the new civil rights law on *both* The Commerce Clause and the 14th Amendment's equal protection clause. In that way, it gives the Supreme Court some breathing space to find the law constitutional. They will dither in private over one or the other possibility of which constitutional provision is more just or appropriate. They will then debate among themselves in their private meetings. The Court always likes to have at least a choice. They call it breathing space or wiggle room. In Brown v. Board of Education in 1954, the Court looked beyond the law to sociologist Gunnar Myrdal for guidance. Myrdal had opined that separating children by color for their early education will "leave feelings of inferiority that may never be erased." That case was decided on a sociological footnote."

RFK: "I like your suggestion, Morris. Let's have two moorings, as you put it."

The other three men in the group agreed. The "two moorings" theory was a strategy to seriously consider as we moved forward in drafting a comprehensive civil rights act. Public accommodation was not the only section to write. There was also Title VI, providing federal funds' cut-off to states and school districts that failed to comply with equality of treatment and immediate desegregation provisions. The Feds were cutting off federal funds. That got state attention and compliance quickly.

RFK: "Well, Morris, it appears that you have survived my first grilling. You test well under fire. I threw you a curveball, and you handled it well. You have a good background of knowledge. We will have other sessions where you can educate and inform your team and me. Welcome aboard. You will bring a fresh and younger creative perspective to the writing of this new law. I want the team to make it tight and precise, something the public can read without hiring a lawyer. I am sure the three career lawyers will welcome you into their inner sanctum of legal experience."

We finished the meeting. I left the Attorney General's office and began to walk down the hall with Nathan Segal and Sol Lindenbaum, two of the four Jewish lawyers in the OLC. "We will help you get acclimated," said Nathan. "You will get used to the AGs hard questioning and his fast pace."

As we walked back to our respective offices, Nathan Segal, the soft-spoken and shy one, took me aside. "Morris, just a few words to the wise. Bobby can be easy to work for, as long as you come prepared. You were good today. Bobby can be a monster if you come unprepared. He likes candor, honesty, and brevity. In other words, get to the point as quickly as possible. He prefers you to say, "I don't know the answer, but I will find one," rather than fudge an answer to a question when you are not absolute. When you are not sure, just say so. He protects his loyal staff. He is also very protective of his brother, the President. He wants the public to see him as tough, fair, and independent, not as the little brother."

Nathan Segal became my new mentor. He was to become my "go-to guy and guide" whenever I had an intractable legal question. A few days later, I got another 9:00 a.m. call from our 33-year-old Attorney General Kennedy.

RFK: "Can you stop by? Do you have time? I need another tutorial."

MHW: "Coming right over!" I straightened up my tie, put on my jacket, and walked down the short internal direct corridor to the AG's office.

Bobby: "I want you to tell me the pertinent civil rights cases since Lincoln's emancipation of the slaves that have affected black people's rights. Please highlight each case, with a brief explanation of Supreme Court decisions held to be the law at that time."

Morris: "We need to start with Dred Scott, which was before the Emancipation Proclamation to give a full picture."

Bobby: "That's fine. Start with Dred Scott and then follow down to today. Update me on developing civil rights laws meant to protect black people in America and cite the pertinent cases. I never took civil rights in law school. My knowledge of black legal history is fuzzy." We worked together until it got dark. This time Bobby took notes, and I spoke.

RFK: "Give me a short history of the 'Stretch Cases,' like Hammer vs. Dagenhart."

MHW: "In Hammer vs. Dagenhart, in 1936, the Supreme Court saw fit to 'stretch' the flexible and elastic Commerce Clause a little bit to allow for social legislation, involving the prohibition of child labor throughout the United States. In 1936, during FDRs administration, Roosevelt stirred up the conscience of Congress to outlaw child labor. Congress based its social action on The Commerce Clause, saying that children were like chattel or goods moving in interstate commerce. Congress can regulate that movement or prohibit it. The power of Congress in this area of commerce management is plenary."

RFK: "What does the word 'plenary' mean in the present context?"

MHW: "Plenary means that the power of Congress is complete and pre-emptive. Congress occupies the field and knocks out any state's effort to try to enter and regulate interstate commerce. In controlling interstate commerce, Congress and Federal Law are supreme. Like Alabama or Tennessee, no state can interfere, nor can citizens who own big hotels like the Marriott or Howard Johnson's claim standing in Court to defy the power of the federal government in this area."

RFK: "What if Governor George Wallace sues the federal government for 'overstepping its power' in regulating the discriminatory behavior of hotel owners in rejecting black customers?"

MHW: "Then we will end up being in Court as a defendant. It won't be the first time. We should prevail and win. No guarantees. By hooking this power to force or oblige a social acceptance of intermingling onto the powerful Commerce Clause with the federal government's plenary power, it preempts state involvement by federal law, and it is indeed an awesome grab of federal power. The southern senators in the U.S. Senate will be ready to filibuster and debate the law to death. They will argue 'states rights' and say that the federal government has no right or business to be "dabbling in this social behavior area." They will argue that Congress has no influence or authority to overpower the states' jurisdiction to regulate social behavior. They will say that no one can force people to eat dinner at a restaurant with other people. They will stand on chairs and assert 'states rights' and 'the right to privacy.' They will impede and obstruct. You will have your hands full and can expect a strong and massive opposition. The constitutionality of the law will be severely tested in courts throughout the South. The law might fail. It will be up to the Supreme Court to serve as 'the final word' after the cases make their way up through the federal district courts and appeals courts."

RFK: "Getting the law passed will be the job of the Senate. We might lobby and try to influence, but we cannot control them. We can give them some good constitutional arguments for passing the law. Getting it upheld in the Supreme Court will be for you and our legal scholar Nick Katzenbach to argue before the nine justices."

MHW: We will have to write the new law in a way that the Supreme Court will accept and sustain it based on positive precedents we cite in our brief and oral arguments. The commerce clause is ironically the most substantial basis. It dealt in Hammer vs. Dagenhart in 1936 with children's rights to be protected against outlawed child labor. That was a social and political issue that the court was willing to deal with as a legal issue. It will be harder to suggest that the Supreme Court's regulation of discrimination and discriminatory practices can be reached as a legal issue. That is both the question and the task at hand for me to research and fashion a persuasive argument. I will be exploring the history of The Commerce Clause and its past applications to complicated questions. The Commerce Clause typically deals with the regulation of goods moving in interstate commerce and not with regulating the treatment of human beings stopping for the night at the Waldorf Astoria, the string of Marriotts along the major highways, or the Holiday Inn, or for an ice cream treat at Baskin Robbins. Regulating people's behavior and discrimination by law, particularly in Florida, Georgia, Alabama, Mississippi, and Louisiana, would prove revolutionary and dangerous.

MHW: "You see, sir, where we are going with this — possible interposition and armed conflict. There is a separation of powers. We have our job to enforce the federal law, Congress has its role in making the law, and the federal courts, especially the Supreme Court, have their job to interpret the law and the Constitution."

RFK: "We have our job as part of the judicial branch. Then the Senate has their duty to review, revise, and to pass the bill into law. We can only advise."

MHW: "During the past two days, I have read every civil rights case since the Dred Scott decision in 1857. In that case, Justice Taney made a foolish decision that led to the Civil War. Taney held that a white slave owner could take his black slaves as property with him as he moved from a previously slave state into a 'free' state. That decision caused a riot. I buried myself in the stacks at the Library of Congress and went back to read the civil rights cases of the 1870s and the Jim Crow laws of the1910s. I traced the thread of civil rights laws going back to 1803, allowing for slavery in the colonies and Sweatt v. Painter."

RFK: "Professor McDougal tells me you have a good sense of history. Where do you think we stand today in terms of American history? What did we do wrong? And I mean, where do we stand right now?"

MHW: "We have a potential second American revolution on our hands. Our black communities in Atlanta, Los Angeles, Chicago, and Houston are unhappy with the roadblocks preventing their people from reaching full equality. They do not trust white people at all. Some of the angrier ones are reverting to self-help and destruction, setting fires to stores, breaking glass in storefronts, looting, and injuring people, and stealing goods off the racks once inside the stores."

MHW: "We are seeing Freedom Riders going from North to South on Greyhound buses to Montgomery, Alabama to remove 'sitting in the back of the bus,' and as a reward, getting their heads bashed in free of charge."

"Students at lunch counters are pulled off their stools in the middle of being served at Woolworths. They are being dragged and forced out of the store. Both young and older adults are standing up for their rights all across America in big and little cities. We need to do something, or we will have riots in the streets. We need him to lead. People need a message that there is a change in the wind."

MHW: "Integrating the University of Alabama is in your plan. When do you plan to do that?"

RFK: "That is tops on my agenda for action. I want to integrate the University of Alabama peacefully. We need to live up to Brown v. Board of Education at the university level. We are in the third year of our administration. We promised black supporters we will live up to our campaign promise and achieve integration at college and university levels. Black people have been incredibly patient. They want what is part of their legal entitlement as citizens; they want what is theirs by law. The White Citizens Council in Birmingham is dead set against this idea. The integration of the University of Alabama could become explosive. We gotta make it happen. There has to be open access to universities."

MHW: "The law already supports you in Brown v Board of Education for opening up both the public schools and the universities. The justices ruled: 'separate but equal cannot be equal' in 1954. That time has come and gone, but the dream remains, and so does the law, and we have not implemented that decision. Black people see this, and they become cynical about the rule of law. They wonder how many decades will go by before they see enforcement of the law. They see a stop and go hesitancy and reluctance by white leaders to stand up to the plate and deliver. Feelings are building below the surface."

RFK: "Once more we have completed a session, a tutorial I like to call it with an abundance of new information and insight and knowledge but no final answers or policy."

MHW: "I beg to differ. The answers are clear; the question is whether the public is ready to accept and enforce the law. Thank you, Mr. Kennedy." I got up, shook hands, smiled, and left.

A few days later, I was the guest speaker at a Yale Law School luncheon for new students held at the Hay Adams Hotel in Washington, D.C., just eight blocks away. The invitation honored me. I somehow kept my remarks from that day and found them among my papers recently. I read them over before writing this chapter. My words rang true then, and they ring true again today. The very same remarks were pertinent to our nation's challenges in 1963 and are still timely and relevant today.

"You are a fortunate lot indeed to be accepted by my beloved alma mater, the Yale Law School. You will find teachers who care deeply about your future success and that you will find something socially responsible to do with your chosen career."

"As a national community, we are surprised by the evil of racism, when it has been with us all along. Every 40 or 60 years, our country is confronted openly and rudely by systemic racism. It starts with Dred Scott in 1857, and then with President Lincoln signing the Emancipation Proclamation in 1863, freeing the slaves. Well, they weren't really free."

"They did not suddenly share equality of all legal rights. Things stayed in the dark ages for blacks with racist laws reinvented to keep them down. The Dred Scott decision of 1857 said that 'The Negro is simply property belonging to his owner who is free to take him along whenever he moves, even to a free state.' These cruel decisions helped fuel energy for racism and for keeping black people hostage, with few possessions and no right to own land for the longest time."

"Plessy v Ferguson in 1898 was another confirmation of the "separate but equal" myth as Mr. Plessy, 7/8ths white, was ejected from an all-white railroad car. He sued and took the case to the Supreme Court and lost."

"This was a call to racism and humiliation as sanctioned again by the Supreme Court. That decision enforced discrimination as a national policy for 56 years until Brown vs. Board of Education in

1954. The Court ruled that railroad car owners and railroads could segregate blacks from whites in different cars without violating the 14th Amendment. Ironically, Mr. Plessy, an octoroon, had initially 'passed' as white and was seated in the 'whites-only' car when he was forced to move. "

"Then came Sweatt v Painter, which allowed the University of Arkansas to park its one black law student out in the corridor, listening to the law professor through an open classroom door. How humiliating! What was the University President thinking? Perhaps the black student had a positive virus of deep intelligence that would infect and overwhelm and even benefit the white students. So, keep him separate but equal in their hallway with the classroom door open. That was in the early 1950s. Then came the historic and groundbreaking Brown v Board of Education decision in 1954 with the Supreme Court voting 9-0 to end segregation in public schools. The ruling prohibited segregation among young people seeking an education in public schools, but is not yet fully followed as the 'supreme law' of the land."

My remarks were well received with a spontaneous standing ovation. I shared the positive reception that I received with the Attorney General the next day. Fortunately, he was supportive.

RFK: "It sounds like you gave them the stimulation needed to become great lawyers one day. Now, let's step away from speeches and focus on building a real law with enforcement and punishment for those who fail to follow the law. Insurrection, rebellion, and challenge is something I now anticipated at first throughout the South."

MHW: "I think you are realistic. The Kennedy brothers will not be popular in the South when you face reelection in 1964. That is just a year away. How will you deal with that?"

RFK: "To be discussed at a later time. It is now April 1963. We still have work to do to get the bill ready for Senate debate. Black communities must receive decent housing, genuine equality, and actual desegregation. It must become accepted as law. Also, equality of access must become our national policy in hotels, restaurants, theaters, and other places where the general public can relax and enjoy life. Why should they get anything less? They want their share of the fun. Now is our time to help make this happen and give Congress all the credit even though we write the law. We will get an awful lot done if we don't care who gets the credit."

RFK: "Everyone in our Justice department cares deeply about this issue. President Kennedy made a promise to achieve civil rights for every citizen during his first term. He ran for office on this promise. He committed to doing something major and earth-changing on civil rights. People treat black people like dirt. They go and fight for our country, lay down their lives, and risk death. They then return home to Georgia, Louisiana, Alabama, Mississippi, and even some places in the north, and are turned away. It happens right here under our noses in the District of Columbia. They are humiliated, insulted, and degraded. They are allowed to sleep in some fleabag hotels off the main highways, but not three or four-star hotels. They can't even eat at the lunch counters at Woolworths after shopping there and spending their money. It's not right, it's not American, and this is no way to treat people."

MHW: "We will make it happen."

The "team of four" drafted the proposed law during February and March of 1963, debating and arguing the precise words for precise meaning. Then I hand-carried the draft to the White House for review by White House Counsel Lee White and his Presidential advisers' staff. That took three weeks in April and then back to the OLC for final review and editing. Then, in May, it was sent to the U.S. Senate for committee review before presentation to the whole Senate.

Still today, I am amazed by the assignment of working with Attorney General Robert F. Kennedy during this historical period. Sixty years later, I see this was an invitation to walk within the corridors of history as our nation moved hopefully to end racism. We did not get there in 1963 and 1964.

Perhaps we can get there now. A significant battle remains, a battle of wills and intellects between those who want America to live out our manifest destiny as the nation of equals. In this extraordinary land, we live up to the original "pursuit of happiness" of living. Brotherhood and kindness and genuine acceptance lead us to live up to these values. That under God, "all men are created equal and endowed by their creator with certain inalienable rights." That among these are "life, liberty, and the pursuit of happiness."

In the 1960s, we were even against the diehards and white supremacists raising the Confederate flag and asking that we march backward into our past. In 1963, one could feel the buzz in the Justice Department and knew that regression would never happen. We were doing serious things with long term consequences. I faced this dilemma of choosing either The Commerce Clause or the Equal Protection Clause of the 14th Amendment. It seemed to me that equality of treatment had more to do with equal protection of the law. And that, in fact, appeared to be the most appropriate basis for the new civil rights law. However, I also had to consider historical precedents, and which choice between the two by Congress would survive a Supreme Court review. The legislation would be challenged as "illegal" in the Supreme Court as soon as it became law. It would be attacked and savaged by southern restaurant and hotel owners and other influential voices and interests, including Governor George Wallace, who wished to see it destroyed as a "violation of states' rights" and as "unconstitutional, an overreach by the Congress into states' rights."

As Bobby Kennedy indicated, earlier social justice legislation for protecting children, as in the Hammer v. Dagenhart prohibition of child labor case, in 1936, had been determined by the Supreme Court to be "a proper exercise of congressional power under The Commerce Clause." The Supreme Court was comfortable, as I had suggested at our first meeting in his office, with that section being plenary and powerful.

Kennedy was right about immediate testing of the legality of the new law. After Congress passed the Civil Rights Act on June 17, 1964, the Act was tested immediately by small hotel owners from Atlanta in "Heart of Atlanta Motel v Katzenbach." The nation waited for the Supreme Court to rule, and finally, the Court held the law valid under The Commerce Clause.

Research by the gang of four on The Commerce Clause proved sound and well-founded. We prevailed. The members of the Supreme Court had two choices: They chose the time-tested Commerce Clause and held the new civil rights law to be constitutional. Hotels and restaurants and other places of accommodation across the South began slowly to open up. It was an evolution rather than a revolution. And the change was achieved without bloodshed or demonstrations; it just happened. People accepted the change. Black families were now free to plan their summer vacations without going many miles off the main highways to find a place to eat or sleep. The Rule of Law prevailed.

The new Civil Rights Act of 1964 became a significant step forward for black people.
- **Title I: Voting** that prohibits unequal application of voting requirements. No more poll taxes or "tripwire word tests "or guessing the number of jellybeans in a jar" for blacks.
- **Title II: Public Accommodations** that prevent private businesses that serve the public from discriminating based on race, color, religion, or national origin.
- **Title III: Public facilities** that created a cause of action for those denied access to public facilities based on race, color, religion, or national origin.
- **Title IV: School Desegregation** gives the federal government more power in encouraging desegregation in public schools. Withholding of federal funds as a "source of inspiration" and motivation for integrating public schools.
- **Title V: Commission on Civil Rights**. The Commission was created in 1957. Title V gave it additional aggressive subpoena power and obligatory hearings attendance power

where civil rights violations in employment and housing and other matters were found.

On signing the Civil Rights Act into law on July 2, 1964, President Lydon Baines Johnson remarked that "the purpose of this historic new law is to promote a more abiding commitment to freedom, a more constant pursuit of justice and deeper respect for human dignity."

Senator John Sherman Cooper

John Sherman Cooper

My lucky conversation with Senator John Sherman Cooper of Kentucky began in Senate chambers, just off the Senate floor, soon after President Kennedy's death in late November 1963. I was eager and ready to move on from my position in the Office of Legal Counsel of the U.S. Justice Department. My boss, Bobby Kennedy, was in such a state of grief and shock that working at Justice had suddenly become quite depressing and painful. Life and dynamism had gone out of the office. It was like working at a morgue or living with a family in grief.

The draft of the Civil Rights legislation, written by four lawyers in the Office of Legal Counsel, was prepared for Senate debate. It was now completed, after a nine-month incubation period. Harold Reis, Sol Lindenbaum, Nathan Segal, and Morris Wolff — four Jewish lawyers dedicated to the Rule of Law and Justice — had written the omnibus Bill in Seven Sections or Titles.

I wrote Title II, both the history and the actual text. The title "Public Accommodations" was clear and without ambiguity. The new and revolutionary law would create significant changes in our fundamental way of life, especially in the American South. The new law affected businesses, such as hotels, restaurants, or movie theaters throughout the country. The new law said that "any place of business open to the general public as a public accommodation may not let some folks in and keep others out based on skin color or religion." Open to one: open to all.

We meant to bring a sweeping end to discrimination in hotels, restaurants, movie theaters, schools, public playgrounds, swimming pools, and other places generally open to the public. The reference for these places is "public accommodation."

I completed my job at Justice. It was time for me to move on to work in the United States Senate to ensure the civil rights law that we wrote was passed and enacted into law in its present inclusive form without delay. We did not want to see it end up in the trash bin or killed by an endless filibuster debate on the Senate floor. This bill would require strong bipartisan leadership, with two-thirds of the Senate willing to break a filibuster by recalcitrant southern senators. We needed a team of eight senators ready to show moral and political leadership and with the courage to serve as captains of the new law driving and steering its passage through the shallow and bomb-laden waters of the U.S. Senate.

Cooper, a fellow Yale graduate, was willing to risk his political life to do the right thing and become lead captain. The others were Hubert Humphry of Minnesota, Paul Douglas of Illinois, Joe Clark of Pennsylvania, Clifford Case of New Jersey, and Phillip Hart of Michigan. That is why I wanted to work with John Sherman Cooper. Plus, fortuitously, there happened to be an opening that the public never knew about. Mike Peertschuk of Senator Warren Magnuson's office called and told me about it. Mike had been my preceptor at Yale Law School and always looked out for opportunities for me on the Hill. He was selected by President Kennedy to serve as Chief of the Federal Trade Commission.

Across America, black people were angry and tired of waiting. There was severe tension in the land and the threat of riots as tempers flared in street protests. Expectations were on the rise. There was both robust support and powerful opposition to the bill. An influential group of powerful segregationist senators wanted to see the bill die a quiet death on the Senate floor and never come to a vote. These included John Stennis of Mississippi, Allen J. Ellender and Russell Long of Louisiana, Spessard Holland of Florida, Harry Byrd of West Virginia, and others from Arkansas and Tennessee, including Albert Gore Senior, former Vice President Albert Gore's father.

The state of Kentucky, a so-called "border state," was split with Thurston Morton, a rabid segregationist, and my future boss, John Sherman Cooper. The latter was willing to stick his neck out to support civil rights, even though his constituents were against it eight to one according to reliable statewide polls. I met with Cooper, "knees to knees" in the cramped and busy Senate chambers on my birthday, November 30, 1963.

I wanted to move to a job as an assistant to a U.S. Senator with access to the Senate floor. I wanted to be there when the debates about the constitutionality of the bill were about to begin. That is where the excitement and action would take place. The bill was not going to the committee. It was historic and significant. Thus, the bill was headed directly to the Senate floor. A moment in history was about to unfold! I had read, studied, and researched the major and minor civil rights cases from Plessy v. Ferguson in 1898 down through Brown vs. Board of Education in 1955 plus all relevant cases from 1955 to 1963. I was ready for the next step. I prayed for a position with a gutsy and principled senator willing to risk his political life for the good of the country. America was ready to live up to her original promise that "All men are created equal" and enjoy equal rights before the law.

Senator Cooper and I were sitting in a place generally reserved for senators, just off the Senate floor. He briefly reviewed my one-page resume, and after a brief discussion, he hired me on the spot and asked when I could start. Attorney General Robert F. Kennedy gave me a good recommendation. I had gone to Kennedy and asked for his permission to interview. He said, "Absolutely, yes. I want you to do this!" In a light and bright moment, Kennedy was incredibly supportive and warned Senator Cooper, in a letter, "Morris is bright and devoted to civil rights and the rule of law. He wants everyone to have the same chance, the same rights. If you decide to hire Morris, expect to have your point of view and core belief system actively challenged. Morris will challenge your ideas and the status quo. He has an ingrained habit of hitting the ball back hard and within the lines."

Kennedy demonstrated his astute political skills to Cooper and to me, "This will be a good deal. You are getting one of my bright young lawyers from the Office of Legal Counsel. You senator, in exchange, have agreed to work on members of the Senate to help us achieve passage of the 1964 Civil Rights Act."

The trade turned out to be a great move: It was deemed fair by both men. It proved to be an excellent step for me. Things were changing extremely fast around the country. Freedom rides from north to south were breaking up the stronghold of Greyhound Bus systemic segregation. People traveling from New York to Alabama could sit integrated for the first 100 miles but had to move their seats when they reached the Mason-Dixon line. Riots in Birmingham and the police brutality of "Bull" Conner by using robust stream hoses in the streets forced blacks to skip, dance, and be humiliated. Unequal and discriminatory treatment was rampant throughout the south and parts of the north, including at Woolworths, where blacks could buy food to go and were not allowed to sit at the counters. De facto segregation remained in schools, restaurants, hotels, lunch counters, balconies of movie theaters, and other places of "public accommodation."

The '64 Civil Rights Act — with broad sweeping consequences — was intended to end injustice and inequality. I was privileged to work with the team writing the law at the Office of Legal Counsel, the cockpit of the U.S. Justice Department. I argued for placing the constitutional basis of the bill firmly in The Commerce Clause, Article I, Section 8, Clause 3, "the regulation of interstate commerce," and in the 14th Amendment guaranteeing equal protection of the law. It turned out to be a smarter choice to have more than one basis for the constitutionality of the proposed legislation. The U.S. Supreme Court, in the case "Heart of Atlanta v. Katzenbach," made its decision upholding the law and chose only The Commerce Clause as a basis for finding "the exercise of Congressional power to be reasonable." Word at the time spread rapidly from the Justice Department to the Senate on Capitol Hill.

There was to be a full-scale knock-down-drag-out debate in the Senate. I was chosen by Senator Cooper to be his legal counsel during the Warren Commission hearings devoted to finding out the truth and the full circumstances of the murder of John F. Kennedy. I was also chosen to serve as Cooper's constitutional law advisor.

Working in Washington during the years 1963 -1964 was an exciting time of change, a rare opportunity to do historic work, and walk in the corridors of history. Few other periods in American history saw as much major decision-making accompanied by civility, dignity, courtesy, bipartisan consensus building, and gentlemanly debate. There was no belittling of other people or name-calling. Despite strong, and at times, rigid differences in political points of view, constituencies, and belief systems, the nation became healed and came together under bipartisan leadership. Statesmen such as John Cooper, Jacob Javits, Phillip Hart, Paul Douglas, and women like Senator Margaret Chase Smith of Maine gave their support freely to the "common good."

The work of the Warren Commission was completed, albeit with flaws, and the Civil Rights Act was passed by a 2/3 majority, as required to cut off prolonged debate. America survived, and the nation moved forward to a gentler and kinder period of putting up with each other and getting along together. Wounds healed with handshakes, dinner parties, and inferred agreements between men and women who put the nation's needs first. During that historic early summer of '64, before passage, I witnessed passionate and vitriolic debates on the Senate floor. Stubborn southern segregationists sought to kill the bill by an endless filibuster. The futurists confronted the segregationists and said it is time to move on. Segregation must be set aside in the interest of justice and the nation. This arguing lasted for two months from early May until June 17, 1964, when the bill was finally voted on and passed. "There is nothing as powerful as an idea whose time has come," intoned Senator Dirksen as he led the final arguments in favor of the bill. Ever the crafty politician, Dirksen of Illinois had opposed the new law but changed his vote when other senators promised the chance to give him the last speech. "Dirk" had an excellent sense of timing as a political opportunist with few bedrock principles. He confided to me, while in chambers, "One must, at times, change one's vote when you realize the tide is turning ineluctably against you. When they are getting ready to ride you out of town on a rail, get out in front before they tar and feather you and make it look like you are leading the parade." Cooper of Kentucky and others had done the heavy lifting. For Cooper, coming from Kentucky, a border state, to lead the fight for civil rights was tantamount to political suicide. The polls back home all said no. However, for Cooper, the maverick senator, whom one of his colleagues, John Stennis, called the "second Abe Lincoln," the answer was yes.

Cooper, Jacob Javits of New York, and Hubert Humphrey of Minnesota created a bridge of understanding and consensus among 67 senators. These senators came from different political backgrounds and passionate beliefs to force the passage of the historic Civil Rights Act of 1964.

I watched and listened with keen amazement at these critical moments in United States history. It all took place while I was working on the floor of the Senate. Like watching a movie, I watched, listened, and learned. It was a bipartisan group with Javits and Cooper being Republicans and Humphrey being a Democrat, an interaction not happening today.

A few months later, as winter set in on January 17, 1965, Senator Cooper stormed out of the Supreme Court's front door and walked gingerly down the icy steps towards my car. He is pulling up the collar of his overcoat to ward off the cold wind and icy conditions. He had just been attending a meeting of the Warren Commission. He was troubled by the superficial slapdash work of the Commission and its effort to paper over the facts. Commissions are of importance at some moment in history. They are formed to find out the truth. A commission is essential today in May 2021 to get to all the truth and facts related to the mob breaking down the front doors to the House of Representatives on January 6, 2021, to disrupt the electoral college meeting and the electoral process.

His first comment: "They are getting it all wrong. It is a whitewash, a rush to judgment. Justice Earl Warren is acting crazy and dictatorial, just like a banana republic dictator. He is not the moderate and patient man I knew from within liberal and moderate Republican circles. Warren is not his usual calm and temperate self. He is acting more like we are not to ask questions but be puppets on his string. I was carefully selected as one of two senators to deliberate as a member of this commission. I want to get down to the true facts. Who killed Kennedy? How many were involved in financing and backing this terrible moment in our history, this heinous assassination and put there as window dressing? He runs the hearings with an iron fist, speeding it along a fast track in an ungodly hurry, a rush toward judgment. This 'single bullet' theory is phony. Everyone on the Commission, including Senator Russell and Jerry Ford, believe it to be a clever, even ingenious, cover-up invented by a staff member, Arlen Specter of Philadelphia. President Johnson called me today, knowing we had a Warren Commission meeting, and he told me not to interfere, but to encourage. "Do your country judge thing," he said, "Get the facts. Make a case for the two killers — gunfire coming from both directions."

My answer: "Senator Cooper, why not slow things down, and insist on a careful collection of all the facts and a due process series of testimonies from all the witnesses? Just ask for more time and additional on-site investigations. You need more information on the separate direction and angles of the bullets. Someone must mark out just where they think the shooters were standing. That part is crucial; you are the only trial lawyer with courtroom experience. It is an honor and a duty. You were selected by LBJ to investigate. You aren't there to take part in a cover-up or slipshod work. You will look back and be ashamed of your work and your service if you assist their effort to throw a cold, wet blanket over the investigation. You are one of only two senators selected for that Commission to determine the circumstances of the death of President Kennedy."

Reply: "You are right. I am part of the Commission by order of the President. LBJ told me by phone, "do your duty, stay in the game, and make sure the outcome is honest and correct. Find both killers, or all three, and their identity if you can. I do not want this matter closed prematurely. If we do that, the results will come back to haunt us in years to come. I will follow the President's directive. That's what I will do."

He was freely disclosing confidential information. Cooper gave me prohibited information that the Commission marked:" confidential" to keep it from leaking or going beyond the walls of the investigation room.

However, Cooper felt compelled to discuss his plans and strategies for his work on the Warren Commission with someone. I was his lawyer. Being legal counsel to Senator Cooper was an honor and a stepping-stone. Lee White, my predecessor, "graduated" from Cooper's office directly to the White House. He had been snatched or stolen by JFK, with Cooper's complete approval and tacit agreement. Lee White went directly from working for Cooper into the inner sanctum of the White House. White became a counselor to the President, where he first served as lawyer to President Kennedy and, upon his death, was inherited by and kept as White House counsel by LBJ.

Lee White came at times to Cooper's office to coach and educate me in the diplomacy of my position with Cooper. White trained me to understand Cooper's quirky individuality and his courage to take up unpopular views but geared genuinely to the general good. Cooper became an active captain of the new civil rights law as it made its way through Congress. He ignored the mail from his Kentucky voters that ran against civil rights in a reliable poll. His only reaction: "They did not send me up here to be a rubber stamp. They sent me here to do what is right and best for the nation. Eight to one odds mean they will vote me out at the next opportunity. That's a definite sign they will choose to dump me out at the next election. I do not care. If I cannot do the right thing for now and future generations, then I do not belong here."

This position was not the first time Cooper faced a significant chance of political execution. He had lost before and served as Ambassador to India and then returned to win back his Senate seat. His devotion to principles and ideals cost him politically. Even though the white nationalists raised a big commotion and stuffed the polls, they could not stuff the ballot box. After championing and guiding the civil rights law through the Senate, Cooper amazingly was returned to office with the largest majority ever recorded in Kentucky history.

"Goes to show you," he commented on my visit with him in his living room at 2900 N Street shortly before his death. "When you choose to do the right thing, compassion, and respect come into play. People will admire you for standing for something. They admire a man or woman of principle, even though they might disagree with you. They will still grudgingly give you their vote if you are honest, reliable, principled, and consistent. They admire you when you stand tall. When you help the little people in the impoverished hollers of Appalachia, you must go to Congress and get the money for their programs. Stand for something special and good."

Cooper's gentle temperament, his remarkable intelligence, his ethics, and high-level core values were born and bred into him by his father, a minister, and a man of honor and backbone. Working with Cooper was a win-win. Men trained by Senator Cooper in the pitfalls and overarching purpose of public service and politics were winners. He wanted me to go to Kentucky and run for mayor of Louisville and eventually run for the Cooper Senate seat when he retired. Sounded like a great idea. I should have taken his advice.

We chatted further on the way back from the Warren Commission to our first-floor office at 103 Old Senate Office building. Cooper's coveted office space on the first floor of the old Senate building made it easier for him to answer roll calls. I opened the door to my tiny Fiat 600, and the senator unbent his long legs and stepped out. "We gotta get you a new car," he said. "This one is too tiny. We'll never survive an accident, and I want to live." We never located that new car. The jitney service continued in my pint-sized Fiat 600.

He was still upset by the cover-up as we walked into the Senate office building and headed down the ultra-polished floors of the venerable old office building. We walked through the Hall of Presidents with historical portraits of Washington, Adams, Jefferson, Lincoln, Wilson, Taft, and Roosevelt, with the most recent addition: John F. Kennedy. I took out my keys and opened the door to his private sanctum office at the back where he kept his

Jim Beam. He was still upset by something that had just occurred, and he sputtered, "They have it all wrong. They refuse to look at the facts. The forensics are right there. One bullet came in from the front, and the President grabbed his neck, and his head shot back in the open limousine. The car had slowed down in front of the Texas Book Depository. The next shot came in from the back, from a window on the 7th floor, the top floor of the Book Depository building on Dealey Plaza. A third shot came from behind the motorcade, jerking his head backward as he slowly passed the area. It was the shot fired by Lee Harvey Oswald, one of two or three killers. At least two were active that day, one from in front and the second from the back. The forensics clearly show there were at least two separate shooters, and they were standing in different places, one from the grassy knoll and one high in the office building. Our new President, Lyndon Baines Johnson, now wants to cover up and move on. I want to delay and get all the facts. They are covering the facts and putting their collective heads in the sand. LBJ pretends to give me the green light to press forward with the investigation. But he is secretly telling the others to bring the hearings to a quick close."

Senator Cooper was boiling mad, somewhat out of control for the only time that I had ever witnessed. "They want to bury the truth under a pile of stones. I think Lyndon Baines Johnson was involved in the planning and execution of Kennedy's death."

As his driver to and from the Warren Commission hearings, I got to hear the latest scoop on the way back. I was not just his legal counsel but also had become "Maxie the Taxi." Cooper selected me to convey him to and from the Supreme Court building for the hearings headed by Earl Warren, and that was a lesson van. On this Wednesday, Cooper emerged from the office building with a deep frown and tight-lipped. He opened the door of my little car and squeezed in. An angry scowl etched across his face. He ran his fingers through his gray hair and mumbled to himself, loud enough to hear.

"The last witness this afternoon told the truth," the senator said. "It was Mark Lane, a brilliant private investigator with integrity. He showed diagrams of how the shooter fired two crucial shots from in front of the cavalcade of cars. The shots came from the grassy knoll on a small hill in front of the caravan. President Kennedy was struck in the throat by one shot, and it was fired from in front and not behind, hence the presence of more than one gunman. Lee Harvey Oswald firing from the fifth floor of the Texas Book Depository building was not alone. I am being silenced and ridiculed by the other members of the Commission. They do not want to hear the truth."

I replied, "It seems the whole thing has gone political. There is a rush towards justice, and no one on the Commission wants to take time to study the facts and determine what really happened." He smiled. "They want to get it behind us as fast as possible. "

Cooper: "Even Senator Richard Russell, the only other senator on the Commission, wants to bring a swift end to the deliberations. LBJ is twisting his arm. He wants to get on to other matters on his agenda. Johnson and Russell are good ole boys from the south. They are part of the network, LBJ from Texas and Russell from Georgia. They want to use raw power to shut down the investigation. They could care less about finding out who was working with Lee Harvey Oswald to gun down the President in broad daylight. It's like a joke, and what is worse, it is a cover-up. The American people may never know the truth unless I can stall their efforts to end the hearings abruptly."

We drove on in silence. The trip from the Supreme Court building back to the office took only five to ten minutes. Five minutes on a good day, but this was a bad day. The senator trusted me with confidential information. I had access to the floor of the Senate, a privilege given to very few. Over the past six months, we had worked late in the Senate office, crafting Title II of what would become the "Public Accommodations" section of the Civil Rights Act of 1964.

In addition to our daily meetings in his office, we would meet each Sunday afternoon at his spacious red brick with black shutters home at the corner of 29th and N Streets in the Georgetown section of Washington D.C.

On one Sunday, we wrote "a letter of inquiry" to Attorney General Kennedy asking for a more in-depth explanation of sections of the new civil rights law draft. That letter and Bobby Kennedy's answer became the official reference for the Supreme Court. They used this letter and the Attorney General's reply for interpretation when it decided the legality of the '64 Act in the seminal case of Heart of Atlanta Motel v. Katzenbach, Attorney General.

My lucky conversations with Cooper continued for many years after his retirement. I would get phone calls at home, asking for my opinion on a myriad of different questions. Cooper wanted a sounding board, a place to bounce off his ideas. He was busy writing his autobiography and talked with me to fact check moments of our work together on the Civil Rights Act of 1964. He recalled our many quiet Sundays at his home. That was where he could let his mind relax and carefully evaluate legislation for Appalachia and "the poor folks back in the hollers of Kentucky." "That is why I served," he said. He was midway through his book when he passed away in 1991 at age 90.

The Chitlin' Circuit

The Chitlin Circuit was created for black people. It was an informal map charting out all the places in the segregated south where black people could eat or stay during the 1940s and 50s. It was a time when blacks were systematically being turned away from hotels and fine restaurants that catered to "whites only." Traveling black musicians like Duke Ellington, Dizzy Gillespie, and Louis Armstrong helped develop the circuit as a matter of necessity before America's civil rights days. They had the money to pay, but they were turned away.

This piece of information about a unique practice and clever necessity was brought to my attention in the spring of 1963, at my midterm early graduation from the Yale Law School. Why did I choose to graduate early, you might ask? Because there was no time to waste. Attorney General Robert F. Kennedy was assembling a small group, a team of just eight lawyers, to work within the U.S. Justice Department to write a significant new law. I was to become the youngest member of that law team to sit at the end of a long mahogany table with his top career assistants in the Office of Legal Counsel. Our assignment was to debate, draft, and conjure up a new Civil Rights Act. The new law needed to withstand the barrage of attack by a powerful and vocal group of southern U.S. Senators. They had already given notice that they would boycott and filibuster against any new and bold civil rights law conjured up by the Kennedy administration.

Attorney General Kennedy had contacted my international law professor Myres S. McDougal by letter and follow-up with a late afternoon phone call in December of 1962.

I was in McDougal's office at that time. He was known and beloved by his students as "Mac," the professor with a southern drawl and patience for every one of his devoted group of research assistants. He had a deep interest in civil rights, having "escaped from Mississippi," as he put it and "Senator Bilbo and the racists who controlled it politically" as he further put it. I was one of this select group of research people invited to look up good material for footnotes to his next scholarly book.

Mac's door was always left wide open for any of his students. He was a kind and caring human being who never played his high intelligence off against lesser lights, we lucky few who worked as his devoted research assistants. He was severely nearsighted and would sit reading at his desk with a green eyeshade covering his white hair and a large magnifying glass scanning and combing over law treatises and other books and student papers. We were in the middle of a law argument when the phone rang; it was his secretary. "Professor McDougal. Attorney General Kennedy is once again on the phone for you."

Attorney General Kennedy, "Mac, how are you. I need your help again. You were kind enough to send me Assistant AG Norbert Schlei, one of your research assistants. I am happy to report he is doing a great job as my Assistant Attorney General heading up the Office of Legal Counsel of my Department of Justice. The President and I bombard him with work."

I need another one of your talented graduates, like Norbert Schlei. Professor McDougal, might you have anyone else up there at Yale Law School that you can send me who understands the U.S. Constitution and particularly the line of cases and history of The Commerce Clause, especially Article One, Section 8, Clause 3? We are going all the way back to 'Hammer v. Dagenhart.' That is a 1936 case that held that Congress might employ The Commerce Clause as a basis for taking social action to correct and end racial discrimination, as it did in Dagenhart for eliminating child labor? We are working on writing a game-changing new civil rights law to stop the mistreatment of our black U.S. citizens. I met with Rev. Martin Luther King and Roy Wilkins, head of the NAACP, just this morning. The pressure is on within the black community to end The Chitlin' Trail and get some real changes fast. We are working on a tight time schedule. I need your help right away. They are arguing quite correctly that black young men can be drafted and go to war and lose their lives for America. Still, they can't come home and rent a room with their black family at the Marriott Hotel or Howard Johnson's or eat lunch peacefully at the Sheraton and Hilton restaurants or even eat at lunch counters at the five and dime at Woolworths."

Myres McDougal: "Mr. Attorney General Kennedy, I grew up in Mississippi. I know all about the infamous Chitlin' Trail. It was a makeshift necessity and a scandal. It was a well-planned means of survival for black men, women, and families, and especially black musicians playing at different jazz locations throughout the south. Black musicians would keep a notebook of hotels and restaurants where they could be served in peace without any hassle in Alabama, Louisiana, Mississippi, and other parts of the south. The Chitlin Trail is a paradox; it is a story of abuse, practicality, and survival. It was the only way black people could move about the south. We need a new law that gives black people the same freedom everyone else has to stay at hotels for the night and restaurants without being told to go around back and order from the window.

If you really plan to draft a law to eliminate this discrimination in public places, I will find you one of my best to come and work with you. That's a deal."

Myres McDougal: "The Chitlin Trail continues as a rotten and undeserved form of acute humiliation and racial discrimination. I am still angry as someone who had to flee the south to get a good job teaching law. I needed to get to Yale to maintain my own sanity and freedom of thought. I was a pariah in the south, and Senator Bilbo wanted me long gone from the University of Mississippi. There was no due process. The police were like vigilantes beyond control. They arrested and harassed blacks and invaded their homes with no search or arrest warrants and without probable cause. People were thrown in jail for months and physically and mentally abused while awaiting 55 days and longer for a hearing. They were thrown in jail on a whim or if they were "uppity" and spoke out for civil rights and to stop the lynching and false arrests. It is still quite dangerous with a ton of different lynchings that have never even been reported or investigated by the state of Mississippi."

"I am glad, Attorney General Kennedy, that you are sincere in writing a new civil rights act that will also deal with police abuse of the innocent."

McDougal: "That Chitlin Trail, incidentally, do you know how the name of the circuit came about? Chitlins are the intestines and guts of the pig, a dish that black folk love. So, the roadmap was like a delicacy among black people — everyone to their own taste. But for blacks, it is a symbol for a survival circuit like the underground railroad during slavery as an escape route to the north. It is a different secret map for survival and opportunity. It is a different map but under the same plague of discrimination perpetrated by the majority."

Kennedy: "Let me describe the lawyer I need, and it can be a man or woman. He or she needs to be creative and bright. I need someone who talks back. He can be a bit abrasive like me as long as he makes other people around the table sit up, think, ponder on his ideas, and take notice. I need him right away. He must know The Commerce Clause and its flexibility in being used to regulate all kinds of activities. The law team is being formed by Norbert Schlei. You recommended Norb to me. I want another person like him with a sharp, quick sense of humor and diplomacy. Can you help me?"

McDougal: "I have some good candidates I might recommend. In particular, I have one bright young maverick, a contrarian, a left-handed tennis player who is very competitive in the field of new ideas. He is sitting in my office right now, debating and actively disagreeing with me on the reach of international law and a couple of points of law. He is a hard worker and an idealist who hates injustice and bullying. He hits the ball back hard, and he loves to play devil's advocate."

McDougal: "I think he might be your man, and I will talk with him about it after we get off the phone. He happens to be a Jewish boy with plenty of brains and chutzpah."

Kennedy: "That's fine. Actually, I can tell you the rest of the team is Jewish and very bright and hard-working. He'll feel and be right at home. Assistant Attorney Generals Norb Schlei, Harold Reis, Sol Lindenbaum, and Nathan Segal are the working team. This "Jewish mafia" has a passion for civil rights. These men could quit the DOJ, form a Jewish law firm, go out in private practice any day, and make a bundle. Fortunately, they prefer working on this exciting new law."

McDougal finished the chat and hung up the phone. He turned to me with a smile, took off his green eyeshade, and laughed. "Timing is everything. You're going to Washington, Morris. You will be privileged to be working with Attorney General Robert Kennedy and his elite team of Jewish lawyers. They are all the cream of the crop, career men with 15 to 20 years of Department of Justice law experience. They have worked their way up the ranks over the past 20 years. The Office of Legal Counsel is the top spot, a place where government lawyers dream of reaching. You are one lucky man. You will be arriving there by express train. I will see to it."

I was stunned. I could never imagine this kind of lucky opportunity falling in my lap. I took my final exams early and boned up on The Commerce Clause and its potential place in Civil Rights Law along with the 14th Amendment focus on due process and nondiscrimination under the Equal Protection Clause. I took the train to Washington, D.C. in early January and went right to work with Bobby Kennedy and his civil rights legislation team.

That is how I got to help write the Civil Rights Act of 1964. My assignment was Title II, "Public Accommodations." Public areas and water fountains were now open to everyone. The south removed signs that said "Colored" or "For Whites Only." We had a strong new federal law that made America reach towards greatness again.

Passing this Act was the start of a long and creative law career. Seeking fairness and justice was to become the hallmark of my career through 40 years of human rights litigation. When the American Bar Association called, I went to Chile and rescued five women from jail, held without trial and without bail. I did this by going down there at my own expense and interviewing them with my law partner Juan Laredo, Esquire, of Philadelphia in the dungeon prison in dangerous Santiago in 1985. Then, I came home and persuaded and lobbied Congress pro bono to pass a law boycotting and prohibiting the importation of grapes from Chile ("Los grappas") into the port of Philadelphia and elsewhere in the USA until the innocent women were released and due process restored. They were quickly released three days after the actual boycott, and prohibition of import went into law and practice.

I sued the Soviet Union for the release of Raoul Wallenberg. I wrote a book about my unpaid efforts to gain freedom for Wallenberg, the Swedish diplomat hero of the Holocaust who courageously rescued 100,000 innocent Hungarian Jews from the Holocaust. On January 17, 1945, Wallenberg was kidnapped by the Russian 18th Red Army in Budapest and criminally assaulted and taken to the Russian Lubyanka prison in Moscow in January 1945, in violation of his diplomatic immunity and basic human rights and held incommunicado in Moscow and ice-cold Siberian jails.

On February 2, 1984, I filed a federal lawsuit in the U.S. District Court in D.C. and won a $39 million verdict against the Soviet Union. Without law, there can be no freedom. Without due process, there is no law. This applies to Wallenberg and all good men and women who are victims of human rights violations. And without Myres McDougal, there could be no me.

Divine Providence on a Cold November Day

On my 57th birthday, November 30, 1993, the sun came up on a crisp blue sky in New York City. I decided to take a walk and kick the leaves on an autumn day in Central Park. I was walking to work with my law partner and friend, Stephen Beck. We enjoyed these daily walks. We used them as an opportunity to discuss world events and some of our pending international litigation cases. Suddenly, I spied "our first lady," Jackie Kennedy Onassis, walking towards me just a few feet away. She was almost in my lap. I could see her smiling dark eyes looking keenly at me, so I returned the brief moment of flirtation. It seemed like she was giving me a second glance. "In your dreams," I told myself. I had an upfront and personal opportunity to say, hello there and to ignite a brief lucky conversation. "Walk up and just say hello," said my inner voice.

Steven Beck and I were walking towards our Manhattan law office. We had plans to be there as usual by about nine to answer international phone calls. We specialized in global law. Wide-eyed, I breathed to him, "Hey man, that's Jackie Kennedy," I said, pointing towards her as she walked, idly kicking the autumn leaves into the air. He walked on, ever ready to do his duty as my law partner. I, the opportunist, stopped dead in my tracks. I was going to chat up Jackie. Law biz could wait.

She was dressed warmly for a November day. The sky was cobalt blue and the sun shining, with a temperature hovering at 32 degrees. I felt I was back in college again at Amherst College, flirting with this beautiful, high-class coed in the camel hair coat and blue earmuffs. Like a Smith College coed, she was young and vibrant with her jaunty, royal blue earmuffs, and a camel hair tan coat with a Schiaparelli scarf of blue and white to complete her look.

I was excited, transposed as if lifted to a higher level. Time stood still for a moment as I tried to think of something quick and positive to say that might stop her in her tracks. She was like an innocent young and vulnerable college girl, standing there in Central Park. She did not look her age at all. Nor were there any age lines of tragedy in her beautiful face. I felt like I might be falling in love all over again for the first time right on the spot. We had a quick flirtatious smile exchange. Her smile seemed to indicate she knew me. I wanted to meet and speak with her no matter what. So much to share.

"No way I am going to the office, let Steve go," I thought. "I will find a quiet way to approach Jackie and say hello. Hell, I had worked for both of the Kennedys. Why not let her know exactly that? I had met and advised the President. I saw Jackie that day in 1963 out in the Rose Garden when the President met with my AIESEC international student leaders. She was there with John-John and Caroline for our reception in the Rose Garden after briefing the President alone in the Oval Office. "Just walk up and say hello," I mumbled to my better self. "Just say something nice and do it now." Meeting Jackie was an opportunity that would evaporate if I stayed tongue-tied. "Capture this moment, you fool! In a few seconds, she will pass right on by. You will be left speechless, like two ships passing in the night. What is your plan of action? Be quick about it. A beautiful lucky conversation is about to happen!! Do not let it get away." I stood and watched for a moment as the wind caused the flying leaves to swirl back down to her feet. She seemed to be daydreaming, not fully there. She was possibly in another world all her own.

I piped up. "Mrs. Kennedy, I worked for Bobby Kennedy, and I met you briefly in the Rose Garden with the President, and your two children, John and Caroline. They were young."

She stared at me, and her eyes blinked. She was trying to remember the place and time. It sounded safe, and not someone trying to invade her freedom to take a walk.

I continued, "It was in April 1963, 30 years ago. I brought a group of foreign students to meet the President." A serendipity meeting and a lucky conversation was about to happen as if by chance. I walked gently and slowly towards Jackie. I was eager to talk with her and to discover topics to talk about. It was destined to happen. She chose to chat with me.

I seized this opportunity. I admired her and also had a crush on her, as many men did. So, as Steve peeled off to go to work, I quietly walked up and stood in front of her, in effect, gently blocking her way. She looked up and said, "Hello," showing no fear as if flirting and welcoming the chance to speak with me. I said, "Hello, Jackie. I am one of your most devoted fans," I quickly added, "It is true. I worked for your brother-in-law, Bobby, at Justice."

"What kind of work did you do? Was it civil rights or something less interesting?"

"It was civil rights and a lot of research of old civil rights cases dating back to 1898 and coming forward to 1963. I helped to write Title II of the Civil Rights Law, the part about desegregating lunch counters in the south, along with busses, hotels, restaurants, law schools, swimming pools, and everything else." I was somewhat nervous, just standing there in the cold and tried to cut myself off by not rambling too much. Short sentences were best, and sentences that answered her questions posed.

Jackie stood there politely listening, brushing the hair from her face. She was waiting for the next thing in our chat to happen. I saw her smile at my recollection of those historic days of 1963 in both of our lives. She was shy and reserved, not a flirtatious manner at all. She seemed unafraid and was willing to trust me, given my service credentials to her family and the nation.

The autumn sun was shining on both of us, casting our shadows onto the green grass. New Yorkers walked by on their private and personal missions, including walking towards getting to work on time on the East Side. Everyone, like scurrying ants, seemed to have a purpose of greater importance. Most were headed to work on the other side of Central Park. The air was clean, and the wind died down. She smiled and did not move. I searched for something else to say to sustain this fragile conversation. Jackie appeared willing to stay longer and to chat. She seemed to relish the chance to speak with someone who knew her husband. I quickly followed up, wanting her to remain feeling comfortable, at ease, and safe all at the same time.

"You conducted yourself with grace, dignity, and class as our First Lady. I admired how you refurbished, redecorated, and brightened up the White House with the help of others." I was now gasping for air and standing next to her. I then quickly uttered more personal words, "I enjoyed working for your brother-in-law, Bobby, in the Department of Justice. It was my first law job out of Yale Law School. He selected me as one of ten lawyers to be on the Attorney General's Honors Program."

She stood still, poised, and smiled. Her dark eyes glistened and focused, like a shy and timid but feminine doe in the woods caught in a moment of chewing, while looking up from foraging for greens on a winter's day. She raised her eyes quickly at the mention of Bobby Kennedy's name. "Oh my, Bobby was my favorite of all the Kennedy boys. He took excellent care of me right after the assassination. He visited me every day for six months. Without his support, I would have checked out. "

I was amazed by her candor and truth. "Bobby was exceptional and caring. He was the best. I trusted him. He was a warm human being. Under that make-believe stiff upper lip shield of toughness, there was a sweet and real man." I agreed with her.

"My office was next to Robert Kennedy's on the 5th floor. He was all business; he was devoted to the President. He kept his social distance until he felt he knew you, which took several intimate conversations until I was allowed into his inner sanctum. Conversations after working hours, often going into 9:00 or 10:00 p.m., helped. The mutual feelings of confidence in each other grew bit by bit, as we worked on projects together."

Jackie: "Were you aware of the tension and distrust between Bobby and FBI Director J. Edgar Hoover? Hoover tried to blackmail Bobby after the President died."

Morris: "Most definitely. Hoover was partial to Vice President Lyndon Baines Johnson. We were aware that Hoover tapped Bobby's phones and reported directly to Johnson. Hoover's office was in the same Department of Justice building, just three floors above. Bobby knew that J. Edgar was wiretapping his phones and planning to blackmail him. He had tapped and tried to blackmail Martin Luther King to stop the Civil Rights March on Washington on August 27, 1963."

I continued, "One rarely saw Bobby's warmth. He was always on guard, rarely relaxing. During meetings in his office, Bobby was always careful to avoid any reference to J. Edgar. The enmity between the two men was huge. We knew it was always there beneath the surface. Bobby was loyal and caring. He cared about his staff, the people who worked for him. Bobby also cared deeply for the poor people of Appalachia in the bituminous coal country of West Virginia. Bobby worried about those who did not have enough to eat and suffered from poor hospitals, poor housing, and dangerous jobs. He cared about the poor elsewhere in the nation, as well. He spoke about his feelings constantly."

"He was all business; very focused. During our working conferences drafting the Civil Rights Act of 1964, there were great exchanges of ideas but little room for his ironic sense of humor, his needling of us, his political charm, and warmth. In my time with him, he rarely relaxed or told jokes. We saw Bobby's tenseness, focus, and devotion to his brother every day. We were obliged to wear the same serious face."

Jackie: "What were your happiest and most fulfilling moments of work with Bobby?"

Morris: "He had a great feel for people and what they wanted and needed. He deeply cared about injustice and people getting less than their fair share of the law's protection. Bobby was a tactician and strategist. He knew how to take complex and tense confrontational human situations and make them peaceful with no bloodshed or heads beat and people injured and humiliated. I worked with him in developing the strategy for the peaceful integration of the University of Alabama. My most fulfilling moment was sitting with him on the same tan leather couch in his office on the day the University of Alabama was finally integrated, on June 10, 1963. It was an act of statesmanship by Bobby to avoid bloodshed during the University of Alabama's historical integration in the spring of 1962. The iron fist in the velvet glove. That was my happiest and most rewarding moment. It went like this. I researched the federal law giving him the power as Attorney General to co-opt and federalize the Alabama National Guard if needed, to avoid bloodshed under 28 U.S. Code 1331."

"I sat next to him on the tan leather couch, placed in front of his desk. We watched together the events unfolding at the University as two black students approached the enrollment office. It was all carefully staged."

"There was a black and white television screen set up just for that day placed in front of us. It was 11:00 a.m. as planned, and the moment that Nick Katzenbach was to walk with the two black students towards the door of the University of Alabama. Hundreds of blacks and whites were on the scene, standing there in the hot sun, quietly and patiently watching, and waiting for the potential drama of confrontation and bloodshed to unfold. Governor George Wallace, at 5' 8," was standing there truculent and defiant at a podium making a speech and barring the door as he had promised his supporters he would do. We sat and watched in silence as Wallace finished his racist/white supremacist "whites only" speech. The two brave black students began walking toward the front door of the University."

George Wallace standing defiantly at the University of Alabama

"Then, Bobby, sitting in his Washington office, carefully and quietly said into the microphone wire so only Nick could hear, 'Nick, remember our plan. Let the Governor have exactly five minutes to make his little speech of defiance about segregation now and segregation forever.' We will let the Governor save face by defending segregation. When finished, ask him politely to step aside and allow the three new black students to enter, go to the admissions office to enroll, and attend their first classes.'

"It was carefully planned and staged in advance with all parties and with the police precisely knowing what was happening. It was a masterful moment of political theater and acumen. Both sides promised there would be no shooting, bloodshed, or violence. It was all staged, and it went off as planned. I watched, sitting with Kennedy, and holding my breath, in his office. We cheered as the young black people with quiet dignity and grace walked towards the door and into the University. Governor Wallace kept his word. He made his political points and stepped back. This successful handling by remote control was diplomatic and peaceful. We helped students of color to achieve their civil right to enter and study at the University of Alabama."

"What was one other top moment of satisfaction in working for Bobby?" We stopped for a moment on a stone bridge in the Alice in Wonderland surreal section of Central Park. We were crossing a stream and pond where kids were floating miniature sailboats, their white sails shining in the sunlight.

"There were several; I will choose one. We made a trade of pharmaceuticals for the rescue of our heroes from the Bay of Pigs fiasco. We rescued our citizens from the Bay of Pigs swamp, a poorly planned mission by the CIA gone awry. Their landing crafts never reached the beaches of Cuba. They were captured and dumped into filthy Cuban jails, and the President ordered us to find a way to bring them home. We had to bring them home. The public was on our backs, along with residents in Miami and other Cuban strongholds in Florida. We created an ingenious barter deal, drawn up by our internal tax division head, Lou Oberdorfer."

"Lou and I took off on a two-week trip around the nation, visiting major pharmaceutical companies. Lou was a talented genius and an unsung hero. It was a secret mission approved by President Kennedy. We persuaded these companies that it was in the national interest that they give Cuba a share of their second-generation products or drugs. In return, the companies received a significant tax write-off. Baxter-Travenol, Merck, Abbotts Labs, Warner-Lambert, and Smith Kline volunteered. They gobbled up the opportunity and shipped old but non-expired drugs, no longer favored but still marketable in the USA, down to Cuba. They took their significant write-offs over a three to five-year period, and we got our boys' home. Everyone won. Fidel and JFK were happy."

"At last, there was something on which they could agree. The deal was kept secret until all the young heroes were safely back home in the USA. I worked on that deal from day one with Lou. It was satisfying being a part of the success in bringing these good young men home."

"My other top moment, as mentioned before, was researching the law and persuading Bobby and Nick to federalize the National

Guard of Alabama to protect the new students and avoid bloodshed. Wallace had no power left. The power was on our side entirely. We allowed him to make his little speech and then step aside."

"We made history that day, right there in Alabama by remote control from Washington direct by phone to Birmingham. We achieved a peaceful integration, and I researched the federal law allowing for the deputizing of the Alabama National Guard to persuade the Governor to stay calm and allow the University's integration. Coach Saban still thanks me for that day."

Jackie smiled and stared at me quietly as her eyes filled with tears. She began to cry. "I was alone after the President died. No one seemed to care. Bobby was the only one. He was loyal and caring all through the terrible days of trauma. I was in an extended period of mourning." She shared vulnerable and intimate moments of her life as she was still recovering from the awful memory. It was something we all felt.

Brushing back a tear, she dried her eyes with my handkerchief, and she continued, "I do not understand how we met, Morris, but it has been a perfect moment for me. I have reconnected with some terrific memories just by your being here. I was down in the dumps for the past few days. Now I am happy and walking in the fresh air and sunlight here in my favorite area of Central Park. I usually come here from my apartment near the park. Do you think this is just a chance meeting? Do you believe in spiritual coincidence? I was wondering what this nice man is doing here on this nice day in Central Park. Are you still working? Here in the city? Are you playing hooky from work and out for a walk in the park?"

Morris: "Well, it just happens to be my 57th birthday. I am giving myself a birthday present of being with you." We both laughed. "Maybe this walk with you is my surprise birthday present."

"Normally, during the week, I am at the office practicing law with Trien and Beck, a boutique international law firm on the east side of Central Park. I walk for my daily exercise each day through the park for 45 minutes on my way to work. Normally I go straight to work. Today I saw you and was stopped in my tracks. I always wanted this to happen."

"I am also writing a book. I sued the Soviet Union for the release of Raoul Wallenberg and won a $39 million verdict. I also won a judicial order from Judge Parker for his immediate release. We intended for the 39 million to be a proper penalty for their kidnapping Wallenberg from Hungary. The Judge asked, and I said 39 million for the 39 years of imprisonment in the Soviet Gulag. Wallenberg was a brave Swede who saved 100,000 Hungarian Jews during the Holocaust in Budapest."

"I am taking time from my law practice to work on the book on Raoul Wallenberg and my efforts to rescue him from Russia. I was honored to be his lawyer, and I worked pro bono for his release. I sued the Soviets in U.S. Federal Court in Washington, D.C. I am still waiting to receive the judgment and the money. My satisfaction is in winning and having the world know and remember Wallenberg's plight. I doubt we will get any money." We laughed together.

"Be patient. The Russians must pay you. You earned it."

Jackie continued, "I know about Wallenberg. I am interested in your book. We are looking for new books at Morrow and Company where I am working as an editor and a judge of new books. When you finish your manuscript, please bring it to me. I want to read and possibly edit it and see if Morrow might publish it one day." I brought her some chapters the following week.

I was thrilled by her generous gesture. It was more than a gesture; she was serious. My Kennedy connections were paying off finally. This offer of assistance was unexpected but welcomed. This opportunity to work together thrilled me.

I noticed a man standing 15 feet away outside the park and leaning on a green four-door Mercedes Benz sedan. The man was waiting for her and keeping a close eye on Jackie. We were walking together along a quiet path. Jackie was kicking the leaves again like a teenager.

She continued, "Thank you for your kind comments about my fixing up and refurbishing the White House with new furniture and stuff. It was my dream, my mission as First Lady. The people's house needed sprucing up. It was falling apart, and the people did not know it. When they knew, the contributions poured in. There was a sad and old atmosphere to it when the Eisenhower's left — dowdy and waiting to be reborn. We brought new life with concerts by Pablo Casals, and with Henri Matisse and French impressionists in a White House art exhibition."

"It was different when Jack was President. The White House was in a miserable condition when we moved in. The pipes were old and rusted. The place was freezing, almost without heat in the family quarters the night we moved in. The walls everywhere needed painting. I put in all new furniture in the Oval Office and kept the Lincoln desk there. I worked with colonial-style authentic cabinet makers to restore the furniture in the main rooms."

She continued, now with a smile returning, "Lincoln was my husband's favorite President, along with Franklin Roosevelt, Thomas Jefferson, and John Adams. I studied the taste of these three presidents. It was a lot of work, but I loved it. I only stopped after they shot the President."

She began to cry again, and I handed her a clean, white handkerchief, which she kept. She wiped her eyes and laughed, "I will return this to you, both clean and new." I said, "Keep it," and she did.

We walked towards the end of the path. We were coming out on the east side of the park. "I have to go. Please stay in touch." She reached in the pocket of her coat. She gave me her card with her business address. And then she was gone with a wave of goodbye.

The following week Jackie and I met again to discuss my book on Raoul Wallenberg. I had finished the first three chapters. "This book of yours has great promise," she said. "Leave this copy of these first chapters with me. Trust me. I will get back to you." This meeting was the last time we met. Our lucky conversation is a happy memory, and I think of her on my birthday every year. She was a 1993 birthday gift, and I am grateful even for that brief shining moment of our sharing sunlight and conversation in Central Park.

Jackie Kennedy was already ill but hiding it. She was diagnosed with incurable cancer the week before our first meeting. There was no way to save her. She put up a gallant fight, only to succumb a few months later. I believe it was by Divine Providence that we met in Central Park. One minute one way or the other, or if we took a different path or a different day and we would not have touched each other's life. Jackie is my most lasting and happy memory of all the Kennedys. She was a refined, gifted, and beautiful lady with class, style, wit, and courage.

I hope we meet again one day in heaven. Perhaps we will have another chance to kick the leaves like we did in Central Park and swap stories and memories. This time we will walk hand in hand. It will be playtime with Jack and Bobby also there.

If You're Black, Step Back

Malcolm X was an angry, bitter, and fiery young preacher with a noisy message. I debated with him for an hour in Washington, D.C., in front of the Justice Department in August of 1963. This meeting was a few days before the "I Have a Dream" speech of Martin Luther King on August 27, 1963. At the end of our debate, I found I had made a new friend and had a lucky conversation.

My first job out of Yale Law School was with Bobby Kennedy. They chose me as one of ten lawyers from across the country for the prestigious Attorney General's Honors Program. This selection was in January 1963. I worked on briefs and questions sent over from the White House. I received a private office in the Office of Legal Counsel (OLC) on the 5th floor, just thirty yards from the Attorney General. The position was power. I was next to the second most powerful man in the United States. In my first month, I met J. Edgar Hoover. His office was on the 7th floor. He and Bobby did not get along well at all.

It was part of my job to review the legality of FBI actions, both before and after the activities took place. It was also part of my job to write the first draft of the 1964 Civil Rights Act along with Harold Reis, Nathan Segal, and Sol Lindenbaum of the OLC. A triumvirate of three white Jews wrote Title II of the Civil Rights Act. African Americans can now eat lunch in public restaurants, sleep at a Marriott Hotel, and buy one of the twenty-eight flavors at Howard Johnson's. This equality was after putting their lives on the line in World War II and the Korean Conflict. The battle for equality is not over.

 One day on the way to lunch with my friend Marty Wagner, I was stopped by a young light-skinned black preacher, with rimless glasses and a Bible in his hand as I came out of the building.

"Do you guys work up there?" he asked, pointing back to the Justice Department Building. "Are you working for Justice?"

There was an ambiguous, combative, and cynical tone to his question. I didn't know if he asked philosophically or to gain his bearings at the corner of 10th and Constitution.

"Why did you come here?" I asked him.

"I am looking for a man for a debate. My name is Malcolm X, and I don't believe you can achieve justice or that anyone can grant it to you. I believe a man has to fight for justice."

"You can't just carve the word JUSTICE on a building and then go after achieving it by passing a bunch of laws. You need a revolution to achieve justice."

And thus, we began our unexpected debate on the Justice Department's steps on a hot summer's day in August 1963, just two days before the March on Washington. At this moment in his life, Malcolm X was a bystander, one of a million black men who came to the capitol for the march.

Years later, in 2003, my students at Morehouse College, a black men's college in Atlanta, could not believe that I debated Malcolm in the summer of 1963, but I did. And I recorded it. Malcolm is MX, and I am MW. It went like this:

MX: "Passing new civil rights laws will be a new cover-up for keeping the black man down. Jim Crow laws were passed back in 1898, telling black folk where they can sit, travel in separate railroad cars, and not eat in your restaurants. Black men still come to the back door for 'take out.' We don't get to sit down inside next to y'all for a hot meal."

MW: "We're working to change that. That is what Title II of the new law is all about. Ending discrimination in places of public accommodation is the title. From now on, black and white and everyone in the United States can travel anywhere, stay overnight in a hotel, eat, and go swimming where you like, and sit anywhere in a movie theater."

MX: "Are you kidding me? There will be riots in the streets if you try that." He shifted his Bible from one hand to the other. His dappled brown skin was a very light shade, and he spoke quietly. There was no ruckus during the hour of our conversation. We missed lunch that day, but it was worth it.

MW: "That's why we're trying to do this by a set of new laws. Title II will make it unlawful to discriminate in places of public accommodation, such as places normally open to ten or more people. It will apply to restaurants, hotels, movie theaters, schools, shopping malls, and any place open to the general public. We can then prosecute any violators."

MX: "Laws will accomplish nothing. You need power and violence. You can't legislate human behavior. Equality through laws? That's a joke."

MW: "First, you need a legal framework for social change. Laws and lawyers can assist in the process. Discrimination is an insult; it's a slap in the face. It's unfair. The time to end discrimination has come."

MX: "The question is how. You can't just pass a law and, with a snap of the fingers, make it happen. People won't change. They'll dig in their heels. There'll be more people joining up with the Ku Klux Klan. You can't even go in through the same doors to a so-called public library in parts of the South, much less a restaurant or a hotel. Schools? Housing? Forget it. It will never happen. It's all based on the color of your skin." A crowd began to gather to witness and listen to our impromptu debate. "My people are angry," he continued. "If you're black, step back, if you're brown, stick around. If you're white, you're alright." The crowd laughed at his rhymed poem. That's the way it is, he went on. "You guys upstairs in this building won't even make a difference. Fifty years from now, it will all be the same."

Over the next 50 years, Malcolm was proven to be wrong. Through the power of the Civil Rights Law of 1964, places of public accommodation were forced to change their segregated practices. If they wanted to stay in business, they had to open their doors to everyone with a warm welcome to all people, regardless of color. It took the March on Washington, Martin Luther King, and many peaceful student protests for the new law to take hold. It took preachers, lawmakers, and presidents to make it happen. I was one of the writers of the new law, a small part of the process. My debate with Malcolm X was part of the process, as well. And yet, so much more needs to be done in light of the George Floyd, Breonna Taylor, and other tragedies. System discrimination in housing and work opportunities remain to be solved. The peaceable kingdom has not yet arrived.

MW: "There are rising expectations, and the creek ain't goin' to stay in the same place. We know that. That's why Title II of the new law will start the ball rolling. We will eventually eliminate discrimination in schools, restaurants, swimming pools, libraries, buses, hotels, all places open to the public at large."

MW: "My work will not be a waste of time," I answered. "Marty and I, we're trying to write a law up there," I said, pointing to the windows on the fifth floor. "That's where we are working with Bobby Kennedy to write the Civil Rights Act of 1964."

Malcom X

Young Malcolm X was not yet known. He was just a young black preacher, soft-spoken, chiding in nature, and a cynic. He was carrying a book in a black leather case with the word "Bible" inscribed in gold. This meeting was before his trip to Africa, which set him on fire and turned him into a noisy demagogue. He was shot by one of his followers at a prayer meeting in Harlem a few years later.

Two days after my impromptu debate with Malcolm, I was marching alongside Martin Luther King, I marched to the Lincoln Memorial. I sat in the fifth row, next to John Lewis, to listen to King's speech.

Marching with Representative John Lewis

Rep. John Lewis (D-GA)

On a hot, historic day in August 1963, I met John Lewis while marching next to him towards the Lincoln Memorial. Congressman John Lewis from Atlanta was a great man and he became a close personal friend. He had unbelievable courage to march across the Pettus Bridge in Alabama and risk his own life for the courage of his convictions. His recent death on July 17, 2020, wounds me directly as a profound personal loss. We had a deep respect for each other. We were there for each other whenever needed. We stuck up for each other when it counted. I have lost a good friend and a hero, a man of deeds, never given to small talk. He risked his life for his beliefs.

On the front line, I marched with John Lewis, right next to him on the famous march in Washington on August 28, 1963. We walked together to the Lincoln Memorial to hear Martin Luther King deliver his historic "I Have A Dream" speech. We marched together again over the infamous and dangerous Edmund Pettus Bridge on the way to Selma in 1965 for voting rights. John got his head cracked, free of charge that day by the brutal and racist local police. There was no quit in this brave man. He had a focused and definite mission, and he cared deeply about poor people and their God-given civil rights to live free and vote.

At the March on Washington, John Lewis and I marched in lockstep and sat together in the fifth row, right behind Martin Luther King, Jr. We marched together arm-in-arm with dignity and grace up the marble steps of the Lincoln Memorial. John Lewis had a firm and most definite grip. He told me where to sit. I was going nowhere without him that day. We listened to Martin speak of his dream.

King stood tall at the podium, and in mellifluous tones bellowed, loud enough for Lincoln and everyone else to hear, "I have a dream. I have a dream, Lord, that one day, little black children and little white children will sit down together for a picnic in peace on Stone Mountain in Georgia." The dream was realized many years later. Martin's "I Have A Dream" speech for civil rights ranks right up there with the Gettysburg Address and the Sermon on the Mount.

My friendship with John Lewis lasted 58 years, from August 1963 to July 17, 2020, when he died. We spoke by phone many times, and I could reach him at any time. Our last phone call took place on March 17, 2020. He was beginning an investigation of human rights and systemic abuse and brutality of the elderly here in The Villages, Florida. He asked for new information. I had called him in 2018 to ask him to look into the severe violations of human and civil rights of the elderly in nursing homes plus police violence in The Villages.

"Are you still gathering information about the awful systemic violence on the elderly in your Villages nursing homes," he asked. "I plan to start hearings in April on the national scandal of mistreatment of elderly patients in substandard nursing homes. Many are unlicensed. There are several in The Villages. They come nowhere near meeting the standards necessary for getting a license to do business. There is no licensing procedure in place in The Villages. Someone must be paying off the Florida authorities to look the other way as old people suffer, are abandoned, and die. Your Governor DeSantis was here in the House of Representatives with me a few years ago. I plan to call him, and we will find out the facts. I will continue to need your documented evidence for our Congressional federal probe."

"Also, are you still teaching?" John asked. "I remember when you were awarded a Rockefeller Fellowship in the 1990s and spent a year teaching Constitutional Law at Morehouse College in Atlanta. The students there loved you. You should have stayed longer. It was valuable having you for many reasons. You were cherished as the token white man on the faculty." The Congressman put down his phone and laughed at his choice of words — token white man. "You were a role model for black students. They could see you were a reformer and practicing lawyer who worked hard to change discrimination and any form of mistreatment. You are an example of goodness with your work in public service for the Kennedys and for helping write the Civil Rights Act of 1964."

Morris: "I loved teaching at Morehouse College in your home district there in Atlanta. I learned so much living within an intelligent black society of warm and good people. It was a warm, friendly, and welcoming place, and fun — great stories with humor and learning together. I did not want to leave. I was accepted and made to feel comfortable. I was ready to stay if invited. That's when the edgy elite on the all-black faculty stepped in. That is when I was bruised by the academic politics of racial discrimination. I was white and being Jewish did not help my application for tenure either. The students were furious. They wanted me to stay. They challenged the faculty, saying, "What do you mean he is not a good role model? He picks up the phone and gets us into interviews with top law schools, which y'all cannot even approach." I remembered how vital the right phone call from an Earl Latham could be. "And he is a great and dedicated teacher with a good sense of humor. He knows his stuff and has been out there in the real world with Bobby Kennedy and other leaders." They argued their hearts out, and I loved them, but I left without a fight just that one time.

"I had a good year of teaching. I learned a lot by being "inside Morehouse." I loved playing tennis with the young men on the team and with Professor Tobe Johnson, their coach. I loved going to Morehouse football games, joining hands with students, faculty, and alumni, and swaying back and forth while singing "Men of

Morehouse" at halftime. I was accepted as a Man of Morehouse in every way, save one. I came out a better man for all that."

John: "That was Martin's school. He was so proud to be educated at Morehouse College, the best historically black college in the land. He loved that school. So, what's new on your docket in Florida now? Are you really retired from teaching? Have you found any more 'good trouble' for me to use in our probe of the nursing homes in The Villages?"

Morris: "I am still digging deep so we can make what you famously call "good trouble" together. I'm going to each nursing home. Some do not want my visit. They threaten right away to call the cops and have me arrested for "trespass." It is not funny. I am fighting for civil rights for elderly friends in substandard nursing homes. Sometimes our Shakespeare Group reads plays there, especially Julius Caesar, Hamlet, and Romeo and Juliet. I play the part of Marc Antony, just as I did on the stage at the Germantown Friends School in Philadelphia in 1954. Fortunately, I still remember my lines. I have been drawn towards trying to protect these warm and decent poor lost souls in nursing homes who have been abandoned by their families and left in horrible conditions. I am focusing on protecting the rights of elderly residents living here in The Villages."

Morris: "John, you would not believe the awful treatment some old folks receive in our nursing homes. They are abandoned, left to sit in the corridors in wheelchairs in their own shit and urine, staring at a blank wall. They call that daily exercise. What a crock! They just wheel them out from their room into an empty corridor. They have no activities, so we need to save and protect these poor souls. It's just not right. Some are World War II heroes who fought to protect and save America in the 1940s."

John: "I will do what I can within the halls of Congress. We will investigate. Their civil rights are being violated, and I am your man. But pancreatic cancer is eating me up. I am sometimes dizzy, but my mind is still clear. I am still on my feet, but a little woozy at times. We are now in the midst of the Covid-19 pandemic. I will survive to convene these hearings even if we do it by Zoom. As long as I can breathe and walk, I will definitely help you, my friend. I promise I will help you and your people there in The Villages."

Morris: "We need a careful investigation by a Congressional committee into the abuse of the elderly here in Florida. We must protect the elderly as an endangered species from harm and harassment. If we have a Protected Species Act, we can stretch it to protect the elderly. If gators, deer, chipmunks, and squirrels are protected by federal law, we can also protect elderly people. We are also a vanishing breed needing immediate protection."

I had introduced and discussed this novel legal idea of the elderly as a protected species under federal law during my Washington visit with John Lewis in early January 2018, a cold day in D.C. with a ton of wind. We discussed the plight of elderly people and their right to be outspoken and enjoy the freedom of speech, and a life free from harm, brutality, and misconduct by nursing homes and the police.

Morris: "Our police and sheriff act like criminals in concert with The Villages management. Today, I am following up to report to you some new information to add to my original report on constitutional violations and police violence on old people. I am doing this as I promised I would do when I came to talk with you in January 2018 and again in 2019."

I had gone to Washington to educate and brief Congressman Lewis on lawless police violence in The Villages. I gave him details on the constant after dark home invasions without advance notice or search warrants. The pattern of illegal late-night home invasions after 10:00 p.m. without warrants has not ceased. It happened to me in my home. It is a nasty and illegal weapon used by Sumter County sheriffs, directed by John Rohan, Recreation Director of The Villages, Dan Marchande, an assistant golf pro at Mallory Hill golf club. There are also other sadistic anti-Semitic leaders on the Villages Management Team. They want to create a witch hunt with tension permeating the once peaceful atmosphere. They laugh and enjoy defying the aging villagers' constitutional rights and love to intimidate, terrorize, and shut people up. Residents are victims of arbitrary and unpredictable police violence if they are gutsy enough to speak out about the conditions of the nursing homes in The Villages where the elderly are left to sit for hours, sometimes days, in their own urine and feces. They have physically attacked me for speaking out. One incident involved the Recreation Center Manager, John Rohan, Sergeant Sarkanis, and Deputy Sheriff Blankenship. Rohan hired police officers to assault and beat me. The three men threw me down harshly onto the Paradise Recreation center cement tennis courts' ground on a Monday morning in February 2018 during my 9:15 a.m. tennis game with no warning, no reason, and no apology. It was an act of intimidation and retaliation for speaking out on the local nursing homes' conditions. The attack was brutal, swift, and unannounced with no papers of the arrest.

Eight Sumter County deputy sheriffs, at the direction of Sheriff Bill Farmer, broke down the door of my home at 10:00 p.m. on November 19, 2018, in black SWAT jackets. They entered without a warning or warrant or any semblance of due process. They pulled me out of bed, took me in pajamas, and locked me up for 55 days in Bushnell Prison. They were planning to kill me without anybody knowing where I was. They put me in solitary. I never got a hearing."

John: "That's awful that you suffered. 55 dangerous days in jail for simply speaking the truth to power? You can never get those 55 days back again. They are gone. At your age, they are especially precious. And for them to put your wife through the two-month absence, and she actively fights and begs Judge Hallman for your release. He does nothing. She had no way of knowing when and where and if you would ever be free again. They were obviously trying to kill you. They were hoping you would die or get killed by another prisoner in an alleged scuffle. Jail is a dangerous and deadly place. Believe me, I know firsthand what jail can be like, living in a hostile environment, not knowing when and if ever you will be released, and see your loved ones again. This deserves a Congressional investigation. I am on the right committee for opening an investigation. We will invite you to be our first witness and explain the situation, and we will look into the lawless behavior affecting seniors in substandard nursing homes across the nation. We will couch this as a broad national inquiry, but with your help, we will focus first and foremost on The Villages as our "poster child" as an example of terrible behavior. The public will eat this up. We all get old. What will happen to us? There will be a Congressional investigation that leads to the prosecution of the guilty. Hang in there. I will get it started. This is a matter of deep concern across the nation. Every state has nursing homes, especially the retirement states of Arizona, Georgia, and Florida.

John: "Morris, at age 84, you are entitled to the protection of your rights to privacy, freedom of speech, and guaranteed personal safety in your home. You spoke out honestly about these matters, and you were thrown on the ground and handcuffed and jailed for 55 days without a right to bail or preliminary hearing. That is a scandal of the worst kind, and it undermines the whole system. That's unbelievable. It sounds like the cops in Selma, Alabama, in 1965, when we marched for voting rights and got brutally attacked with nightsticks. That is when they cracked my head wide open and blood gushed forth just for marching peacefully across a bridge, and we got jail time just for being on the Edmund Pettus Bridge. We were going over to Selma to register to vote!"

Morris: "I got involved when a young lady came to me and told me of the neglect her parents suffered in the local Villages nursing home. For over a year, she goes every day and changes their diapers. She came up to me and asked for my help. This was after one of my book lectures on "What Happened to Raoul Wallenberg?" and my efforts to rescue him."

John: "And what did you do?"

Morris: "I said 'Yes.' First, we invited her over to our home. Patricia made her a nice hot meal, a chicken dinner with matzo ball soup as a starter, and she told us the details. We adopted her and treated her like a daughter."

John: "In other words, you cared for her plight and powerlessness. You showed mercy and concern, and you offered hospitality and compassion to someone who was down and lonely and had no one to turn to for advice and to help her in taking care of her elderly parents."

Morris: "Yes, she was living all alone. We had her over for dinner twice. We were concerned. The very next day, I went to the nursing home with her and observed the horrible conditions. Then I went to The Village's management the same day and registered a written report and complaint. I simply wanted to see some change or reform. A few days later came the retaliation and the abusive police conduct on the tennis courts where my three buddies and I were in the middle of a quiet tennis game. Rohan organized the police attack and led it himself."

John: "And when they attacked you on the tennis court, did they give you any papers? Did they give you a reason for jumping on you with aggravated assault and battery by throwing you to the ground?"

Morris: "No, no explanation was offered. Sergeant Sarkanis ordered them to cuff me and then uncuff me after a brutal half-hour of pain and humiliation as all my tennis friends came over to witness the event. Sarkanis ordered Blankenship to uncuff me and let me up after a half-hour face down on the cement. Both my arms were severely injured. I went to the hospital for treatment and then directly to Rohan at The Villages management and filed a written complaint. A few days later, in the morning, I was again attacked on the tennis courts, this time at Tierra del Sol. They also had no papers to serve, no charge, no warrant, no nothing, just a raw attack."

"And that was the second of four separate attacks. Two additional attacks, both without warrants or cause, occurred at my home on September 13, 2018, and soon after a nighttime attack on November 19, 2018. They jumped me, forced me down, cuffed me, and dragged me off to Bushnell Jail with no time to put on my shoes. Patricia came running after them in the dark, begging them to give me my shoes. I went shoeless to prison. No arrest warrant, no nuthin', just like in the Ku Klux Klan's brutal night raids. Sumter Country is where the Klan has had its headquarters in Florida for the past 100 years."

John: "I'll bet I know what happened. They pretended you did not cooperate when they busted down your door in the dark. They knew there was no crime. To cover their ass, they invented a fiction story of trespass or resisting arrest. That's an old and completely illegal trick still used in Florida, Georgia, and Alabama. The police are embarrassed. They find nothing to justify their home invasion, and Chief Sheriff Farmer said, 'go out and work him over.' Beat him up a little. Rough him up and terrify him and his wife. Make them start thinking about moving away from The Villages. These are all Klan tactics. This is nothing new, but it never gets old. They want you to stop being a pest and a whistleblower. There is big money for The Villages in those nursing homes. They are all substandard, and the Florida licensing bureau gets paid off by The Villages to look the other way. The cops answer to Farmer, who is the pet dog of The Villages. He does whatever they say. The Villages say, "jump puppy dog," and Sheriff Farmer answers, "How High!" The cops don't care. They are "bad dude rejects" from northern urban police forces where they have been arrested for George Floyd beatings, police violence and deaths, and they have been ultimately fired. They are the human dregs, the detritus, and the bottom of the barrel. And so, they act like well-paid robots."

John took a breath and continued: "You were punished for whistleblowing, wanting to reform things and for exercising your right to free speech and for seeking humane change."

John Lewis got to the point. That was his best quality, along with backing up his talk by deeds. He was a man of courage and leadership walking across that famous bridge in Selma, Alabama, and getting his own head busted by police while fighting for civil rights. His angry efforts were ceaseless, and I loved him for that.

"You spoke up, Morris. The Villages can't handle that. The Villages management retaliated really fast and worked with the Sheriff's office to throw your ass in jail without a warrant or even a bail hearing. You were the victim of a systemic pattern of lawless activity by Sheriff Bill Farmer. That man owns the county and has served unopposed for 39 years. That ain't a democracy; it is fascism and an extremely dangerous place. Rohan apparently can do any damn thing he wants, just like Bull Connor in Birmingham back in the 1960s with dogs and strong water hoses making the people skip and dance. He and Bill Farmer are a team of evil masochists and anti-Semites."

Lewis continued: "That situation is hazardous. When free speech is not encouraged or tolerated, The Villages is a corrupt company town. No due process: it is obviously way out of control and deeply corrupt. They are greedy bastards out to make money off innocent and naive old people. They don't give a damn about how residents are treated in nursing homes. They're in it for the money and don't give a rat's ass about you or anyone else. It is about profit at the end of the day, the so-called bottom line. If they have to, they'll use the Klan to clamp down, frighten, and terrorize troublemakers like you. They don't want the Jews or Blacks there either. Just look at the numbers. You and the three newly elected reform commissioners of Sumter county represent a real threat to their fascist power. How else do you explain their dragging you off without your shoes in the middle of the night like some major criminal, a dangerous bank robber or drug king? It's no joke. Just think about it. Right here in America, we have night raids like Hitler's brownshirts in Germany in the 1930s on the Jewish families in Berlin, Cologne, and Niedermarsberg, where you tell me your dad comes from. And then, after they frighten you and scare your lovely wife to death, they pretend they do not have you, or that you are in protective custody. And then held for 55 days in the Bushnell Jail from November 19, 2018, until your release on January 14, 2019, without any preliminary hearing or bail hearing. They wanted you to die. This is 55 days of pure evil."

John Lewis: "Are you kidding me? You have no framework of protective laws for the innocent adults you have living there. They want to run you out of town, my dear friend. We must act before they kill you. This Farmer is a carbon copy of "Bull" Connor from Alabama, who turned the hoses on little black children, made them fall and break bones, and ordered the bombing of churches."

John Lewis: "You have in The Villages a 'corpocracy.' It ain't no democracy. It is all about the money, how much the developers and the corporation can make. They are saying 'the hell with the damn nursing homes.' It is a terrible use of arbitrary and arrogant power to victimize elderly citizens who live in The Villages. Brute fascist force is being used by a handful of money-hungry white bastards. They use arbitrary power to crush people. No one controls them, there is no restraint, and there is no democracy when Sheriff's run unopposed for reelection for 39 years. It is obscene, and it is not America. To incarcerate the innocent; that's what they did with you, Morris, for no damn reason except to shut you up. Soon it will be happening to your friends."

John Lewis continued: "That's what happened when the white supremacists in Alabama and Georgia, after Edmund Pettus Bridget, put me in jail a total of 40 different times. They dreamed up fictions about "trespass." or "resisting arrest without violence" or some cockamamie phony charge. We never trespassed, and we never resisted. Martin taught us not to resist and not fight back. Peaceful non-violence at all times, just like you. We had a legal right to be there, and phony political charges can put you in jail without any hearing. I was in prison 40 times, and it was never about trespass. It was about power: theirs or mine. I had none until the publicity began running our way, and the media came to our rescue. I am going to get you scheduled to meet some members of my black caucus to discuss holding public hearings on this matter."

I responded: "Holding open Congressional hearings on police violence and brutality on our elderly is vitally needed. We also need social media and public opinion involved. Too many older people are dying. They call it "risk-averse." They do not want to take risks anymore. Finding a way to end those police practices is long overdue."

I continued: "Common courtesy would be great too. If you suggest someone has trespassed on your lawn, then have cops place a courtesy phone call. Make a gentle inquiry. Don't overdramatize or criminalize innocent behavior. The night raids remind me of Hitler's brownshirts. Just grabbing people and throwing them in jail and later on dreaming up some excuse. They made surprise raids on innocent Jews in Berlin in the 1930s. and during the war."

Morris: "We do not need violent attacks by squads of eight Sumter County police, dressed in military SWAT jackets, I watched them drag me, an 83-year-old resident from my home in the dark. I have lived there quietly for a decade. I have the date, time, and place, which was 10:00 p.m. on November 19, 2018. I have a record of all the abuses."

John Lewis: "Keep that information carefully recorded. We want you to testify as to the details. I am opening an investigation into these matters. If anything happens to me, the file will be right here in my desk, in the middle drawer. You know my medical condition. I have pancreatic cancer. I am winning so far."

Congressman Lewis opened a file for a Congressional investigation of abuse of the elderly in The Villages, including but not limited in any way to the nursing homes. He promised to have his subcommittee investigate and document what he called "atrocious home invasions," including a record of all of the break-ins and the dragging of innocent elderlies in their nightclothes without shoes or dignity intact off to jail at night."

Congressman Lewis asked, "When are you going to move out of what they call Trump City?"

Morris: "I won't move until we restore the legal protection of the elderly. We clean the stables of the accumulated corruption and restore democracy." I answered. "I will fight these matters with you from within my violated home. We will investigate all of the violations and restore due process and the civil rights of the elderly. We need to live without anxiety and peace of mind and genuinely protected safety with no more nighttime raids. We need new laws and practices to protect the elderly from the police."

John: "How ironic is that? A guarantee of personal safety. New practices taught and learned to protect old people who gave so much in three wars to protect our nation!"

John quietly corralled support for a congressional investigation into elder care and elder abuse. He was looking into taking action to clean up these nursing homes and restore dignity to the elderly in The Villages retirement community in Florida and elsewhere in America at the time of his decline and death. John called me one last time on May 20, 2020.

John: "Morris, my dear friend, this is our last conversation. I am dying. You have my word. My colleagues in Congress will listen to you. Contact my staff. They have the names of the three Congress members, with two from Florida. We will make good trouble."

Morris: "I'm delighted. I know they will. You always keep your word." A week later, as I was writing this chapter, I thought back to our first days together.

John and I were the youngest in the group in the 1963 march on Washington. We marched right behind Philip Randolph, head of the railroad Pullman workers, and Martin Luther King in careful rows of six right down Constitution Avenue and up the Lincoln Memorial's podium steps.

John said to me, just before he got up to speak: "I am angry. I am on fire. I want to make my pitch for Freedom Now. I cannot abide even one more day of delay. Mr. Randolph, head of the railroad Pullman workers, and Martin Luther King have asked me to temper my remarks, so I must protest, how long oh Lord, how long?"

Morris reminiscing: "We were in our twenties, the youngest men on the podium. Our chemistry was instant. John was an impatient firebrand, and everything was black or white. There was no middle ground. He wanted to be hellfire and brimstone, placing blame, and fighting for the rights of his people. I was the calm, steady shield, the steadying hand. He needed that."

Morris: "I was the shield, in more ways than one," I recalled. "Martin said to me after the speech was over, and we were leaving, "Now John Lewis and Morris, you two younger men, please walk in front of us. If they start shooting, just jump right on top of us. Be our shield. Take a bullet."

John: "Why did Martin say that?"

Morris: "For his own protection. Martin felt if anyone tried to pop him with a bullet or two that you and I could bravely become young martyrs, standing in the way, and bravely taking the bullet for him."

After the march on Washington ended, the next day, I took John Lewis to lunch in the private dining room of Attorney General Robert F. Kennedy. We broke bread together in a quiet, peaceful place, with white tablecloths, silver cutlery, and privacy — just the three of us, a special lunch.

Bobby Kennedy questioned John Lewis regarding his next steps, plans, and strategies for achieving civil rights and voting rights without violence. John Lewis, the youngest member of Dr. King's team —the boy from Troy — was articulate, precise, and determined. His honesty and integrity permeated the conversation. He laid out just what he wanted to achieve. "The next step is to achieve voting rights for black people and every American."

John Lewis, arrested for "trespass" and "disturbing the peace," endured, and he prevailed. He was thrown into a variety of filthy southern jails 40 times on his way to personal freedom. He gained everyone's respect for his constant commitment to civil rights for all — young and old. He wanted to end the disgrace of police violence and home invasions. He was outspoken in arguing for full respect for the powerless, the frightened, and the voiceless.

He hated bullying and the "macho arrogance of cops" who, like the killers of the murdered George Floyd, thought they were actors "above the law." John Lewis hated brutal and violent police conduct. He was a devotee of non-violence. "We all live in the same house," he said, "the world house." It was that common sense and belief that inspired him and me. He got his skull cracked while marching on a bridge by brutal police action. It was unwarranted, undeserved, and permanent. He proved his point in favor of love, patience, and inclusivity.

In February 2020, he told me again by phone, "Morris, I am totally against those horrible home invasions on you and your wife in the middle of the night. There is no excuse for this activity by your police at night. Someone could be shot by accident. Older people are in bed, and they need their sleep to live. That is lawless and absurd. You must continue to fight and eliminate lawless reptilian activity." I had John's support right up until the day he died.

Through the years since 1963, we stayed in close touch by phone. John matured and mellowed, but he never changed his zeal for equality. He grew from being a firebrand, ready to fight and die as a young man at 23 on the Edmund Pettus bridge, fighting for voting rights in 1965. John gave years of honest and compassionate public service to our country. He reached 80 years of age by working for his beliefs in honesty and equal justice for all.

He has now gone to heaven to receive his reward. He worked his whole life in God's vineyard for civil rights. We were brothers to the end, and perhaps beyond. He is still sending a strong message: "Finish the production; create a better product, a better wine in my vineyards."

John was setting up hearings focusing on "The importance of Civil and Human Rights in Nursing Homes" when he died. His unfinished agenda will hopefully be picked up and implemented by designated members of Congress. His investigation will occur, especially as the COVID-19 pandemic shows that our nursing homes have already had a higher risk of contagion and an embarrassing record of high mortality rates, much higher than the rest of our communities.

Morris: "Rest in peace, John Lewis. You have done so much good, my friend. Your work will be carried forward by others. They will be bold men and women with the courage you have inspired."

A New Day Was Coming

I loved and believed in the value of the AIESEC student exchange program since 1959, when I was privileged to win a travel grant to work in Cologne, Germany, at the Chamber of Commerce ("Industrie und Handelskammer zu Köln") for a life-changing and transformational two months.

My transformation from hatred to love began in 1959, a mere 14 years after the Holocaust wiped out six million innocent Jews in Europe in the evil genocide.

My mother, with great foresight and spiritual awareness, said, "Morris will go to Cologne as a peacemaker and as a healer. He will bring young people together as friends and will let them see what a good young Jewish man can do in the land that killed six million." I was warmly welcomed and accepted, plus I learned German, and now French and Spanish. Six months later, I was miraculously elected head of the entire program with a mandate to work towards world peace. Why this miracle? It was ridiculous. I wasn't even in Rotterdam in October of 1959 when I was nominated at the AIESEC Presidents' meeting. No one knew who I was, yet Norman Barnett argued so strongly that they developed faith in my ability to lead.

I was elected President of the program in February of 1960 at the Barcelona Congress. I went immediately to Geneva, where I built the International Secretariat and served as the first full-time leader of the 33-nation program. Today AIESEC is still active and vibrant, with 89 member nations built on the solid structural foundation that my eight-member cabinet team and I created.

In 1993, 30 years after my two-year term as AIESEC student leader, I volunteered to help reestablish the moribund South Africa national committee when I should have known better. I journeyed to South Africa on a so-called courtesy voyage (or free air flight) with a brand-new upstart airline. The new company put together a few dollars to challenge South African Airways' monopoly that fought to immediately trash and kill the new competition. The flight left New York City at night and successfully arrived in Johannesburg, South Africa, the next morning. The arrival did not equal the reception I received when I first brought AIESEC to Ghana in West Africa. At the airfield, I met Kwame Nkrumah, the President of that young baby nation, just three years old at the time. It was a chance meeting where I was able to expand AIESEC into Africa.

My mission in South Africa was to galvanize and reawaken the AIESEC business student exchange program.[4] On my first day, I visited the University of Witwatersrand Economics Faculty to raise AIESEC traineeships. Students would go abroad for international business experiences of three to six months. This program was vital for the new economy under Nelson Mandela. I moved between the universities of Cape Town, Durban, and Johannesburg.

Globally, 531 member universities were waiting for South Africa's AIESEC Program rebirth. I returned from "AIESEC retirement" to find businessmen and economic/business students to lead a revival of AIESEC in South Africa. AIESEC was here once but closed up as the political situation moved from tense to dangerous. There was little will for a volunteer program, even one as valuable as AIESEC in a great nation going through a painful political transition. I was also witnessing the end of apartheid and freedoms for black citizens. AIESEC had been dormant, and a new day was coming. We rebuilt AIESEC in two months. It was time to go home.

I found out quickly that there is no such thing as "a free airline trip." The fledgling airline plane never returned to New York because it was bankrupt with no more return flights! Was this an omen? I could not get home with a useless return ticket — a piece of paper with no value. The planes were seized and sold. I was stranded in a foreign country with no money.

I was high and dry in South Africa, miles from home. I was stranded! I found myself marooned in a turbulent and dangerous

---

[4] The original formation of AIESEC in South Africa was in 1958.

South Africa, metaphorically on an "island with strangers" going through a slam-bang human rights revolution.

I was bereft of funds. I was broke. What to do? I could live and work as an international lawyer in South Africa, especially in Cape Town by the sea. Cape Town appeared attractive, and so was the idea of having money in my pocket to buy breakfast or dinner. I had gained new friends in the Mallinicks Law Firm, a civil rights law firm with a strong Jewish presence. The head of the firm Gerry Mallinicks, a self-made man, admired the fact that I came to South Africa to help young people. Why not settle down in Cape Town, at least for a while? I can work as an international lawyer at the Mallinicks Law Firm, teach law at the University of Cape Town, play tennis on weekends, go swimming and surfing, ride horseback, galloping in the late afternoon in the surf, and attend services at the synagogue on Friday nights? Why run back to America?

I contemplated how I might easily develop a happy life there. The people were cordial, refined, warm, and friendly. The Mallinick's Law Firm of Cape Town stood for character, ethics, and change. I met with their hiring committee. They offered me a job on the spot as legal counsel for international law matters. I became a global law specialist, went to cricket matches, played tennis on weekends, drank the wines of Stellenbosch, and went to Shabbat services on Friday nights with Gerry Mallinicks before a lovely diner at his home. It was a great life of interesting law work and play. I turned to God and asked quietly, "What would you have me do?" And God said, "Stay and play and enjoy yourself. You've earned it. Rebuild the AIESEC program and work with the law firm towards ending apartheid."

Dear reader, does God come on board and do this with you sometimes? God often plays with me the way he played with Noah. He commanded Noah, "build me an ark on dry land. There may be no water in sight. Build it anyway and watch the doubters when my gushing waters begin to rise."

I had the nerve to ask God again. "What exactly should I do? I am happy here. Should I stay, or should I go? What exactly do you require, command, or suggest I do?"

This time God answered: "This is a tough call. I cannot command you to do anything one way or the other. You can do good deeds here or back home. None of my statutes apply to govern your decision. None of my laws are involved."

"I cannot and will not command you to do anything. You have free will. Use it well."

God's gentle hand was still on my shoulder. But he refused to pull me one way or the other. I decided to stay in South Africa and see how things work out. I had no yearning to go home and no plane to fly on. I was in a dry season in my life up until now. I felt alive again. I was starting an exciting new life. So, I decided to stay and to see how things played out.

After working for Mallinicks for two weeks, I was called to a new assignment. Gerry Mallinicks supported me and, like a "mensch," continued to pay my salary. I was suddenly thrust upwards from my "incognito" status. I went from being a nobody to become the mediator, legal counselor, and advisor to Nelson Mandela and Willem de Klerk. I worked with them as they began to pass the reins of power and management in South Africa and end apartheid. How did this happen? I still do not know exactly.

Something about being in the right place at the right time: I was a neutral person with no ax to grind, no agenda, and a good background of human rights mediation in Chile and elsewhere in the world.

It was my job to hold hands and ensure that those two men worked together and in harmony during the historical and mind-blowing first 100 days of transition, a handing over of power from a white minority to the black majority after centuries of suppression in South Africa. It'll never happen again. I was "anointed and

State President Willem de Klerk

appointed" and accepted by both men, yet I represented neither one. I served the interests of the people of South Africa. I became their peacemaker and mediator on all issues during the transition.

My acceptance as a mediator by de Klerk and Mandela began quietly at a sold-out cricket match in Cape Town on a Sunday afternoon. It was an international match between India and South Africa in a vibrant and noisy stadium. At that moment, the teams tied the score, and they called a time-out. I was somewhat bored. Cricket is not my game. I walked up the hard-white cement steps from the Mallinick's Law Firm Elite Box to get a beer.

Suddenly, I saw a man sitting in the Presidential box who looked like me. He was my precise body and facial double. "Who is that man?" I wondered. I asked one of the President's Box attendants and found out he was none other than the State President of South Africa, Frederik Willem de Klerk. The South Africa Secret Service men surrounded the man protecting him from visitors. They hovered over him and scanned the sky and the stands for possible intruders or interruptions. Their duty was to protect the President from harm during a period of severe political turmoil and social unrest. Some citizens said, "things are moving too fast" or "not now; not here." President de Klerk was taking a risk by being outside at an open-air stadium. A hostile marksman could be seated anywhere.

The South African National Party, who helped build the nation's infrastructure, wanted to throttle all efforts to end apartheid. They liked living apart. For them, it was an existing way of life. They had "trekked" and built the nation going into the interior from Cape Town and making fertile farmland out of the jungle. It was like the American South of the 1940s but much worse. Men wanted to hold onto their wealth and the land they had created from the primitive jungle. Blacks wanted some divisions and sharing of the large estates. A possible war and blood bath were brewing if these two leaders failed to deliver a workable compromise and a package of laws on which all could agree. It required real statesmanship and honest leadership with the nation's best interest directly involved.

The coming of democracy and the scary prospect of one man, one vote, gave the white South Afrikaners nightmares. "Blacks will soon be running the government." As one wealthy farmer said, "They will have their revenge." With vast holdings in bottled wine in Stellenbosch, wealthy farmers were selling out their vineyards and moving north to Rhodesia, a place with the same climate. Rhodesia, under Ian Smith, was a black nation still run by conservative whites. Premier Ian Smith thought they would hold out and defeat "the winds of change" as the stubborn Afrikaners called it. However, the change was a reality.

Would beautiful and serene Cape Town become a tragic seat of the revolution, a place of a sudden change from quiet docility and order to become violently overthrown political order? Would there soon be blood in the streets? Or would order, fairness, and cooperation prevail?

I was a guest and not a citizen. Who could I look to for protection? What safety would I have? I began to see a quiet, stable nation suddenly run amok. In my mind's eye and fertile imagination, I saw chaos in the city of Cape Town overrun by armed black men in posse formation combing through the streets, making the whole place free and clear of all white men.

Fortunately, this never happened. It came close. Closer than the outside world ever knew. Mandela was a steady and quieting miraculous force. He urged the crowds of angry blacks, "Let us not lose what we have painfully and patiently gained." He was a constant, sure-handed political disciple of Mahatma Gandhi.

I watched him work his magic in the crowds of Cape Town, in the groups of people outside the stadium and elsewhere. Thousands of angry and uneducated blacks waiting to seize the government and even overrun Mandela, their "temporary leader" if necessary. Chaos was inches away.

Amid this atmosphere of violence at the edges and tension, I was still present at the top of the stadium at the Sunday cricket match. I made my way to the elite boxes' top deck for a breath of fresh air and to survey the countryside. I peered down at the restless crowd attending the cricket match. Gentlemen in long white sleeve shirts, white pants, and white shoes playing cricket below as if nothing else mattered. Little else did matter to them at that moment. They were athletes' intent on winning for the home nation, South Africa or India, and the honor and celebrity attending the bringing home of the winner's wreath and team victory.

Suddenly, I saw President Frederik Willem de Klerk in the flesh. Ever since my arrival at the airport in South Africa, students claimed, "You look exactly like President de Klerk!" He was right there, three feet away, seated in a special box, protected by his secret service, but near the aisle. Immediately, I decided that it was time to meet him. I brushed by his security guards and entered his box and sat down right beside him ("tuchas am Tisch" or "tuchas at the table"). He looked up in surprise. He smiled. Then he laughed, "My goodness, you are my very spittin' image. Seeing you is like watching me in a mirror, eyes, your mouth teeth everything. Did God suddenly decide to duplicate me, and have you arrived here from out of thin air?"

He looked at his security people with a stern glare. "How did you allow this breach of security to happen? Who are you? How did you find me? Who let you in? Well, now that you are here, I'll be my civilized and polite self and let you explain who you are." We settled down, cheek by jowl. We chatted, "who are you and where are you from" for a while, covering the facts of life that all humans have in common. Our country. Our schools. Our feelings about being in South Africa at this historic time.

President de Klerk persisted with questions, getting more curious, calmer, and less afraid. "Did you materialize out of thin air?" He chuckled again; he did this chuckling at his own words a lot. "Did God send you to solve our problems? Why are you here?" Cordiality mixed in with questions. He persisted, "From where do you hail? Are you Jewish? You are aggressive like a Jew. I have many friends here in Cape Town who are Jewish, especially near my home in nearby Manaus. They help me get elected."

I replied to his barrage of open-ended questions, "Well, President Mr. de Klerk, I must admit that ever since I landed at the airport and mingled in Cape Town, people seem to do a double-take, thinking I'm you."

I then became playful. "Who is getting the better deal?"

"I think I'm coming off quite well," he replied. "You are younger, better looking, with a better bald head." Then he added, "And a helluva lot brighter than me, I suspect."

I told him of my work with Attorney General Robert Kennedy in the Office of Legal Counsel of Justice on the Civil Rights Act of 1964, and his eyes widened. "We need you," he said. "We need a good lawyer right now to sort through a whole bunch of civil rights issues like immunity and forgiveness for past criminal conduct. We are working towards reconciliation and away from punishment. We need people with experience in brokering deals and the fine art of reaching a compromise which both sides accept. We need diplomats, people who can help us synthesize what we must face up to from crimes in the past that people feel in the present."

We sat in silence contemplating the cricket match on the field before us but with our minds on a different subject — bringing peace to a troubled nation and overcoming the past's hurts and crimes. He resumed, "We are going through a lot of messy things right now. I have an idea."

President de Klerk stopped talking. He sat up straight and laughed. "Bring this man a cold beer!" he said.

He still had truly little knowledge of who I was, but he offered me his hospitality and a cold beer. I accepted. Wholly composed, he reached into the coat pocket of his dark brown woolen suit and pulled out a blue and white Parliament cigarette package. He lit one up and offered me one. I declined and offered him a mint, which he accepted. I sat next to him as security buzzed around on their cell phones, trying to figure out which man was the real De Klerk. He told them to buzz off. "I am OK with my body double. Leave us alone!"

The security guard was embarrassed and confused. "Which one is de Klerk?" "How did that darn body double get through?" De Klerk waved them off. We had a good conversation about how debates worked in the U.S. Senate as a way to find a pathway to consensus and the actual passage of workable laws of civil rights and fairness. He wanted to know about my work with Bobby Kennedy. I could sense he was thinking about my credentials and the possibility of hiring me as an outsider who might help resolve the negotiations going on between himself and Mandela. "I need competent outside counsel, an adviser who can help me steer through the days ahead." We discussed some of the sensitive matters I had helped to negotiate like the exchange of Bay of Pigs patriots, caught by Castro, for second-generation pharmaceuticals, and the Civil Rights Act of 1964 and its arduous voyage through the U.S. Senate.

We also discussed the AIESEC student exchange program and its direct benefit for the future of South Africa in training black and white students to work together in an integrated society at home and abroad.

"We train young business executives for a global future," I said. "I can bring this idea to be part of the government transition to the integration of government departments."

We need this," he said. "Now that we are no longer officially shunned, we do need to reenter the world economy. You can help us there too."

We chatted for the rest of the afternoon. We both gained value and enjoyed the conversation. It was a long cricket match. President de Klerk had a strong desire to hire me as his lawyer for transition purposes and rebuild AIESEC in South Africa. "You must rebuild it. I will help you," he said. "Black and white students are going abroad as an integrated team and from the new South Africa to the world. They will be our ambassadors and business leaders, and they need sophisticated training in the ways of the world."

He was enthusiastic. Near the end of our impromptu visit, President de Klerk invited me to visit him at his country home in Manaus. He wanted us to sit on his front porch "to watch galloping horses running on the brown sand and splashing water up and down the beach while running in ten inches of the surf."

The following Sunday, his chauffeur came for me at my home in Cape Town, where I stayed with a Jewish family who were saved by Raoul Wallenberg. He drove me along the seacoast to see the wild horses and the surfers. We traveled the 18 miles from Cape Town to the seaside town of Manaus, an upscale suburb with large homes. As we talked and drove quietly and slowly by the beach's long strand, a group of wild horses danced along the edge of a beautiful ocean. With blue skies and a few cumulus clouds on the horizon, all was calm and bright. We headed to Willem de Klerk's country mansion for lunch. Nelson Mandela was already there. Just the three of us for lunch. Three men who were interested in fairness, equality, and the cause of peace. A typical Sunday luncheon!

Nelson Mandela and Willem de Klerk

Two big, black Labradors greeted me, accompanied by two huge white men dressed in white tuxedos with white gloves. They walked me inside and along the white marble floor to the dining room, where white tablecloths and crystal glasses and centerpieces of purple and white orchids awaited us.

I thought that this was to be a simple, informal luncheon and discussion. It seemed more like a state dinner with all the trimmings and protocol. But soon, the atmosphere warmed as both men entered the room.

"President Mandela and I are working together in forming the new government. I agreed to step down as President and become just the Prime Minister in the new government. Mr. Mandela will be the Boss and President," he said, smiling. "Mr. Mandela will be a good President. I will see to it. Power will be changing hands gently for the better. I want you to be my independent counsel for this process."

"Mr. Mandela will be a great leader for all of South Africa. We will work for a new beginning and new transparency in government. We will inform the people, and they will know every step we take together. We will reach out and travel together throughout the realm. We will have regular town meetings to share with the public what we are doing. We want to build confidence, and we will."

Nelson Mandela turned towards me. "We want to know more about you, Morris Wolff. We are intrigued by your background. You are the lawyer in the U.S. federal court suing Russia for the release of Raoul Wallenberg. How can you win a case like that? Every point of contact, everything that happened, was beyond U.S. jurisdiction? Tell me about being the lawyer for civil rights and meeting my civil rights American hero, Rosa Parks. You have an impressive record of accomplishment. You love to be an adviser. When do you sleep? And in which country?" We both laughed.

They asked if I would be willing to serve as an independent legal counsel to the new government to see it through its trial period of the first 100 days.

"It will be good to have an experienced outsider with no personal agenda, no preconceived notions, just an experienced adviser like Harry Hopkins to FDR."

I was surprised by de Klerk's quick comparisons of Franklin Delano Roosevelt from recent American history. That was not de Klerk's public image. The public perceived de Klerk as a farmer of limited intelligence and an ordinary man, not as an intelligent man who read books as his passion and hobby. He kept his intellectual side a secret to get elected. He came across as a tough guy with severe challenges as a nation's leader with a steel backbone but a gentle, quick wit, and intelligence. I saw and experienced a new dimension of this man, and I liked what I was seeing. I wanted to work with him, and of course, Mandela was my idol of restraint and self-control. How did he manage not to go crazy during those horrid 27 years of isolation on Robbens Island, robbed of the best years of his life? I admired both men and their willingness to put everything aside and to work together. They were statesmen and not politicians. They will rank in history with Benjamin Franklin, Thomas Jefferson, John Adams, George Washington, Abraham Lincoln, Teddy Roosevelt, Franklin D. Roosevelt, and John F. Kennedy.

Mandela had done his research and homework. He referred to my education at Yale and Amherst, working my way through college with my own sweater business and my parents as devoted family people. Mandela asked about my civil rights work during a crisis.

He wanted to know more about my effort in 1963 while working with Attorney General Bobby Kennedy. "How did you get Governor George Wallace of Alabama to remove himself peacefully from blocking the entry of black students with no bloodshed?" I answered, "We negotiated with him quietly by telephone through closed circuits. Deputy Attorney General, Nicholas Katzenbaum, was on the scene, telling Wallace, 'Make a short speech, Governor.' Then, the troops started leading students to their classrooms. I said further to Mandela, "This became our model for ending segregation through the South, including Alabama, Mississippi, and Georgia. We integrated the university quietly that day."

"I want to know even more about your work with Bobby Kennedy and the President," Mandela inquired. "What did you learn from them that you can teach us?"

"Service and focus," I answered. "Both men identified the right things to do. They were courteous towards those who worked with and for them. They pursued the right thing to do and stayed focused on the job at hand. They used their advisers well to make deliberate decisions and avoid impulsive action. They worked for the common good. They worked hard and accepted life. The President was exceptional in his ability to analyze complex issues. He had a great dry sense of humor. He was constantly in pain, but he never complained."

"Tell me about your help to write the Civil Rights law. I understand it has worked in protecting the rights of black families to eat, swim, and sleep as they travel. They can stay overnight at the Holiday Inns, the Waldorf-Astoria, and the chain of Marriott hotels across the nation?

"Yes, it does," I said, "It prohibits discrimination, and makes it a federal law violation to turn families away based on skin color. I worked with Bobby Kennedy in helping to craft the language of the Civil Rights Act of 1964."

Mandela replied, "We will need your expertise, Morris Wolff, in helping us during the early days of our transition." You will be our counselor, an impartial observer, and an adviser during our first 100 days. You will see the goodwill the President, and I, have engendered together in our new friendship."

"Once we were enemies. Today we work as friends. Mr. Mandela has no hate or enmity for all the mistreatment and injustice he suffered. He has 'coupons' for the future, he tells me. Every day a coupon is on his pillow, urging him to do something. Mandela made something lasting, enduring, and great today for the future of South Africa and the generations to come after us. We trust each other. Everything is on the table. No secret deals. No side agreements. Just two simple men who are working to establish a legacy."

I was moved and deeply impressed by the actions, the judgments, and the wisdom of both men. There was a lack of ego, a sincere and genuine desire to cooperate, and their unselfishness. They had a divine spark guiding them as leaders in a new arena.

These men were not politicians. They melded together from two worlds of strikingly different backgrounds and were farmers from the land. One descended from the Dutch Boer trekkers who came from elsewhere. The other came from a tribe, a group of warriors and plant gatherers who lived on the earth itself with native dances, voodoo, spirits, and traditions dating back 300 years.

They were South Africans. They were statesmen working together, with a sense of creating history. They strove to achieve and succeed. These two anointed men walked in the corridors of history to make a better world. I was happy to help them as their legal counsel behind the scenes. I helped both men when they called. I was there to mediate and iron out differences and to help both men reach a common goal. They never gave me a title; they just gave me work. "You are here as our behind-the-scenes counselor and advisor."

"Keep the peace, at all odds keep the peace," I could hear God saying to me, and so we did.

I worked with both men equally in terms of heart and concern during those first 100 days. I urged restraint, civility, self-control, and patience. I met with delegations of citizens from different tribes and different cities. All had something to say and to add to the new constitution. It was an eye-opening and diverse human experience. There were constituencies with different needs, wants, visions, and objectives.

One evening, after work was over for the day, I brought de Klerk a small elephant as a gift for his granddaughter. He was very touched that I remembered her birthday. We had met and played together, a beautiful and sensitive, bright child.

I reminded him of that first bold day together when I took a deep breath and bolted into his Presidential Box. I blurted out, "Mr. De Klerk, sir, ever since I got to Cape Town, everyone has been telling me that you and I are spitting images of each other. I want to see who is getting the better deal!" Crazy words that made no sense. He recalled how he had looked me over and laughed. He remembered and still said, "I am coming out, OK."

"Yes," he said. "Morris, you are still my body double, my identical, including the smile and your chuckle, your laugh. But I am still getting the better deal! I think you are better looking. You can play me in the movies!"

That's how winners get to be President; they say nice things. So, my meeting with both men was meant to be. It was not by chance that I was at the cricket match and was brash enough to break the security perimeter set up to protect the President. The Hand of God clapping on the waters of Cape Town and whispering, "You three good men need to get together. You have work to do as a threesome, working closely together."

Ever the diplomat and gentleman, he replied, "I think I am coming off quite well. I could use you as my body double when I don't want to show up for state ceremonies. Or if they make a film of my life."

For challenging the old racist regime, Nelson Mandela, the first black President of South Africa, spent most of his adult life in prison. That was a terrible miscarriage of justice and an unwarranted and unfair deprivation of freedom. Mandela's imprisonment and Wallenberg's 39 years as a Russian prisoner affected me in the same way. That's a big blow. After that, you could easily spend the rest of your days filled with bitterness and regret.

One afternoon, I had a chance to walk the beach at Manaus with Mandela alone. I asked him, "How were you able to keep your sanity? You could see the city of Cape Town from your prison cell with no chance to visit or mix with free people. I would have preferred to be free."

"But that's not how I saw it," Mandela replied, picking up a flat stone and scaling it across the water. "Sure, I opposed and condemned the racist political system that put me in prison. I would have preferred to be free that whole 27 years. But I saw my prison years as a tremendous opportunity. I developed a team of men who would later govern South Africa. Like me, they were political prisoners, jailed after sham trials that proved nothing and had no facts to support unfair outcomes. I read books, gained my voice, and was able to grow and learn. I gained a genuine stature and respect for the cause of equality for all people. The world not only listened to me but, in time, came to revere me. I became a hero of restraint. My voice developed strength and respect in a way that never would have happened otherwise."

Mandela stopped walking and smiled. He understood in his bones that everything happens for a reason, and he shared his inner wisdom with me.

Now our 100 days of working and laughing together were almost over. For once, God did not command me one way or the other. He just hinted: "You have work to do at home."

South Africa in 1993 was a nation undergoing significant trauma and transition. A seismic and cataclysmic change in social philosophy and human relations was taking place. As if overnight, the people were handling it quite well because of the leadership that is shown by the outgoing President Willem de Klerk. He was a smart and smooth old pioneer and trekker and Mandela, the man of honor and fighter for freedom. Six months before, they set Mandela free from the prison on Robben Island, where he spent 27 years looking through the bars of an isolated cell. Mandela could see the mainland to which he would return to govern as President. "Apartheid" and "trespass laws" as a form of legal enslavement were a thing of the past.

Willem de Klerk gracefully handed over the leadership of the country to Nelson Mandela. No war. No bloodshed. Both men, as leaders, set the tone of the day.

God was still at work on my travel plans of return. In 1961, Heinz Albrecht kept my books, kept me on the straight road, and worked with me to build AIESEC's International Secretariat in Geneva from the ground up. We made our headquarters in a two-story building with a garden for children. It stands there today, nearly 60 years later, a quiet reminder of world peace.

My friend, Heinz, worked for 27 years within the ranks to become the President of Swissair in Johannesburg. When he heard of my flightless predicament, he called and teased me, "Next time, Morris, why don't you fly Swissair both ways," he said.

We recalled old times together skiing in the Swiss Alps near his home in Lucerne, and my coming to stay for Christmas Eve with his family in 1961. "I will have a ticket waiting for you at the terminal with the manager of Swissair in Johannesburg. Get up there and keep your mouth shut and with God's help, fly home. Don't tell anyone. I am breaking the rules for you once again. Just like in the old days when I carefully kept your books in Geneva when you served as our leader of the AIESEC program."

Once again, God, with a gentle hand on my shoulder, was actively present in my life! I listened carefully. I tried to serve the word of God and serve the needs of a suffering South Africa. Also, I was able to serve the needs of these decent young people using the opportunity of the AIESEC program. I was on my way home after three great months in the new South Africa. Thank you, God, for putting my friend, my former bookkeeper, and now President of Swissair, Heinz Albrecht, there ready to help.

My work was now complete. I did my best to serve God and young people. It was time to go. I said goodbye to Mandela in his office in the capital. He thanked me for my service and gave me a big bear hug. I feel his presence and warmth, and his embrace still today, 27 years later. He was one of the greatest men of our era. I loved him, and I knew him well.

With the death of Winnie Mandela on April 2, 2013, (just a few days apart from the 50th anniversary of Martin Luther King's tragic assassination in Memphis,) a 40-year chapter of my life knowing and working closely and constructively with famous black people to build, create and preserve civil and legal rights in America seems to have come to an end. But there is much more to do in creating a loving, tolerant, peaceful, and safe environment in our nation and around the world.

As I think back on the Civil Rights movement in America, one of my best moments was serving for one year on the faculty of Morehouse University in Atlanta as the only white professor. I was a Rockefeller Scholar selected as a visiting professor in 1993. I was the single white man in the whole school other than the placekicker on the football team. I had many beautiful moments in teaching a group of young black men and women. At first, they were skeptical. "What makes you think you got something to teach us about constitutional rights from your viewpoint and background?" It was a challenging question on my first day from Darryl Davis, a brilliant and challenging abrasive student who never let me off the hook.

Darryl Davis was simply curious. He wondered how I happened to show up as a teacher on the faculty of his beloved university as if he might be the proprietor of faculty selection in his school. Davis was also a contentious and quite pugnacious person. He had read in the U.S. Constitution, in one degrading section, that black people's vote could only count as 2/5 of the vote of a white person. I admired his courage to get on his feet and challenge the professor and his having read the Constitution word for word in advance and came ready to argue. I did not choose to answer his question immediately. I asked Darryl if I might put his question up in my "escrow account" until a later time. Daryl became a U.S. federal judge and credited me with "being his inspiration and motivation" in pursuing a career in the field of what he calls "justice and the law."

A Chance Meeting in a London Bar

Ray Milland, 1947

I met Hollywood Actor Ray Milland in a London bar one quiet, rainy Friday afternoon. I was staying at the elite Connaught Hotel, London's most elegant hotel. Ray Milland was sitting by himself having a dry martini in the famous Winston Churchill Bar at a small round table with a clean white tablecloth. I walked into the bar, looking for nothing in particular. I was a hotel guest on international business with a client who was buying an English advertising firm to gain access to the European Common Market. It was a long day of negotiations with an ailing English advertising company that I was to acquire for my client "for the lowest price possible." These were his words; he watched me negotiate that morning at Barclays Bank. The English advertising company wanted cash and to strengthen its position as it entered the European market with an American partner.

Ray Milland sat alone, the only customer in a quiet bar at 3:00 p.m., before the evening rush. He caught my eye as I stood there and, with a welcoming wave, motioned with his hand to come over and sit with him at his small table. I was amazed by his invite and his open gesture of friendliness. I took full advantage of the opportunity, dropped my briefcase in the empty seat next to him, and joined him. "I don't like drinking alone," he said, "but I do like having an afternoon toddy and a chat with someone."

I found his brief and cryptic invite quite ironic as I remembered his starring role as a fumbling alcoholic in "Lost Weekend." The part brought him an Oscar nomination and the prized golden Oscar statue as best actor that year. A gold chain crossed his three-piece light gray business suit and cufflinks with the Oscar statuette proudly, but conservatively, hidden. I saw the golden cuff links only when he raised the dry martini with an olive in a chilled glass quickly to his lips for a small sip." Why was I so lucky to be summoned to his table? Did he mistake me for someone else he actually knew and now was too embarrassed to admit it?

Rather than question my good luck, I grabbed at the chance to have a drink and chat with a movie star. I knew right away; it was Ray Milland. I knew his smiling face from the movies. I quickly took my place at his white-clothed table before he could change his mind. I loved meeting and chatting with celebrities. It was my lucky day for an unexpected conversation, and I said nothing to him about my good luck. He was English and reserved despite some of his noisier roles in the movies. I sensed this was to be a one-time experience on a rainy afternoon in London. The oak-paneled bar at the Connaught was empty. Regular drinking hours were at least two hours away. I had him all to myself and his full attention.

"What will you have? Drinks are on me," he said with a quick smile. "I am here on assignment in London interviewing for a new movie." He asked me, "Where are you from?" I answered, "I am from Philadelphia." He said, "That is the hometown of American actress Grace Kelly." Milland starred with Ms. Kelly in the movie *Dial M for Murder*. The movie is about a reserved Londoner hell-bent on killing his naive and innocent wife for the secret insurance policy he has taken out on her life.

"She is from Philadelphia, my hometown," I said. "She went to Ravenhill Academy, a private girl's school three blocks from where I went to Germantown Friends. The Kelly family lived in an all-red brick mansion on Warden Drive, a posh neighborhood. The family has a bunch of stars, including her brother Jack who rowed in the Olympics. They are a famous Philadelphia family." Now we had something in common about which to talk. We broke the ice, and things warmed up quickly.

"Do you come to London often?" he asked. "About twice a year. I am invited to lecture at an annual conference on international law and multinationals at Henley-on-Thames, and the other time just on business. My work with SC Johnson and Sons, a global company with subsidiaries in France and Germany, brings me to Europe quite often. I just made a partner with the Philadelphia law firm of Stassen, Wolff, and Kostos. The head of the firm is former Governor Harold Stassen of Minnesota (at age 29) and one of the five signers of the United Nations Charter in 1945." I was proud of my achievement in being named to a firm headed by 'the boy wonder' devoted to international work. It was 1978, and I was 42.

"Interesting work, I must say," he replied. "Gets you out of the house and away on challenging adventures. "What brings you to London this time?" he added.

"I am here on legal business for a client. He is buying an English company to branch out and get his foot into Europe with his American-based advertising firm. We are both from Philadelphia. He is an unusually generous man. We finished the transaction of buying a company after months of haggling over the purchase price. I received a handwritten note from him when I arrived here. The note says, "Stay for the weekend and have fun. It's on me. I have to fly home to Faith and the children. Roam the city and have fun. Thank you for the great job you did in finding the right partner for my growing business here in London. Thank you for opening your reliable network of excellent people here on the continent. Today we have conquered London; Tomorrow, the rest of Europe and the world. I would like to suggest the new Turner exhibit at the London Museum, and dinner at Wheeler's Seafood in Soho as starters."

I explained to Ray Milland that Roger was generous, mercurial, suicidal, and eternally optimistic. "Roger is in the advertising business and given to exaggeration and hyperbole. He insists on always traveling first-class and staying at first-class hotels even though we cannot afford it. Debt and speculation are his major enemies. He is going towards and through a self-inflicted crisis. I try to counsel him and calm him down. We are the same age and grew up as friends in Philadelphia."

"Roger is naive and in self-denial. He sees only the upside and the positive. He wants to expand his modest advertising firm everywhere. America is not big enough. He needs to be known in Europe too. He yearns for making big money, what he calls 'megabucks.' He has delusions of grandeur. He wants to go global, growing his business without a safety net, without a substantial stash of capital in the bank, and with nothing in a reserve account."

It was May 1978. Everything was rosy and green in London. Roger was flying on a cloud. We were both 42, a vulnerable year for young men beginning to wonder if they had become as successful as they thought they would be after graduating from college and 20 years of toiling in the vineyard. Roger wanted to make his fortune in international business overnight. He was manic-depressive and schizoid with two different large personalities.

"He selected me as his lawyer because he trusted me. We had good chemistry. I knew his weaknesses and cautioned him to take small steps, but he would not listen. Everything had to be right away. Roger was a major risk taker, buying pork bellies and commodities on the stock exchange without research. He also bought other volatile stocks that often went bust and belly up with no financial return. He was not disaster averse — just the opposite. I stood and watched him explode."

"We had good chemistry except for his addiction to risk-taking. I talked to his wife, Faith Whittlesey[5], about it, and she just shook her head. "Roger is a genius at what he does in his field, but we cannot control his financial impulses," she said. "We can stand by as he

---

[5] Faith Whittlesey was a Pennsylvania Republican politician. In the Reagan administration, she was a senior staff member for two years as Assistant to the President for Public Liaison. She served twice as U.S. Ambassador to Switzerland.

flies his own kite in the wind. I pray he stays alive. He is a good father, and the children love him."

He kept his risk-taking behavior with money as far from his accountant and me as he could. I told him to stop his speculative stock buying of mercurial commodities. "Roger, you have no idea about commodities. You are in advertising, not pork bellies, cotton, and the quick buy-sell of grains and other commodities. Get out while you can. This buying is not for you. You are a genius at advertising. Stick to your field!"

Roger kept his addiction for gambling on commodities a secret from his wife and me. He took advances from his advertising clients, money meant for paying the newspapers and TV media, and invested in the commodities' funds. It was secretive and stupid. It was like stealing, and his destructive addiction brought him down. I thought he had finally gotten smart when he said he was "clean" a few weeks before our business trip to London. But he went home to Philadelphia that weekend and committed suicide. He closed the overhead door to his garage, connected a hose to the exhaust pipe of his car, inhaled for a few moments and took his own life. He left a significant insurance policy to cover his debts and take care of his wife and children. His wife and I still mourn for him."

I read the note from Roger to Ray Milland. "Morris, great job on closing the deal with our new British affiliate. As a reward, why don't you stay in London for the weekend?"

I explained my exuberant client Roger to Ray Milland with no awareness that Roger, at that very moment, was flying home for the weekend and to his death.

I asked Ray Milland how he got started. "Well, I was fired from my boring day job and lost my status in the English Royal Guard. A good friend took me along with him on an audition he was having. They saw me sitting in the third row, smiling, and asked me if I wanted to read. So, I got up and read a few lines. I got a part along with him in the film. I fell in love with acting, and the next thing I knew, the parts just started to roll in. I played in a zany, funny film called, *It Happens Every Spring*. It was a baseball movie, but it starts out with a chemist who discovers a substance that has a peculiar aversion to wood. The creative chemist trades his lab job to become a major league pitcher who throws a ball the hitters can't hit because they come to the plate holding a piece of wood, a baseball bat. Each time they come to the plate, they strikeout. It's a little corny, but I had fun making the movie. I got to know all the baseball stars on the Boston Red Sox team. They all had roles as ballplayers in the film."

"Then I made *Lost Weekend* and had to learn what it was like to be an alcoholic. That was a difficult part because the man is in a frenzy most of the time, desperate for a drink." He lifted his glass and said, "I really should not drink alone. That is why I asked you to join me. I drink more slowly when I have someone to talk to."

We talked into the late afternoon. It was now two hours later, 5:00 p.m. People were beginning to flow into The Connaught, one of London's famous watering holes. He told me about his love affairs and different marriages and his favorite stars and movie parts. He was congenial but quite reserved and could clearly laugh at himself.

"It is frankly all so amusing," he said. "Sometimes you have to lose your day job, to find your career."

"I wouldn't trade my place with anyone," he added as he stood up and wished me good luck. As he got up to leave, he announced, "Morris, hopefully, we will meet again on the other side of the pond," meaning America. He was headed home after the upcoming lost weekend. "Until then, all the very best."

Ray Milland was an English gentleman, polished, funny, and quietly reserved. He had a vast vocabulary and was a fascinating conversationalist. Milland was erudite and a good storyteller of his adventures. That afternoon as a quiet and spare conversationalist, he enjoyed drawing me out rather than talk about himself. I felt at home with him at the small table despite the difference between us regarding life achievement. I felt relatively small at the time. Maybe now, 42 years later, I might feel differently. A chance meeting in a bar on a rainy afternoon in London, I learned a lesson about the risk of drinking. Ray Milland inched forward so only I could hear his voice. "It was tough going making that movie, *Lost Weekend.* I was an alcoholic playing an alcoholic. I was scared I would fall back into old habits." The invitation to sit down and talk to a stranger who turned out to be a famous actor was ironic. Life has its pleasant and bittersweet moments. This day was one of them. I met and developed a friendship with Mr. Milland, and at the same time lost Roger to gambling, alcohol, and foolish investments.

Finding Love in Prison

Have you ever come within a hair's breadth of getting married in a maximum-security prison to a beautiful, brave, daring, and courageous woman? I think not! Well, I damn near did! That is almost. Angelina was a vibrant, magnetic, beautiful woman — and a political prisoner. My very own Angelina, or Angel. I was wildly attracted to her, and I was single and very available at the time. It was love at first sight. She was young and vulnerable. I will tell you more about this brief romantic adventure later in this chapter.

God had indeed chosen me for an extraordinary assignment. I was asked by the American Bar Association to fly to Chile and rescue four beautiful women from prison in Santiago and restore their freedom to go home and their First Amendment Rights in Chile to freedom of speech.

I received a formal request from the American Bar Association's central office to rescue these four lovely ladies from their solitary confinement in a dirty, rat-infested Chilean jail. My answer was an immediate "yes, I'll go. You pay the airfare and hotel in Santiago, and I will do the rescue work pro bono. Just cover my expenses going and coming, and I am your man."

Little did I know when I met these women in prison for the first time, that one of them was already seeking to create a legal marriage with me as a way to get out of jail. Little did I know they were arranging for me to fall in love and marry the most beautiful member of their quartet. Angelina was by far the prettiest, and her "mother," one of the other prisoners, looked me over from top to bottom and asked me, "Are you married?" I answered, "No, not at this time." She said, "Then you will marry my daughter?" After speaking with them for an hour and eyeing my "fiancé" Angelina, I knew there was chemistry between us, and good chemistry it was indeed. "Once I get the four of you out of this miserable place, we will seriously consider your generous offer," I nodded to her mother, Francesca. Later, after I obtained their release, we kept a close and friendly relationship, but we were never married, though I was tempted. We sustained our new friendship by mail. I stayed for a week in Santiago to celebrate her freedom. Still, I was never able to return to Santiago, Chile, to consummate our mutual promises. I think of Angelina every day and every night about how beautiful and brave she was, and how I loved, admired, and respected her. Our age difference was minimal. We should have married.

Gestapo[6] policemen of the evil Pinochet government had grabbed Angelina at a podium in a large public park where she spoke to a crowd of 100 women and children. They gathered to hear her report on the Pinochet regime's atrocities, which included dropping pregnant women, babies, and young children alive without parachutes from military airplanes over the ocean and the lands and hills of neighboring Argentina. The children became known as "Los Desaparecidos," or the disappeared ones.

That afternoon in the public park, a posse of the secret police threw Angelina to the ground, manacled her wrists in heavy handcuffs, and dragged her face down through the dust on the square to a white van labeled "Policia." That is the beginning of her story.

My mission was to rescue these innocent women from a harsh sentence with no specified date for release. The women had already been held incommunicado and without legal representation for 18 awful months. My mission included a commitment to report my facts and findings to the American and Philadelphia Bar Association. I kept carefully written notes hidden under my mattress during the entire time I was in Chile. The authorities followed my American Bar Association (ABA)-selected law partner, Juan Laredo, and me during every minute of our 10-day investigation of human rights violations. They trudged behind us throughout the city of Santiago by order of the Dirección de Inteligencia Nacional or

---

[6] Frequently called "Pinochet's Gestapo" the **Dirección de Inteligencia Nacional** (DINA) was established in November 1973. DINA had the power to detain any individual so long as there was a declared state of emergency. They disbanded in 1977 and replaced by the Central Nacional de Informaciones (CNI). The CNI dissolved in 1990 when Chile moved to a democracy after the fall of Pinochet. See Wikipedia at https://en.wikipedia.org/wiki/Dirección_de_Inteligencia_Nacional.

DINA (National Intelligence Directorate). It was also clear that our own American CIA members were on the scene trying to figure out our plans and our loyalties. They couldn't believe we had come all the way from Philadelphia to rescue four women.

Emiliana Cortez came alone to meet us in the evening at the airport in Santiago. As part of her early parole, the authorities allowed her out in daylight. The Episcopalian Church of North America, the Philadelphia and American Bar Associations (ABA) paid our expenses. I arrived with Juan Laredo, my law colleague, on this fact-finding tour. The ABA on Human Rights was asked to investigate significant abuses of women in Chile jail cells. The Association needed facts before censuring President Pinochet of Chile. Also, the State Department was urging President Reagan to install a boycott on all produce ("Los grappas," the grapes) coming from Chile to the USA until after the removal of the repressive regime.

Santiago was becoming as lawless as Abilene, Texas, during the cattle-sheep wars on the prairies in the 1830s. Pinochet had closed the courts and censored the press into submission.

It was winter and cold in Philadelphia when we left, and sunny and warm when we touched down on an open empty airfield. The day before our late afternoon arrival, President Augusto Pinochet arranged the quick and bloodless assassination of Chilean Ambassador Orlando Letelier[7], an opponent of Pinochet, in Washington. A bomb placed in his car went off as he was driving alone near DuPont Circle. He had become a so-called "enemy of the people" by speaking out on the need for human rights in Chile. Most Americans doing business in Santiago had bodyguards, sometimes two or three, to keep them safe from gangs or random assassins.

"Damn dangerous to come here in the first place," whispered the pilot as we disembarked together. "I would not let any member of my family come here for my wedding," said a young American law professor here for one semester. I thanked both men as I made my

---

[7] Orlando Letelier was a member of the Allende administration and one of the first arrested by Pinochet. He suffered severe torture in different concentration camps in Chile for 12 months. He moved to the United States after his release.

way through customs and met Emiliana. The government arrested Emiliana for handing out leaflets opposing the Pinochet regime in the town square. Her crime, you may ask? She operated a printing press without a license. There was no law in Santiago, only power. They made up phony laws and prosecuted innocent people, sticking them in jail for unlimited terms. Many died in prison.

Emiliana said, "Please hurry. I am allowed out during the day after a year in prison. I must be back there before 7:00 p.m. to meet my curfew!"

I did not know who was coming for us at the airport. I thought it would be local lawyers or members of the Episcopalian Church. The local church was the co-sponsors of our human rights investigation with the ABA and the Episcopalian Church of North America. They wanted to change the abuse and tyranny that descended on this once free nation under democratically elected President Allende. Our report would lead to worldwide pressure on Chile to remove Augustus Pinochet, the dictator, from power.

We reached the parking lot where Emiliana's dirty and decrepit old car was. The car looked like a mudslide; it was so dirty. It was hidden from view and parked with her license plates covered.

Emiliana said, "I keep it dirty on purpose, so no one tries to steal it. I park it on the outside of the prison, and I pay the guards to keep an eye out for "ladrones" (burglars). They will steal anything in Santiago these days."

I asked her, "How do you get privileges to come out of prison to gather us at the airport?"

Emiliana said, "They trust me and know that I will return to jail. My three girlfriends are collateral inside the jail, which gives them certain leverage. We are all hostages. They know we will not separate from each other," she replied.

MW: "How were you chosen to be the trusted one?"

EC: "Despite my present circumstances, I have been fortunate. Some might say I have a "charmed life" with a good education. With encouragement, I try to make a difference and to be authentic in my everyday activities. I do not follow the herd and am a political activist with visibility. I am a non-conformist and a confessed change agent. I want to see a different Chile where free speech, due process, and the right to privacy return. We've completely lost our civil liberties. They even put a big black lock on the gates of the Supreme Court with a sign that says, "Not open for business." There are no courts of any kind open for business in Chile, neither prominent nor little. There is nothing to curb the unfettered power of the dictator, General Augustus Pinochet. He rules with an iron hand, and devastating secret police, like Hitler. We live in a police state. I want to live to see that changed. I even flirt and charm the prison guards."

MW: "How do you charm prison guards in a scary environment like that?"

EC: "I work the guards not with money, but with jokes, flirtation, and friendliness. That keeps them happy and their hands off me. The guards treat us with respect. Despite their uniforms, they are also Chileans under siege and deprived of their human rights. They hate Pinochet, who is a cruel dictator. They quietly support us. They tell us that they are proud of us."

MW: "I promised to keep a careful diary for the ABA, a journal of each day's activities. I am taking a few discrete notes for my report. I won't use any names, and the report is confidential. I won't mention by name any of the women. I am discreet in keeping the confidence of clients."

"Tomorrow, we are to meet with your group of defiant women at the prison. I will not compromise or embarrass anyone."

"What exactly did you do as a group that put you behind bars?"

EC: "For me, it was the printing press and handing out leaflets in public places. I was in all the public parks around the city, handing out pages that said, "Stop the killings; stop Pinochet." It was a matter of free political speech, which we no longer enjoy here. I want to throw out the new Nazis. That will be enough."

MW: "What about the other three women? What did they allegedly do?"

EC: "They robbed a bank, actually a few banks, like Bonnie and Clyde. They didn't do it for greed or personal use. They use the money to pay the evil ransoms for members of their families. They wanted us to rescue them from prison before they were unceremoniously dumped to their secret death at 20,000 feet from airplanes by the Pinochet regime."

"We want to get them out of prison. It is very tough to bargain and plead or get prisoners any form of bail while awaiting trial. The women are brave revolutionaries. A guard died in one of their robberies, but their purpose was not greed. They did not keep any of the money. Everything goes to saving lives, to rescue people before becoming "Los Desaparecidos," the missing ones. We have thousands already dumped from high altitudes alive!"

"They give me a day pass and let me out of jail because my only offense was promoting free speech and freedom. I had nothing to do with the bank robberies. The prison authorities trust me."

Emiliana drove Juan Laredo and me to our hotel in downtown Santiago.

E: "If you are hungry, they have delicious fresh fish here. You should try it. The Chilean wines are cheap and excellent."

"I suggest you double-lock your doors tonight. I will come for you at 8:00 a.m. tomorrow to bring you to the prison to interview the three brave women bank robbers. The women suffered torture and beatings to gain information about the ringleaders, who are a group of men. The men stay in the shadows. They let the women do the brave, dirty work. We still have much chauvinism and very few brave men."

"The men mastermind things. They allow women to take over. Things will change one day. Male chauvinism is beginning to fade, especially in the city areas."

MW: "Thank you for bringing us to the hotel. We need to get back right away. Don't waste a minute with good-byes. We will see you tomorrow morning."

We checked into our room that Juan and I decided to share for security reasons. We knew that people broke doors even on the upper levels of the finest hotels. We unpacked and then went for a late dinner. Emiliana was correct. The fresh fish was excellent, and Latin music was a joy to our ears and tired souls.

Juan said, "Mucho Alegria Aqui (much joy here)!" as we took our seats at ringside to the dance floor.

"The music gives the people the liberty of movement, if not complete freedom and full relaxation. They can always go dancing, even under the worst regimes. Music is the language of the Latin soul. No one can repress that," he said as the band played Cumbria and rumba music. I felt like dancing but restrained myself after the waiters served our dinners. Music moves me, especially Latin. The music made me think back to my summer in Guanacaste Province in northern Costa Rica in 1955, teaching English. The teachers included me on Sunday excursions to the white sand beach and palm trees and "la musica."

We danced until dark and then went swimming, with or without, after a few rum drinks. We would watch the full moon rise out of the ocean at eye level in the warm tropical breeze. It was life in paradise, a free and open life under a stable democracy. Costa Rica was light years away from Pinochet's repressed Chile, another Spanish speaking nation that was entirely different.

I took 10 American high school students for the summer to a small town with a plaza and dirt roads, Liberia, Costa Rica, in the summer of 1965. Now, in 1985, I was again back in Latin America but on a different, less pleasant kind of mission. The first mission was to foster close and friendly relations between "gringos" and kids from a high school in rural Costa Rica where horses and cattle outnumbered people.

The people of Costa Rica had Sunday night "paseos" (walks) in the town square, with the girls going one way in the inner circle and the young men going around the other way. It was an early version of match.com. People were in their houses, and the bedtime for students was 9:00 p.m.

Both Chile and the little village in Costa Rica had curfews. One was peaceful, and the other quite dangerous to violate.

The next day, at 8:00 a.m., Emiliana returned to gather us to visit the jail. The guards checked our papers, and they escorted us to a waiting room. It was quite large, with bare white walls and, as we discovered by poking around, totally wired. Whatever we shared was taped and could be used to incriminate the women.

After a few moments, Emiliana returned with three very attractive young women, all dressed in the drab gray, loose-fitting prisoners' clothing. No one was permitted to dress nicely for the occasion. Pinochet's regime did anything to insult and humiliate people. It was the inhumane practice of the day. They were glad to see me, the first man they encountered in three months. However, they were happier that Juan Laredo came with me, especially since Juan was 15 years younger, almost an entire generation. Juan was 34, and I was 49 at the time.

After the women came into the waiting room, the doors closed. We all were aware that it was a trap, a setup. They wanted us to talk, but these women are quite savvy. They realized almost anything they said would be held against them. We did not have privacy; they recorded everything we shared. Quite wisely, the women shrewdly decided to have fun and play games with us, instead of talking about any aspect of their political and legal situation, and their armed bank robberies to raise money or "la causa."

Emiliana looked at me with a mischievous gleam in her eyes and quickly said, "Today, we will have no politics. We will have a wedding instead, right here in prison. Isn't that a good idea?"

I asked, "Who will be the lucky man?"

E: "You are! You are the lucky man, the chosen one. You will be the groom, and we have for you a lovely fiancé, a "prometido" of rich beauty and wealth."

Everyone laughed. There was a collective sigh of relief as we averted a major gaffe in relationship building. We were playing a game, a masquerade. These good women were dead serious. It was a game, for now, to relieve tensions, but after they were released from prison, they wrote and implored me to come back to Santiago and keep my promise.

E: "The youngest member of our group decided she would love to be married to our new friend, "Mauricio," none other than Mr. Morris Wolff. We have seen your handsome face in the paper sent by your ABA to us. We understand you are single again, at this time in your life. You can indeed give here and now your hand in marriage to Maria Carmen, known to us as "Angelina" or angel, this lovely young thing, seated next to me."

MW: "I agree with this proposal. That is an excellent suggestion, although things are happening extremely fast, indeed! She is quite beautiful and will be a very suitable wife. I will do everything to make her happy." I was somewhere between playful and serious.

E: 'Querido prometido' or beloved fiancé, she confided to me she has fallen in love with your photo and is desperate to marry you. We think that she may be merely desperate to marry anyone who might be able to get her out of jail (laughter). She wants to leave us all here as she chooses a better life. We do not mind. We give her hand to you." (Much laughter.)

The lovely and young Maria Carmen stepped forward. She was stunningly beautiful with dark eyes and a beautiful smile. She was quite my junior by 20 years. I fell in love instantly and would have been happy to take her to the USA if the authorities allowed. We talked together about possible plans. It was all a sweet dream, but it was also authentic. These women were finding a way to make their lives bearable behind bars. Humor and laughter are the best palliative medicine. We selected a mother-in-law (suegra), a reverend, and a bridal party, and I was happy to play the part. I was quite glad to take her hand and go through the ceremony. At that time, I was genuinely single and quite eager to meet this new and beautiful love.

The event was an incredible moment for rising above nasty conditions to a lofty place of joy, even for just one hour together.

We did not have a bridal cake or champagne, but I could see just how resilient and determined these women could be. They wanted a new, better life for themselves and the generations to come. They were real heroes and profoundly unselfish. They wanted to get rid of Pinochet, yet his name never came up the entire time I was there.

We focused on the moment of comedy and relief. We all welcomed our laughter and spontaneity together by developing a charade of the marriage ceremony with everyone having a given role in the mini drama. It seemed real. Maria wagged her finger at the cameras up above. It was as if to say, "We know you are there, but we are not going to waste this fun moment for laughter with being serious. We will have some fun with these two handsome men from faraway Philadelphia and confuse the authorities. She wagged her finger again at the cameras as if to say buzz off. We ain't offering you nuthin."

We all signed on to having fun together and play-acting in a somber and repressive environment. The guards enjoyed our pluck and courage under desperate conditions. They watched through the mailbox slot in the door, eyes going back and forth as the wedding ceremony began and howled with their laughter. These women could have been their sisters.

The next day, the four women wrote to me at the hotel thanking me for being there for them, keeping their spirits upbeat, and being a good sport. They told me in writing that I was "married now" to Maria Carmen and that they had several witnesses. I admired them deeply. They were authentic and brave women fighting for freedom, and they were great resilient survivors. We spoke the next day with three courageous local lawyers who agreed to come into the prison with us on our next visit. These attorneys then decided to represent the women and to obtain their freedom. These were brave men, selfless advocates of human rights for everyone, especially the oppressed.

Through our joint efforts, as pro bono lawyers, we got their freedom. Juan and I had to leave Chile. The women, once freed, were protected by the Episcopal Church and two local Chilean lawyers.

The women, especially "mi prometido," stayed in touch with me for a year through handwritten letters. "I am looking for a man like you,

Mauricio," she confided. "I cannot find him yet, but I have kept your letters. They inspire me to persevere."

Maria Carmen (Angelina) was as smitten as I was. Love, at first sight, does not require fluency in any language. As Auden once said, "Love comes in through the eyes, a combination of the eyes" and the brain, with a soft and caring voice. Communication is vital, and it can happen in broken English, Spanish, or whatever language or hand signals are available.

Brain contact and stimulation, or body English, nothing more is required or needed if two people are willing to allow it to happen. "Once you find her, never let her go." It can be the magical chemistry of two people at the right moment in time where needs co-exist.

After our visit together, Maria said: "You are my savior, Mauricio."

This attraction made the picture even more complicated. We had true feelings for each other and deep respect for each other's desire to achieve fairness, equality, and freedom. Maria said, "You're the best piece of luck we have ever had." She spoke about her desire for liberty soon and for all of the poor people in Chile. She wanted to come to the United States.

Maria Carmen was a religious soul, heartfelt, authentic, and real. She is well-versed in her Bible; the only book allowed her in prison. "I read constantly," she said. "Just to keep my positive attitude and my faith." I especially like the story of the Good Samaritan and how Jesus, in the book of Luke, Chapter 10, asks each of us the deep and profound question of 'Who is your neighbor?' Everyone is your neighbor," she said. "You cannot ask for whom the bell tolls; it tolls for thee."

Maria Carmen stayed in my mind for many months after I returned home in April 1985. On that first day back, I went to watch my daughter, Lesley, play lacrosse. She was elected captain of her team at the Springside School in Philadelphia. My daughter's zeal, laughter, and leadership of her team reminded me of Maria's laughter and energy. All the parents were on the sidelines rooting for the team as Springside mounted a 10-6 lead and seemed headed for victory. But somehow, the tide turned, and the Springside lacrosse lost in a heartbreaker 11-10. I watched my daughter Lesley run over, taking her reluctant teammates with her to high-five and congratulate the winners with a handshake, hug, and laughter. It was just a game, not a war. They played the game and took defeat as well as victory in stride. Lesley has always been a good sport. I thought back to the beautiful moment of play, masquerade, and the charade of our engagement and marriage in a prison room with the sunshine flooding in. It was the same as the sunset flooding the hockey field as these carefree young women trudged off with honor intact to the changing rooms. Tomorrow would be another day of learning in the area of political play in Chile and at home.

For a fleeting moment that day, I saw Maria Carmen's smiling face in front of me. It was against a clear blue sky at sunset. The moment was a gift; it told me all is well with "mi prometido." I knew, somehow at that moment, that she was miraculously released and free. A telegram two days later confirmed her release. I do not know how I knew, but at that moment, I knew. It was a spiritual confirmation. At first, it was just blind faith, a certain "knowing" that the message was sent early by a spirit that Maria and her three friends were released.

It took five years for a new democracy to replace the brutal Pinochet regime. It was not until 1990 that the new government removed the large chain lock from the Supreme Court's gates in Chile. Juan Laredo and I were invited back by the new president, Patricio Aylwin Azócar. We went to the capital in Santiago to receive the Chilean Medal of Honor from the Republic of Chile "for the personal initiative and caring you have shown during Chile's darkest hour."

We felt honored to return. Maria Carmen was free, and she came to the ceremony with her mother and father. They also celebrated Maria as a freedom fighter for Chile. Maria beamed as she introduced me to her family. My heart thumped with a mixture of pride and my heart's true feeling of love for this brave and beautiful dark-eyed woman of grit and courage who was now on her way to a new life.

What was my lucky conversation? Well, it was the luck of meeting Maria Carmen. We shared a broken Spanish conversation and a little bit of English with hands in the air language. But best of all, we understood each other quite perfectly. It was a lucky conversation dominated by laughter, comedy, and comic drama. It masqueraded for the moment because of the honest and open dialogue that was not available when the wiretaps and machines recorded every word of our visit together. We fooled the authorities. We had to speak in code and sign language, but we understood each other quite well.

Sometimes the best conversations are with the eyes and heart. "Love comes in through the eyes," as the poet Wystan H. Auden once said. Our discussion on those two visits came in through the eyes, only to become a deep affair of the heart.

Justice Denied for Wallenberg

Raoul Wallenberg, Pre 1945

I deeply believe that our Supreme Court today is corrupted by Chief Justice John Roberts, an opportunist with no moral core. Evil walks the Supreme Court's corridors in the black judicial robe of John Roberts during daylight hours and sleeps in a secure lair at night with protective bodyguards. This darkest of all evil men, in my humble opinion, is John Roberts, the Chief Justice of the U.S. Supreme Court. As long as he sits on the Court, I will not rest in my efforts to stir up public opinion to remove him. He alone is responsible for the detention and death of my hero and client Raoul Wallenberg, consigned by Robert's treason to a death in Siberia in solitary confinement. He was on the edge of rescue and John Roberts consciously prevented it.

President Reagan was ready to demand the release and achieve Wallenberg's rescue at my urgent written request. Roberts sabotaged the plans at the last minute. According to William Colby, the head of the CIA, Roberts acted at the Russians' specific request. He was blackmailed and compromised by the KGB to sabotage the meeting.

Reagan invited me to meet with him in the Oval Office on November 11, 1983. The meeting was set to discuss the details for arranging the surprise release of Raoul Wallenberg from Russin in 1983. Roberts worked with the KGB to make sure my meeting with President Reagan never happened.

Reagan was planning to argue strongly about Wallenberg's humanitarian service in Hungary and our moral and legal duty to bring him home. Before Reagan could do so, Roberts snatched and trashed that written demand off the President's desk and abruptly canceled the meeting without informing the President of "a change of plans." In the press release, Reagan said: "Wallenberg is our de facto diplomat. We sent him there to save the Jews of Budapest. It is our duty and our responsibility to gain for him his remaining years in freedom. He has endured 39 years of pure hell and isolation in Russia and has miraculously survived. It remains our duty to bring him home. Mr. Gorbachev, please open the prison doors and immediately send him home."

At the last minute, John Roberts, White House Counsel, threw a monkey wrench. Roberts destroyed the press release and canceled the White House press conference without notifying me, the President, or anyone. Roberts sent Reagan a memo that said: "Morris Wolff is right on the law. He is our de facto diplomat, and under the U.S. Hostages Act of 1868, we have a duty to bring him home. But Mr. President, for a number of reasons, despite the Presidential power, I suggest we duck the issue."

Chief Justice John G. Roberts, 2005

The President was enraged and chastised Roberts for his cowardly act and insubordination. "Why should we duck the issue?" he said to Roberts. The real reasons for Roberts' calumny and cowardice emerged later in 2005 when he was being elevated to the Supreme Court's Chief Justice. Roberts held the keys to Wallenberg's release and freedom.

That was treachery and treason at the highest level. Roberts deep-sixed the Presidential plans to demand the immediate release and

President Ronald Reagan, 1981

then participated in a cover-up. But he overplayed his hand in a laconic but clear memo advising the President not to take action. Roberts decided on his own with no legal basis to not act on the request for Wallenberg's release. That secret Roberts White House memo was buried in the archives and not discovered until 2005 when Justice Roberts was up for the Senate's advice and consent to be elevated to Chief Justice. Sony Films Corporation wants to make a film tracing my efforts to rescue Wallenberg and the White House blockage and double-cross. They want to title the movie "Duck." Roberts' elevation to Chief Justice should have been quashed. He should have been removed from the Court and stripped of all retirement privileges. He caused the continuation of Wallenberg's unlawful imprisonment without justice or due process.

President Reagan called and invited me to the White House for the meeting to announce our demand that the Russians release Wallenberg immediately. I was also assured by his White House appointments secretary, Faith Whittlesey, that the meeting was on as planned." Be here by 10:30 for an 11:15 a.m. meeting." I arrived by ten to be on the safe side. "Here is the press release from which the President will be reading," she said. "Just look it over to be sure it includes everything you want him to say, especially about the duty to rescue and bring him home."

When my meeting with the President and the news conference was canceled, I was mystified. Faith Whittlesey assured me it would be rescheduled, but it never was, due to Robert's behind the scenes nefarious activities. I went back home and prepared my lawsuit, which I filed against the U.S.S.R. four months later in federal court in Washington, D.C., on February 2, 1984. Through an act of God and a role of the wheel, Judge Barrington Parker got the case. More on that in the next chapter.

In 2005, I received a late afternoon phone call from E.J. (Eve) Kessler, a journalist for The *Jewish Forward.*

"John Roberts killed the meeting," Eve said. "Roberts was acting for the Russians."

That is the terse report I received by telephone when I was in Switzerland on international law business in the summer of 2005, 22 years after Roberts was blackmailed by the KGB to ensure that President Reagan did not meet with me and on November 11, 1983, demand Wallenberg's release from the U.S.S.R.

Kessler: "Morris, I am writing an article on John G. Roberts, on the occasion of his nomination to the United States Supreme Court. I have uncovered some information in the Reagan library in California about Roberts's unusual involvement in the Wallenberg case and his role in the possible cover-up. I thought you might like to hear what I have uncovered. It is a story of scandal and misbehavior by our own government in your Wallenberg case," she said.

Kessler continued in a voice of excitement: "On November 11, 1983, you wrote an incisive letter to President Reagan asking him to intervene in the rescue of Wallenberg, using his executive power under the U.S. Hostages Act of 1868. Brilliant argument. Wallenberg was, by 1983, a citizen of the United States you said, as declared by an Act of Congress in 1981. I have a copy of your letter right here in front of me. I found it in the archives of the President marked 'secret material; not for distribution.' In your letter, you reminded the President of his absolute executive duty and power to demand that the Russians release Diplomat Wallenberg. You urged him to take action leading to Wallenberg's immediate release from Soviet custody. You stated the President's power is mandatory and not discretionary. John Roberts, who at the time was a White House staff lawyer, at first agreed with you. Roberts wrote a strange memo agreeing with your interpretation of the law. He even said you were correct. But he said, 'despite the Presidential power, I suggest we dodge the issue.' The Roberts memo has apparently been buried as 'secret' until now. It has just come to light during the confirmation hearing. Have you ever seen the Roberts memo, Morris?"

I answered, "No, I never did. This is the first I heard of it."

Kessler asked, "Would this have changed things had the President taken the action you recommended?"

I replied, "Why absolutely, yes. It would have made my task much easier. We could have freed Wallenberg even before filing my lawsuit. There were nearly three months between the time my letter was hand-delivered to the President and read by him and my filing of the lawsuit on February 2, 1984. It would have changed my whole game plan; I could have had the power of the President backing my lawsuit. It would have been awesome. Reagan and I going after the Russians on a joint initiative — two branches of government, the Executive and the Judiciary, and his personal lawyer — all demanding Wallenberg's release from Russia at the same time."

"I did not file my Wallenberg lawsuit against the Soviet Union until February 1984. The President's swift use of awesome power in November 1983 would have led to Wallenberg's release. It might have made the lawsuit unnecessary! The Russians would have realized this was the end of the game. And Wallenberg would be a free man today! The President has a duty to use his awesome legal power; this was not a discretionary choice. His legal counsel would have told him so. Reagan had an absolute duty to demand Wallenberg's immediate release as a hostage held illegally and without even the semblance of a trial by a foreign power. I am appalled by this information. I want to come home and ask Mr.

Roberts face-to-face at his Senate confirmation hearing why he took this step in his memo to condone the kidnapping and encourage a 'no action policy.'"

Kessler continued: "Do you think this failure on Roberts' part shows more than poor judgment?"

"Yes, much more than just poor judgment," I answered. "It goes to the very character of the man. It shows him to be weak-kneed, an example of his lack of guts. He failed to do his duty — and that was to advise his President to follow the law. As Assistant White House Counsel, he had no choice. That's why he got paid. He was a coward on this decision. It might be indicative of a pattern of weak thought that might carry over to the Court. No guts, no glory. What if he's a coward on the Supreme Court? Is he going to duck the tough questions like *Brown v. Board of Education* and *Roe v. Wade*? I want to ask him a few questions. One will be 'what did the KGB have to do with your quashing my scheduled meeting with President Reagan?'"

I sat there in a state of shock in the sunlight of a small café in Zurich, Switzerland. I was on a work assignment and a holiday back in one of my favorite places of mountain beauty. Forty-five years earlier, at age 24, in 1960, I worked for two years, establishing an AIESEC exchange program's international office and extending it to universities in Nigeria, Ghana, and Sierra Leone.

No wonder I never got an answer to my letter. Roberts and Fielding had buried it. A quiet cover-up. All I got was a cryptic letter of appreciation thanking me for my interest in the Wallenberg case and an assurance that President Reagan wanted me to know he was "interested" in Wallenberg's freedom as well.

The Roberts memo and my letter were buried in the secret canyon of White House records. These "radioactive" records, like the Nixon tapes, somehow found their way to the surface, and they incriminated Mr. Supreme Court Justice Roberts. Later, these documents were transferred to the Reagan Library to die a natural death. Kessler, an ambitious Jewish reporter, had somehow dug them up and made the memos front-page news. All things finally come to the surface of the lake. It was ironic, discovered by a Jewish reporter — Holocaust survivor — and it was as we say in Yiddish "Bescharet," destiny and simply meant to be.

I wrote a letter to President Reagan in early November 1983 asking him to use the *1868 Hostages Act* as a basis for pressing for the release of Raoul Wallenberg. The law provides that the United States President has an obligation to "demand the release of any U.S. citizen held hostage and in custody without a trial by a foreign government."

Faith Whittlesey, the President's assistant, was entrusted with the fast and guaranteed delivery. "I will stand and watch him read the letter," she assured me. "I am totally in your corner on getting the President to act. It was a good initiative and quite consistent with his signing the law for Wallenberg's full citizenship on August 5, 1981. I attended that Rose Garden ceremony and celebration. I stood right behind the President when he announced: "full citizenship for Wallenberg. We must hasten his rescue and bring him to freedom." She later assured me that she hand-delivered the letter directly to the President and stood patiently by his desk as he read it carefully and grimaced.

The President said to her, "I want to make this demand on the Soviets, and I want to make it now! Faith, this is an important letter from Morris Wolff. I like this kind of opportunity to showcase an issue. We can do something good for human rights and Ambassador Wallenberg. We can use this as a lever to gain Wallenberg's release."

The President instructed her to take the letter to White House Counsel Fred Fielding for immediate follow-up and fast action. He marked the letter "Yes, do this, and do it now," Ronald Reagan. That note and my letter were delivered to Fielding (the same Fred Fielding, who 21 years later served as George W. Bush's White House Counsel from 2004 through 2008, and counseled that waterboarding and torture were perfectly legal activities under U.S. law). Fielding assigned the drafting of an answer to my letter to the future Supreme Court Chief Justice John G. Roberts, who was at that time Assistant White House Counsel working for Fielding.

It is 2:30 a.m. on May 9, 2019, as I write this chapter of my book. Why is Roberts, living proof of treason, dual allegiance, and cover-up, allowed to hear cases of national and international importance on the Supreme Court? The reason is simple. The American people do not know the facts of what he has done — it is treason. I have told you the dual allegiances of his past that should have been explicitly raised and answered at his Senate Judiciary confirmation hearing by Senators Arlen Specter of Pennsylvania, Orrin Hatch of Utah, and others. They protected and coddled him from exposure. They protected his criminal behavior.

I asked the Senate Judiciary Committee for the privilege of speaking to the full Committee as they weighed the prospect of elevating Roberts to the position of Chief Justice. I wanted to ask questions about his secret memo to the President asking him "to dodge the issue." Both Senators Arlen Specter of Pennsylvania and Orrin Hatch of Utah denied me this opportunity claiming, "there was only limited room for witnesses." I was incredibly surprised and disappointed by the response of Senator Arlen Specter because he knew the truth.

They all knew the real story but confirmed him anyway. They did not let me testify. I had gone to Washington on my own dime to meet with each member of the Senate Judiciary before they held their historic hearings on Robert's second confirmation to become Chief Justice. I told them face to face why he was "dangerously and deeply unqualified." They turned a deaf ear and pretended the facts would go away. Senator Arlen Specter, my former boss in the DA's office in Philadelphia, apologized to me in person for his cowardly behavior and lack of backbone a few months before he died.

"We should have let you testify; you had a right to testify," he admitted. "Your words were important for the public and the committee to know the truth." Arlen Specter, in 1965, as DA of Philadelphia and fellow Yale Law graduate, was my boss and friend. He stood up for me as best man at my wedding on May 15, 1965, in Bala Cynwyd, Pennsylvania, but when the chips were down a few years later, he caved in and failed to do the right thing.

Roberts betrayed the people of America. I wanted them to know it through my testimony on his "fitness" in front of the Senate Judiciary televised hearings. In 1983, I was just beginning my work on the Wallenberg case when I discovered a federal law requiring the President of the United States to "demand the immediate release of any U.S. citizen held in jail or custody without a trial or due process of law." This law was good, vibrant, and powerful, guaranteed to get Wallenberg out of the Russian prison if supported by the United States president. Wallenberg enjoyed dual citizenship; he was a U.S. citizen and a Swedish citizen as well. As President Reagan's legal counsel and lawyer/advisor in the White House, Roberts knew this significant fact. That's because I visited the White House and told him, face to face, "The President has the power and the duty to demand Raoul Wallenberg's immediate release under the U.S. Hostages Act." Roberts agreed with my citation of the law. He promised to advise and encourage the President to take immediate action to demand Wallenberg's release. Instead, he deep-sixed and sabotaged my idea. He advised Reagan: "Morris Wolff is right on the law, but Mr. President, I suggest we duck the issue." Reagan was bewildered. He argued back, "I want to do this." But in the end, he did nothing.

My meeting with Roberts at the White House took place on November 4, 1983, exactly one week before my scheduled meeting with President Reagan that was mysteriously canceled at the last minute. I did not receive an explanation. Roberts, unfortunately, was already compromised by Russian intelligence. The KGB blackmailed him. They discreetly let Roberts know, through KGB agents, that they had "very embarrassing information on Mr. Roberts of a personal nature, and would welcome his cooperation."

Roberts sabotaged my Presidential visit. I did not learn about his skulduggery and treason until years later, just before Roberts' second Senate confirmation hearing.[8] Thank God there was the brave and hard-working investigative reporter named Kessler, from the *Jewish Forward*. Was Roberts a spy? Yes, whether you cringe at that suggestion or not, he was a deeply compromised government official in a strategic White House position. The new Alger Hiss. He had dual allegiances. Would the public ever learn the fact of his duplicity and criminal behavior? No.

Roberts should have been disrobed and released before he donned his first black robe. A Senate investigation would have achieved that. Instead, Roberts took his "deeply compromised position" with him as he moved from the United States Court of Appeals District of Columbia Circuit to the Supreme Court. I wanted to prevent the possibility of his becoming Chief Justice and to stop it in its tracks. According to Bill Colby, head of the CIA, "Roberts was a spy." Colby confided that to me during a luncheon in Washington D.C. when the confirmation hearings were going on. They even shut out Colby from testifying. Senators Specter and Hatch, the Republicans of the Senate Judiciary Committee, were contacted by Bill Colby and me. We asked to testify. I would reveal my explosive material to the Committee. I wanted them to hear how Roberts sabotaged Wallenberg's last clear chance for freedom by canceling my appointment with the President. Wallenberg was only 72 and alive, according to sources in Russia. We knew which gulag and which prison he was in at the time. It was on the Volga River near Kazan.

I called Faith Whittlesey. "You must testify," she said. "John Roberts, as White House Counsel, committed treason and consigned

---

[8] Originally, George W. Bush nominated Roberts as an associate justice to succeed Sandra Day O'Connor, who was retiring. When William Rehnquist died, and before Roberts' confirmation hearings, Bush changed Roberts nomination to Chief Justice and then appointed Samuel Alito as Associate Justice. See the New York Times article *President Names Roberts as Choice for Chief Justice* at https://www.nytimes.com/2005/09/06/politics/politicsspecial1/president-names-roberts-as-choice-for-chief.html.

Wallenberg to death when he canceled your White House meeting with President Reagan."

Faith continued, "You were to have met for 30 minutes. Your mission was to give Reagan the facts on the infamous Wallenberg kidnapping in 1945 from his post as a Swedish diplomat in Hungary near to the end of World War II." Faith continued, "I also wanted you to explain Wallenberg's courageous service to the United States as a savior of 100,000 Hungarian Jews from the Holocaust."

"Roberts was in collusion with the Russians, bought and paid for to keep the President's mouth shut about Wallenberg, and to prevent any chance of Presidential rescue. Roberts canceled your meeting, Professor Wolff, without the President's knowledge."

After the disappointment of the cancellation, I moved forward. On February 2, 1984, just three short months later, I filed my lawsuit, suing the Soviet Union in the U.S. Federal District Court for the District of Columbia. "That's the first time in U.S. history that someone sued Russia in an American court," said Professor Jordan Paust of the University of Houston Law School.

We won our lawsuit. Judge Barrington J. Parker wrote the courageous, groundbreaking opinion in the Wallenberg case, ordering the Russians to release Wallenberg immediately and pay $39 million in damages to the family. He issued his opinion on November 17, 1985. But the treasonous collusion that was first in play in 1983, between John Roberts and the Russian KGB, continued. A few years later, Roberts again intervened unlawfully and prevented the heroic Parker judgment from being enforced. Roberts found a Washington law firm to fight the favorable ruling I had won. They filed a "notice of interest" appeal to delay the enforcement of Judge Parker's gutsy and well-written opinion and verdict. A copy of the ruling by Judge Parker is at the back of this book.

After November 17, 1985, to keep Wallenberg in prison and under wraps in a Soviet jail, Roberts directly interfered again with our ability to enforce Judge Parker's judgment. His destruction of my visit with the President was only step one. In step two, he tried to get the verdict and judgment quashed and set aside. This action was a second and separate part of his desire to cover and protect Russia's political interests. The Russians would have been embarrassed and humiliated by the judicial opinion revealing their crime. The judicial opinion had the power of legitimacy. No longer was it just me as an advocate. Their crime of kidnapping Wallenberg from his diplomatic post in Hungary and other criminal behavior was to become known to the world, including the rebels in Belarus and Ukraine. They would use this as part of their propaganda as they sought to break away from Russia and secede.

The Soviets were prepared to do anything to avoid these breakaways and a continuous bright light shining on their blatantly unlawful behavior in the kidnapping and holding Wallenberg in solitary for 39 brutal years of confinement.

The major heroes in this story are Judge Barrington Parker and Professor Myres McDougal. The following chapter contains my conversations with Professor McDougal and Judge Parker after the verdict.

After the Wallenberg Verdict

Raoul Wallenberg

Judge Barrington Parker helped me by ruling Wallenberg's way. He informed the Russians to take immediate action and release Wallenberg, citing his age and the fact that he had been criminally kidnapped and detained. That is when the Russians contacted "their friend" John Roberts who intervened behind the scenes. The delays in enforcement of the verdicts began. Our law team had trouble understanding why the Russians were flouting Parker's explicit order that they take action and release Wallenberg within 90 days or be held in contempt and fined with further penalties.

Parker was angered by this back-alley action. We both were determined to get the "notice of interest" delay tactic thrown out. We were on the same side. Parker was known to be an unpredictable but highly principled "moral maverick" as a federal judge. He did things his own way. Parker went against all the odds, and precedents, and all the other 11 federal district judges on his D.C. District Circuit Court to step out on its own and decide in favor of Raoul Wallenberg's freedom. He held the Soviets criminally liable for kidnapping Wallenberg from his diplomatic post in Budapest, Hungary. Judge Parker slapped a $39 million fine on the Russian government and its 18th Red Army who captured and took Wallenberg from Budapest's consular position, breaching existing U.S. international laws, and consigning Wallenberg to years of a living death in a series of Russian prisons. Parker rendered a historic decision in Wallenberg vs. USSR. This towering and persuasive decision should have resulted in his immediate release from barbaric custody in Moscow's evil and dangerous Lubyanka prison, and the other places in the prison system where they moved him. They made him "disappear" into the "gulag archipelago" in rural Russia and Siberia, and lied to us incessantly about where he was hidden.

Judge Parker and I started out as advocates and a compassionate federal judge willing to listen. Now he was as upset by the injustice and mad as I was. The back of the hand treatment, given his carefully reasoned opinion and decision to punish the Russians and demand Wallenberg's release was undeserved. He worked hard legally to gain Raoul's freedom, something Reagan should have done two years earlier before the litigation. Parker and I became close friends with a mutual goal. We wanted to achieve Wallenberg's freedom through the US federal court system. We were both trained and educated at Yale Law by Sterling Professor Myres McDougal. "Mac" was our shared mentor. We remained among his favorite students and devoted ourselves to his ideals for compassion, fairness, and justice.

Mac, early in the Wallenberg litigation, became our go-between, our mail drop, and our secret meeting ground. Mac was our undisclosed back channel of quiet communication. No one knew of this extrajudicial channel of communication other than Parker, Mac, and me.

I filed the complaint and supporting brief in the Wallenberg lawsuit in Washington, D.C., on the morning of February 2, 1984. I walked up the courthouse's snowy steps with Wallenberg's brother, Guy Darden, who flew in from Sweden just for this historic occasion. We received nationwide coverage by the press and ABC, CBS, and NBC TV. Later that morning, by a spin of the wheel, Barrington Parker was selected from the judicial panel to be the one and only trial judge entrusted with Wallenberg's chance for freedom. Barrington was a winner, like the Kentucky Derby longshot. We had the best and sole judge willing to listen.

Parker was the grandson of a Carolina slave who fought for civil liberties and freedom from enslavement. Parker had the same fight, and nothing would drive either one of us from the case. God bless the active backchannel to McDougal. He had his own contacts to help us. The Wallenberg case was my favorite in 50 years of practice. By the grace of God, Parker and I were now joined at the hip and joined in court. We were also spiritually united through Mac, who wanted to make new laws and new precedents in the burgeoning fight for human rights in federal courts. Wallenberg was our world. We shared that passion. *Human rights everywhere* were Mac's motto.

I went to New Haven to see Mac soon after discovering that Parker was the judge in Wallenberg and Mac's former student. Mac raved about his fairness and integrity. I told Mac about the Wallenberg family's fateful telephone call, asking me to accept the case against the Russians. I wanted to learn from Mac about Parker's nature and biases. All judges have their partiality. I wanted to know in advance what to expect, and what Parker's soft spots were as a listening judge and as the ultimate decision-maker on Wallenberg's fate. I also wanted to probe with Parker all of a Russian-USA collusion possibilities in keeping Wallenberg on ice for 39 ugly years.

The following is how my conversation with Mac went back then:

Mac: "So, by the luck of the draw, you landed Barrington Parker as your trial judge in the Wallenberg case. Congratulations! The fates are working in your favor already. He is the only judge on that panel with the guts to listen to your first word. He might even rule your way if you follow my advice. Remain patient and argue with diplomacy and tact in his courtroom. Barrington is an autocrat. He runs a tight ship. Etiquette and good manners are vital. Your soft voice will "turneth away, wrath." Let Barrington Parker do all the talking. You are ready to listen. Be brief, in your response to questions, even terse.

Morris W: "Good advice, Mac. I plan to do exactly that; I will listen and learn. Two ears; one mouth. He is the one judge with the backbone and balls to engage and tolerate our arguments based on international law protecting diplomats, and the Alien Tort Statute of 1789, Thomas Jefferson's expansive jurisdiction baby. This case is just like the international law assignment you gave us in your seminar on human rights litigation and international law. Thank you for continuing your guidance at this moment in history."

Mac smiled. He removed the green eyeshade visor he wore while sitting at his oak desk reading law books and related articles. He had trouble seeing with his eyes but not his mind.

He listened well and took everything in. That includes the original March 5, 1983, 4:00 a.m. phone call from Raoul's brother Guy von Dardel in Sweden to my filing of the complaint in 1984. And then, I learned two days later that Parker was assigned to my case. I needed Mac to review my complaint and motions on jurisdiction and become the trial judge for a moment.

Mac: "The Wallenberg family trusts you. It has extended an honor in asking you to serve. I am glad you will do it pro bono and that you trust in the pure goodness of the cause. You will meet important people. It will be like walking in the corridors of history. You will be arguing in Parker's courtroom. Relax and trust him. This is a rare opportunity that few lawyers ever receive. It is unique, so use it well. You will have an opportunity to create new international human rights law in front of a distinguished jurist in the highly respected District of Columbia federal courtroom. A lot of history is going to be made. What you do will be remembered for 100 years at least, plus you have an opportunity to expand international law.'"

Mac: "This also allows me, as a scholar, to break new ground. We don't have to stand in awe and do nothing when nations misbehave. Nations cover up their evil deeds — like kidnapping and keeping Wallenberg on ice in Siberia."

"We can start writing about our choice to limit the evils committed by barbaric governments in the name of sovereign immunity. The Soviets can no longer hide behind words like 'immunity' or 'acts of state.' They can't engage in collusion and the raw politics involved in a secret conspiracy with our federal government. Russia and other foreign states mean us no good. With new laws, these foreign governments risk becoming subject to our federal court system's jurisdiction and accountable for their brazen kidnapping of Raoul Wallenberg and other foreign diplomats. The KGB's criminal wrongs in Hungary leading Wallenberg to brutal solitary confinement prisons of Siberia will be exposed by you and other activists in U.S. courtrooms. Your landmark case will become a precedent for others down through ages to come."

Mac: "The global reach for taking human rights issues like environmental change and barbaric treatment of innocent people in foreign courts of law will be extended within the U.S.A. first, and then everywhere, such as in China, Burma, Iran, Argentina, and Venezuela as the result of this one case. It will be like a rolling stone that gathers no moss. Wait and see! You, plus all my students, will develop this creative and expansive concept of international law as the supreme law of the universe. You will be a visionary architect, building a new structure of law and justice in an old building. Justice Justice, shalt thou pursue. It says so in the Bible."

MW: "Or better yet, like Frank Lloyd Wright, we will build new and controversial tools for the young architect of tomorrow with new uses and applications. We will reach out for creative new jurisdiction theories to serve a new global world for the next century. We will invent new theories of international law and national accountability for human rights — like the right to clean air, and personal privacy and safety in our homes, and we will argue for the establishment of these basic rights in the U.S. federal courts."

MAC: "You will need Professor Fred Rodell. He is a great writer and thinker. He smokes too much, but he writes and thinks brilliantly. He remains very proud of you and your work."

MW: "I will work closely with you and Professor Rodell. We will build an outstanding permanent law team. We will gather together with other tough litigators like Professors Jordan Paust and Anthony D'Amato, lawyers Nathan Posner, Leo Weinrott, and Murray Levin of Philadelphia. These are tough, brilliant, and creative lawyers and jurists. They will be part of my team, a team of gentlemen, to persuade Judge Parker to stretch and reach out and create a new law for the 'Rescue of Raoul Wallenberg.' Parker will be under pressure from conservatives from the White House to 'not to touch this case with a ten-foot pole.' They like to step away, take no position, and abstain. They don't want to ruffle the feathers of the Russian bear. They will label this case as 'far out' and undecidable by judges. They will call it a 'political question' and not for judges to decide. They will place imaginary 'Do Not Decide' and 'Too hot to handle' stickers on the case, and also seek a dismissal."

Mac: "We won't let that happen. Parker is your selected judge. It looks like a random choice, one out of twelve in the lottery. Five of the twelve judges in the District of Columbia are my former students. They all drink the Kool-Aid of liberal progressives, fighting for human rights, and support your arguments and your case."

Mac laughed. "My work for human rights was good for something. I originally wanted to stay in Mississippi and fight for human rights right there in the Delta, in the cotton fields where blacks earned next to nothing, still working as near slaves and living in dirt floor huts with no windows or toilets. That, Morris, is where I was born and raised in the cotton fields of the Delta. My smart parents rushed me out of there before I could get my ass lynched. I arrived in 1926, too early for civil rights in the state of Mississippi. They sent me north to live with my aunt, where my noise about civil rights would be safer and fall on deaf ears. I would not suffer the same assassination fate as Emmett Till or Medgar Evers."

Mac became an information back-alley bridge between himself, me, and Parker. We shared an architectural imagination of what the law should be. We loved the due process and making a record. We believed in fairness and justice and hated the abuse of power in the hands of bullies, cowards, and tyrants. It was inbred.

Parker and I were both idealists and realists. We were eager to create new law, anchored to old precedents. This willingness to look forward to making the legal world of the 1980s and the next century was the air we breathed. Our commitment to building new courtroom precedents, plus our willingness to consider making new law, and not just being stymied and hogtied by old preexisting law was our binding characteristic. It was like a marriage of true minds. Of all the judges on the panel, God gave me Parker to rule in my Wallenberg case. There are no accidents in life. And this was my lucky moment. First, I had a new blessed conversation with my beloved Professor MacDougal (Mac). I am convinced that God sent this man Barrington Parker to decide Wallenberg's fate, even as an evil and compromised man in the White House, John Roberts, was sabotaging my planned meeting with Reagan. That meeting would have led to Wallenberg's freedom, and it was crushed by John Roberts. Reagan was crazy about Wallenberg and wanted to rescue him. "I have the power and duty under the law, so let's do it," Reagan said.

Mac: "All that is left for Wallenberg's freedom is the federal court system. The rest is raw politics. That's your only avenue into legitimate power and honorable decision making. The executive branch has failed Wallenberg time and time again, starting with Roosevelt and then Harry Truman and up through Eisenhower and Reagan. They left him to rot after enticing him to serve. They have ignored him, except for Reagan, whom I truly believe wants him out and back home with a ticker-tape parade down Broadway. Perhaps with the two of you and Reagan seated comfortably on the top edge of the back seat of a Lincoln Continental convertible waving to the crowds, with confetti flying down from the tall windows above, just like a Hollywood movie. That is just perfect for Ronnie."

A year later, in 1985, after obtaining the verdict in the Wallenberg case, I visited with Judge Parker. I wanted a lucky conversation to reveal the details of why Judge Parker ruled our way and chose to severely punish the Russians for their criminal behavior. None of the other judges in the D.C. Circuit Court would touch the case. They ducked out, went on vacation, and dismissed it as a political question. In the courtroom victory, Parker demanded Wallenberg's immediate release. Finaglers from the U.S. State Department managed to delay the release at the meddling Russians' request. Finally, the promised release was delayed and delayed and never achieved, and this burned me. So near and yet so far. There was evil power at work behind the scenes with no explanation. I called Mac and went up to New Haven to see him again and stay for three days.

Mac: "By filing a notice of interest against your favorable verdict in Wallenberg, the State Department thoroughly destroyed the most important human rights verdict of the century. It was underhanded, done in the shadows, and involved work of the KGB and John Roberts. 'It was evil and not legal, Mrs. Segal.' Evil is what evil does, and it is a dirty tactic, like the Mafia."

Mac was as furious as I was with the outcome.

Mac: "The State Department is cozying up to the Russians, just like Roberts. This is not a good thing. It is a bad sign of things to come. Do not trust the Russians. That is the mistake made by FDR at Yalta in 1945 just after the war. FDR trusted the Russians to keep their promise not to meddle in Poland and the Baltics. It was written in the treaty signed by Stalin, Churchill and by FDR in a weakened state near death at Yalta. He should never have gone in the first place. We won the war but lost the peace. Stalin refused to respect the freedom of Poland and the Baltic States of Estonia, Lithuania and Latvia that bordered on the USSR. A sign of our weakness. The Russians have compromised Roberts and even your Wallenberg verdict. The Russian government has forced our State Department to oppose your lawsuit and file a so-called "Statement of Interest" seeking a dismissal of your hard-earned victory in court and the verdict of $39 million.

Mac: "Leave it to the State Department to sneak around your back and file a statement of interest against your verdict with a different judge. The only judge of record is The Honorable Barrington J. Parker. Morris, you are gaining national media and international media coverage with your exposure of the Russian's infamous behavior. Keep your foot on the gas pedal and accelerate."

Morris: "The forces of evil wanted time to think up new underhanded ways to destroy our landmark verdict and prevent Wallenberg's release. Lawyers from Baker and McKenzie have taken on the USSR as a client. They are in it for the money. Plain and simple. They are whores. Guns for Hire. They don't give a damn whether Wallenberg lives or dies. Just show me the money. They have been hired to create roadblocks and to delay enforcement of our verdict."

Mac continued his quiet rant. "These well-paid lawyers admitted to me they were in it for the money and not the principles of freedom and justice. They formed an unholy alliance and a cabal of legal talent similar to the stormtroopers and Gestapo "einsatzabteilung (operations department)." The worms came out of the woodwork from the U.S. State Department, acting in concert with members of the extremely well-paid private law firm, Baker and McKenzie. Russia retained and paid the law firm, located at 806 Connecticut Avenue near the State Department and the Russian Embassy, to make sure your verdict got derailed. Roberts arranged the hire at the Russians' request, a real conflict of interest if I ever saw one. They were feasting like hyenas on the remains of your excellent verdict knowing that delay and more delay was their only avenue for accomplishing an end-run around enforcement of the decision."

Mac continued, "They were in it for no damn reason other than money. There was no alternative principle of altruism or pro bono involved. No patriotism or doing the right thing involved either. How could lawyers from good law schools do this? These lawyers functioned as hired guns, moving back and forth from being State Department and White House Legal Counsel to the private law firms to make a bundle and then return to governmental positions. It's like getting on and off a moving trolley in San Francisco or the merry-go-round at Disney World. These hucksters simply go through revolving doors, in and back again in different years. They followed the money, not a love of justice, and ran the meter at $400 per hour."

Morris: "Both the State Department and Baker and McKenzie fought hard against Wallenberg's release. After hiring Wallenberg to go to Hungary in 1944, and guaranteeing his protection, Roberts made sure he stayed alive in a Russian prison. It was like a terrible morality play — a real fight between good and evil, all twisted up and complex. A team of pro bono idealists lined up against the evil empire."

Morris: "The raw use of evil power used to keep Wallenberg in his KGB cell at Lubyanka by U.S.A. abandonment, was involved, plus U.S. taxpayer dollars funding the Soviet effort. Where is the Congressional investigation of collusion when and where we need it? This was actively led by John Roberts and his lame successors. Roberts was paid off by the Russians to put a damper on Reagan and to make sure Reagan never met with me in person. This was even though I had a confirmed scheduled appointment with Reagan, two months before filing the federal court lawsuit, in Washington D.C. Raw, amoral power defeated a moral and legal initiative. The Russians paid this prestigious law firm to meddle and file a Notice of Interest against our winning verdict. It included a motion for a new trial to set aside the favorable Parker decision. I considered it treason."

Morris: "How ironic and scandalous that our most celebrated hero of the Holocaust, created by America, funded entirely by the U.S.A., is still in chains and not free due to the concerted effort of our own State Department? Wallenberg's brother and sister were outraged. So was Nils Lagergren, a Justice on the International Court of Justice, the husband of Wallenberg's sister. You'd think they and the Wallenberg Empire in Sweden would use their awesome financial and international political clout."

Morris: "The State Department, in the act of betrayal and treason, wanted to destroy my verdict, and prevent Wallenberg's freedom. They were afraid Wallenberg would embarrass the Russians if and when the full truth of his illegal detention was fully revealed. Can you imagine Raoul Wallenberg telling his story on talk shows with Johnny Carson and David Letterman!"

"Rather than bring Wallenberg home to personal freedom, John Roberts was content to let him rot and eventually die in the hell of solitary confinement?" Mac grimaced and nodded.

I left Mac after three days of shared discussions, and a wailing and gnashing of teeth. Then the following day, I called Mac to ask for his diplomatic help in arranging an in-chambers meeting for me with Judge Parker. A particular sensitivity and protocol was to be followed for this in person unique conversation. Lawyers do not usually meet with their judge when the case is over. I did not want to be turned down. I wanted to talk with Judge Parker and try to piece together the cryptic reversal of his final judgment. What happened behind the scenes after the winning verdict for the plaintiff was entered. Parker was the striding giant in my case. Mac pitched the idea to Judge Parker as "please do me a personal favor and meet with Morris."

Mac made the call to Judge Parker as soon as we hung up. The meeting date was set for the following Tuesday afternoon in Judge Parker's federal judicial chambers at the courthouse in Washington, D.C. The resulting conversation with Parker took place after I entered his judicial chambers.

President Richard M. Nixon appointed Judge Parker to the federal bench in 1969, an unusual move by a Republican President. Judge Parker was noted for his courage and boldness. "He had no hesitancy in coming forth with controversial decisions," according to his friend and fellow federal Judge Robert Carter. Parker was well-liked and respected. He was also black.

A warm, hearty, friendly, and deep bass voice answered my knock on Parker's judicial chambers door: "Yes, come in; the door is open, wide open." He sang out, "We are always open for men of goodwill who pursue justice on a foolish pro bono basis. You are one of them,

Mr. Morris Wolff, a fearless fighter able to reach great victories in seeking justice for others. You never give up." He got up from behind the desk with the help of a cane to greet me.

Judge Parker had retired from active duty on December 19, 1985, right after delivering his magnum opus on the Wallenberg case. He was given permission to keep his office at the courthouse for three more months. I came in response to Parker's telephone call from "Mac." It was now one month after the verdict. I thought it would be a short, superficial, and perfunctory visit. It turned out to be quite in-depth, open, and candid, beyond all of my expectations. It turned into an exciting hour, with many new revelations and pathways.

Roberts' effort to kill Parker's winning verdict became clear as we spoke. It came through in the words, emotions, and hand movements of Judge Parker as he reported to me how his ruling was quickly trashed by the U.S. government. That includes the State Department and John Roberts, the yellow-bellied goldfinch, seated safely on his golden perch in the White House.

Parker rose with the help of a cane and motioned for me to sit next to him. Arthritis and advanced age now paralyzed his leg. "Now, I am free — as a retiree — to speak candidly with you and to the listening public on the lecture circuit. I expect to be heard. You are my first post-retirement visitor."

MW: "Judge Parker, I am honored to be your first guest in chambers. I want to know more about your thinking of the skulduggery behind Robert's continuing effort to derail the Wallenberg case and verdict. The Wallenberg case decision had become final. The Soviet's refused to appeal and allowed the period for appeal to expire. You demanded, in your opinion, that the Russians release him within 90 days. They refused and are in contempt of court, your court as we speak to each other here this morning. How can we use this contempt tool and lever to force them to release Wallenberg to us in Moscow, bring him out of the Soviet gulag, and bring him home? We have waited for 39 years. Let's do this together as a team."

The judge, with his cane by his side, smiled. He recognized our unusual triangular friendship with Mac at the apex. He shifted in discomfort and moved his left leg. He mistook my deep respect and admiration for him as false flattery. "Don't kiss my ass. Don't kiss up to me. There's no need for flattery. Morris, you knew the law, and you were prepared and professional. I just had to listen carefully to your brilliant arguments and do the right thing. I respect your courage in taking on this dangerous case. The Russians could have shot you, or put some poison pills in your coffee, or left some poison or a bomb trap on your front doormat when you least expected. They have no shame, no scruples and no limits."

JP: "Now that I am retired, I am free to talk openly and candidly with you. You did a brilliant and professionally creative job, in writing the persuasive complaint and supporting brief in the Wallenberg case. Your arguments in favor of his freedom are compelling. Wallenberg was the most important case I have ever heard, even above the Hinckley case, where I had to rule either sane or insane for President Reagan's crazy shooter. Thank God the President survived that awful moment."

JP: "You did some very unique and positive research, breaking into new territory and resurrecting old wine for placement in new bottles, so to speak. Your first Saturday with Rare Book Room Librarian Marie Arnold proved to be vital in your personal discovery of the Alien Tort Claims Act of 1789 as your basis for asserting jurisdiction over the atrocious behavior of the Russians in burying Raoul Wallenberg alive."

JP: "You did the digging in the law library and made my job easy. You hung in there and held control over the Wallenberg litigation process even when you were all alone, and stood tall in the saddle while being teased, humiliated, and even bullied by your arrogant, smart-ass know-it-all colleagues."

He shifted his body to ease the pain in his left leg that was forcing him to retire. "Don't forget that you and I share Professor Myres

McDougal as our permanent mentor for achieving justice. You know that "Mac" is devoted to judicial realism, that is, using progressive and expansive interpretations of the law. Mac wants us to be judicial activists, to find our own way to do the right thing, to do justice, and then find a precedent or an existing statute to fit what needs to be done. This is Legal Realism at its best in the old Yale Law School tradition of Jerome Frank and Myres McDougal. That's what we learned at different times as law students. We come from the same training in the law of judicial activism versus judicial restraint."

MW: "Your readiness to consider my new theories of U.S. federal judicial power and its reach across national boundaries when an innocent man, like Wallenberg's life, is at stake was crucial to my success. During opening arguments about the jurisdiction, I felt you were chafing at the bit to be on our side of the argument. You wanted to assert the power of a U.S. court to take possession of a case of criminal kidnapping against Russia, the "evil empire," and to hold them accountable. That took courage. I looked up to the bench and saw you listening, with patience. You were fair to both sides, but you were kinder to ours. You used your honesty, patience, and passion for justice to make a great decision."

JP: "My traits of seeking fairness come from my ornery father, beating up on me to 'make me a better man.' He was always pushing me to do better, 'do your best, nothing second rate.' My father always talked about opportunity and 'the road not taken,' and striking out on the 'road less traveled by' to find one's way through the woods of life. My dad was also a maverick, a self-made man, like you. He was the victim of hatred and discrimination. He was pursued, harassed, and threatened with death by the Ku Klux Klan. He had to hide under a bushel of potatoes in the storeroom once. He was Mr. Civil Rights well before Martin Luther King and Medgar Evers."

We shifted to other subjects. I was curious and wanted to learn more about Judge Parker as a person. "What led you to a life in the law and to becoming a federal trial judge?" I asked.

JP: "Good question. My family heritage and background accounts for everything. My father was the Dean of the Terrell Law School for Blacks in Washington, D.C., which has since closed. I practiced law with my father in the firm of Parker and Parker until I was appointed to the federal court by President Nixon. I went to Dunbar High School in Washington, where I met my wife, Marjorie Holloman. We met at a dance, and she became my tutor on social behavior. I graduated in 1936 from Lincoln University in Pennsylvania, where Kwame Nkrumah, the first President of Ghana, learned how to be a leader devoted to his country. I received a master's degree from the University of Pennsylvania; your hometown and the university where you still teach," said Parker with a wink of his eye teasing me with the coincidence and research. He knew facts about me from Mac and had read my resume with care. He continued, "I earned my law degree from the University of Chicago in 1947 and plunged into private law practice and active politics in the Republican party. I always wanted to be a judge, and in those days, elevation as a black man in the system came through the Republican party. My oh my, how times have changed."

MW: "I want to know about your maverick part, the man who stakes out a territory of concern, decides legal matters on his own, and refuses to follow the herd." He smiled at my recognizing this unique trait, which Professor McDougal had pointed out to me before presenting my courtroom arguments to Judge Parker in the hot and humid D.C. federal courtroom in the summer of 1984.

JP: "Too many public servants, especially federal judges, are too cautious, both cowardly and careful. Too many judges are looking out just for themselves, and for the next step up on their career ladder, from federal district court judge to appellate to the Supreme Court itself. They become careful careerists; they fail the public. They fail to remain independent and to have integrity, and the guts to decide something new and different. They become like puppets on a string, wielding their own strings, and avoiding a lot of unleashed power, and yet afraid of their own shadows."

MW: "That's what John Roberts was doing when he canceled my meeting with the President. He misused his power and overstepped the boundaries of the President. Roberts sabotaged my meeting with the President without Reagan ever knowing it. He was deceitful and intent on sabotage for some reason, and the Russians had him under their thumb. He was not helping the President; he was committing common law treason."

"Roberts ignored the President's passion and desire to rescue Wallenberg, and he committed perjury. He lied to the President. President Reagan gave Raoul Wallenberg a special status as a United States citizen on purpose. He revered Wallenberg as a hero and as one of the Righteous Gentiles. Reagan made Raoul a gold star citizen to make it easier for us to rescue him. Roberts blocked the President's desire when Alzheimer's disease was beginning to cloud the President's mind. It was a tragic and very intentional mistake. He has never admitted his reasons."

Two years later, John Roberts jumped like a frog from his lily pad as White House Counsel to a series of intermediate jobs leading finally to his judicial appointment to the Supreme Court.

JP: "Roberts is a crook, and controlled by the KGB. He must have done something awful and the KGB nailed him with that information. Roberts was a careful tippy-toe careerist. He is weak and fearful as a jurist, always looking for where the majority is going and then hopping on their train at the last minute so that he can write the majority opinion. Very clever and very political with a small p. His day of removal or early retirement must come soon. He must be defrocked and be disrobed; mark my words. He is just one of the J. Alfred Prufrock's who get ahead as frogs by not making waves in the pond. He worries, as the poet TS Eliot suggests:

Do I dare to eat a peach? I shall wear white flannel trousers and walk upon the beach. I have heard mermaids singing, each to each. T.S. Eliot weeds out the brave from the cowardly with biting sarcasm."

MW: "I am surprised by your knowledge of his poem, *The Lovesong of J. Alfred Prufrock*."

JP: "Eliot's brilliant poem focus on the malaise, and lack of leadership in 20th-century man, just before World War II. We had an emergence of tyrants like Hitler, Mussolini, and Tojo in Japan. Nobody spoke out. Everyone cowered and prayed that hell might blow over. Well, it did not, and Wallenberg, if he was here with us, could tell us that in spades. We have no more heroes with backbone and courage except people like Churchill and Raoul Wallenberg. You indeed did as Hamlet said:

Take arms against a sea of troubles,
And by opposing end them? To die: to sleep;
No more;

JP: "I am paraphrasing a great quote from Hamlet and his Prufrockian inability to make up his mind in a time of moral crisis. 'The hottest places in hell are reserved for those who, in times of great moral crisis, maintain their neutrality,' according to Dante. The key verb is to suspend, to stand back, not get involved, take the easy way out, and by doing so, avoid risk in the ranks. That's Roberts and many other careerists like him too. He committed treason. Don't rest until you nail him. He is running away from you, won't even meet with you, I bet."

JP: "*Alfred Prufrock* by T.S. Eliot is typical of 20th-century men of evil and inaction. They hid behind lace curtains, looking out on the street as the Nazis came to carry away innocent Jews. Or the Klan, the night riders in white, that come to lynch an innocent Negro one night in Alabama. That is what happened to my uncle, and I watched it happen. These feckless men, as judges, are willing to hide behind the myth of judicial restraint. They include Justice Felix Frankfurter. What they really mean is just don't rock the boat; don't take any chances. Follow politics and pressure. Had I done that, there would be no Wallenberg decision."

MW: "Judge Parker, thank God you are not a timid soul or a Milquetoast or a Prufrock. You are bold, confident, and determined. Now I understand just why. You have seen the ultimate injustice of death without due process before your very eyes. I resonate with you. You are my kind of human being, my kind of judge."

JP: "Those traits of self-confidence and ornery behavior that you call maverick, come from life and also from my father. My father was a nonconformist. He was always working against the grain, a contrarian by nature. I inherited core values and traits from my Dad." Parker stopped for a moment. All was silent. I could see a faraway glint and daydream in his eyes as he thought back to his own father and the examples of manly behavior he inherited.

JP: "My Dad was a unique black man. He set out as one man to solve inequality, discrimination, and the evil practice by police of terrifying blacks in America. Dad went out and raised money in small amounts from black families. He established Terrell Law School for well-mannered, civilized, bright, and high-quality blacks who could not attend white law schools. If admitted to white law schools, they had to sit in the corridor outside the classroom and leave the door open so they might hear the lecture but could not participate in asking questions in class. There would be no Q & A. The Supreme Court opinion in Sweatt v. Painter cured that. A black student in Arkansas got tired of sitting in the noisy corridor. He sued the University of Arkansas for the humiliating practice of shoving black students out the classroom door into the busy corridors where they could hear only a small part of the lecture. 'Separate but Equal' has never been equal. Everything was segregated, and that meant no law school was available. My father was a man who refused to take no for an answer, just as I did in the Wallenberg decision. He went out on his own, like Johnny Appleseed, spreading the news and planting seeds of his new school and recruiting students; black men and women who never dreamt they might one day become lawyers."

JP: "He paved the way for all black lawyers and judges. He handpicked high-spirited and passionate people. His motto in 1928, even during the Depression, was, 'don't just sit there: attack!' He was my hero. He taught me to go against the establishment. Morris, I want you to know that John Roberts came in person from the White House to my chambers and put pressure on me to reverse my decision in Wallenberg. I refused."

"They never mentioned his secret and unethical initiative in the papers or on the record. He came unannounced to my chambers one afternoon and offered me a 'special deal.' I could not believe my ears. Roberts said, 'I can make you a Court of Appeals or Supreme Court judge if you reverse yourself on Wallenberg.' I threw him out on his ear, told him, 'never come back, or I will report you for prosecution to the Justice Department for tampering with a verdict.' What Roberts tried to do by pressuring me was a violation of the separation of powers. He consciously violated our most fundamental law and should be impeached."

MW: "You have some of the passion and orneriness of your Dad. You won't be pushed around."

JP: "Yep, got those traits by direct transfusion from my father, and never knew I had them in me until well after age 40 when I first became a judge. I had to do some serious introspection before ascending to the bench. So, when I saw the barriers of so-called 'jurisdiction' in your case, of nations like Russia trying to build a fence around its borders and call it 'sovereign immunity' I just revolted. I tore down that argument of immunity as a sham. No one has freedom from accounting in court for their own criminal behavior. No government official, such as the KGB leader Lavrentiy Beria, gets a free pass for his own sadistic misbehavior in locking up Raoul Wallenberg and beating him and chucking the key away for 39 years. These Russian KGB operatives are human garbage. There will be one day no place to hide for people like John Roberts. He can never justify what he did to Raoul Wallenberg when he canceled your meeting with the President. That meeting would have changed history. It would have opened floodgates of deserved freedom for political prisoners."

JP: "My father was self-reliant. He went out on his own with almost no help to start that first black law school in the South. I hate barriers like the blankets of Sovereign Immunity and Act of State, allowing governments to do anything they want and call it an untouchable act. I hate unlawful barriers like those faced by black law students. Barriers to law school admission and barriers of Sovereign Immunity are related. That is why you found me soft on Jurisdiction in Wallenberg. I allowed you to haul the Russians into U.S. Federal Court at your request, and also because I detest false barriers of discrimination. '***Fiat Justitia ruat cœlum***,' or 'Let justice be done though the heavens fall.'"

The Judge shifted his weight and took his cane to lift himself for a brief moment of relief. Parker was against judicial restraint and creativity. I believed he was the only district court judge in America with the courage to face injustice in the Wallenberg case. Others would have ducked the issue and characterized it as a political matter. With his grandfather as a former slave, Parker was able to sense Wallenberg's pain as he sat in solitude, enduring years of barbaric treatment in Russia or Siberia.

JP: "I admire what you are doing, Morris, in not giving up on Wallenberg. As long as there is awareness of his plight, he is still alive. You have earned my respect. You have become my esteemed good friend and new colleague for justice. I wish you the best and god's grace."

He teased me and called me 'Mr. MW Esquire,' and we laughed together, more with a sense of quiet understanding and mutual respect, than anything else. There was no meanness or pettiness to this man. Parker had respect for men and women who stick their necks out to do the right thing.

JP: "Use my opinion as a cudgel and as a tool. That's why I made it a direct demand on the Russians. I specifically said $39 million in damages, at your request."

JP: "I have tried to get the State Department and President Reagan to demand his release now. For some reason, the White House is still stonewalling. They do not answer my letters. I get delay letters from White House Counsel John Roberts claiming, 'we are looking into this matter.' They want to wash their hands, as if Wallenberg is of no importance as if he is the man who never was."

We returned to questions aimed at finding out more about Judge Barrington Parker, a bold and brilliant African American. Parker had a giant ego, pride, and a firmly rooted moral compass. Before his historic Wallenberg human rights decision, Parker was the man who found President Reagan's would-be assassin, John Hinckley, insane and unable to stand trial.

"There was a public clamor for my skin. There was a big outcry for a public lynching of Hinckley," commented Parker. "Members of the public wanted me removed from the bench. They were outraged with what I thought was a fair and honest decision. I had no bone to pick in that case. John Hinckley was clearly insane and unable to stand trial. He was nutty as a cuckoo. He had no idea who or where he was. I caught a lot of grief about my decision in that case."

"By comparison, I received a lot of public praise from Jewish survivors, both here in America and Israel, for my decision in Wallenberg. They were grateful. I still have handwritten letters from them." He reached into his desk and pulled out a portfolio of letters. "There are more than 300 letters in my file from all over the world."

We commiserate as we read a few of the heartbreaking letters, and then he returned them to his file for safekeeping and future use. "I plan to give you these letters from the people Wallenberg saved and who wrote to Wallenberg in Russian prison between 1945 and 1963," Parker commented. "There was no support or applause for my Wallenberg decision to punish the Russians from our State Department. They were completely quiet. There were no roses, no congratulations from anyone. That was quite ironic since key figures like Cordell Hull at State seduced, selected, and sent Wallenberg into war zone danger never to return. He went on June 6, 1944 — D-

Day exactly — with no security cover or plan for his retrieval from danger as promised. It was reckless, a scandal of inaction and abandonment by our government. They left him to twist in the wind, alone in solitary from his kidnapping on January 17, 1945, right up to the present day. We know the Russians have him, and we know exactly where."

Parker shifted away from his amputated leg.[9] "The war is over. Why did we not speak up candidly and boldly demand his freedom as a diplomat at that time? We needed to demand his release from the Soviet Union!"

Parker turned towards me as if I might know. Was I the custodian of Wallenberg's interests, possessions, and unanswered questions?

MW: "I have no answer, your Honor. I was nine years old at that time and in third grade in America just discovering human rights."

It was indeed a mystery. The Russian Ambassador to Sweden, Alexandra Mikhailovna Kollontai, told Wallenberg's family "Schrei nicht" or do not scream. We will see that Wallenberg is released and sent home right away." It was a lie, coming from Russian officials through the Ambassador's lips to the family, and then nothing but silence for weeks and months.

I walked over to look briefly at a large Map of World hanging on the Judge's wall. It showed how close Sweden was to Russia, just 45 minutes by a comfortable air flight. "Scoop him up at the airfield and bring him home," I thought to myself. "So near and yet so far." There was no real full-throttle effort by the wealthy and influential members of his banking family to rescue and bring him home.

We moved on to a new fascinating area of legal concern on the question of jurisdiction. I asked, "Judge Parker, why did you finally decide to grant us jurisdiction over the Soviet Union? That must

---

[9] While crossing a busy Washington D.C. street, Judge Parker was hit by a car and had his left leg amputated in 1975.

have been a hard decision since the mainland of Russia is thousands of miles away. That is quite a stretch."

I continued to probe. "You could have washed your hands of the case before you started. You could easily have ducked the issue and deemed this a political rather than a legal question for the courts. You could have dismissed our complaint and labeled the matter a "question for the President of the United States to take care of within the State Department as a matter of international relations and diplomacy with Russia?"

JP: "That is one real question that deeply concerned me. You had tweaked the nose of the Russian bear with your lawsuit, and the Soviets were hopping mad. Backchannels from the State Department let me know exactly that. I never told you at the time. I knew I was making a new precedent with your case, a kind of global reach to deal with human rights violations by a foreign government, a government with which at that time, we were on the edge of doing battle and going to war. It was the era of the Cold War with plenty of tensions, enough to go around. It is not an easy question of why I took up the case on its merits. I already knew the State Department wouldn't touch it. They lobbied and pressured me, saying, 'this one's a hot potato. Please do not touch.'"

"The Soviets were angry that you had even filed the lawsuit. They even thought someone put you up to it. They had no idea how independent and cussed you are."

"I knew that you were cussed and aggressive and a smart ass even before you stepped into my courtroom. I did my own research on you beforehand. I knew that Mac got you your first job working with Bobby Kennedy in the Office of Legal Counsel on the hallowed 5th floor. You became a member of the inner circles around Kennedy over at Justice." He smiled, "I like to know about my lawyers before they enter my courtroom, so I know how to deal with them during arguments and cross-examinations at trial. I called Mac to get the skinny on you before you popped into my courtroom all full of passion about Wallenberg."

JP continued, "Mac was my mentor too. He told me plain and clear, 'Morris Wolff has integrity and brains. Morris would not have filed the suit if he could have gotten Wallenberg released earlier through Reagan and the White House. The White House road, and especially John Roberts blocked Morris. That's Mac's word, and I trust it." Parker got up with the help of his black cane.

JP: "Mac told me you scheduled an Oval Office appointment with President Reagan, all carefully arranged by his assistant, Faith Whittlesey. Mac said that 'John Roberts and Fred Fielding killed, kiboshed, and deep-sixed' your scheduled meeting with Reagan. John Roberts and Fred Fielding were two of Reagan's chief aides. Mac read your research memo for that meeting of yours with President Reagan. He approved its soundness, and the President was ready to endorse and present your position as his very own at a news conference scheduled for the same day as your November 1983 meeting at the White House. Had that meeting with Reagan taken place as planned, Wallenberg's release could have happened by direct Presidential demand. We had the law — the Hostages Act of 1868[10] — clearly on our side. Wallenberg was in good health and only 72 according to CIA sources and our spies working inside Lubyanka prison in Moscow."

"When I learned from Mac that you had been stonewalled by aides at the White House and forced to file a lawsuit, I reached out for it and took it off the docket of new cases. I did not want it going to someone else. The others would have kicked it out as 'a political question.' Not me. I was ready to decide on the merits when I learned fully from Mac what the case was all about. I asked the Clerk of the U.S. Federal District Court of the District of Columbia

---

[10] For more information about The Hostages Act, see *Executive Power Under the Hostage Act: New Life for an Old Law* at https://heinonline.org/HOL/LandingPage?handle=hein.journals/cintl14&div=20&id=&page=

to make damn sure that the case came to me. He complied with my request. And so, we met in court!"

He laughed again, the same belly laugh as before. "We give forum shopping a new twist here in D.C." President Reagan was obliged under law to demand Wallenberg's release as an American diplomat and citizen, and he dropped the ball, based on Robert's treasonous advice: "Don't do it, Mr. President. Morris Wolff is correct on the law, but I strongly urge you to respect the Russians' Cold War interests and the present tensions and let them release Wallenberg when they are good and ready. Don't rub their noses further in the mud by exposing their criminal behavior in kidnapping a Swedish diplomat who merely saved a whole bunch of Jews."

Roberts added, "The Cold War is cold enough already. Let's not rouse the Russian bear at this time."

"But Roberts was serving two masters, two different countries, and that is treason," said Judge Parker. "How he got away with it, we'll never know until Roberts tells us."

Parker got up, went to the refrigerator, and opened two Canada Dry Club Sodas. "Good for indigestion," he said. "And I have indigestion for what happened to you."

After a rest period for his leg and age, we continued our conversation. "Once I learned you got a raw deal and were shut out by the White House, Mac alerted me that you would be filing your lawsuit in the first week of February 1984. I kept an eye out for it. I pretended that the case just fell in my lap by chance. I was committed to doing the right thing by taking your case off the list and appropriating it to myself. I would hear the case and make a decision. Simple as that."

I asked, "As an international lawyer, I was amazed that you defied the time-honored precedent that U.S. Federal Courts refuse to not take jurisdiction in cases where the crime involved takes place beyond the water's edge. You chose to upset and reverse that long-standing precedent of territorial jurisdiction. You shook their rafters, and you ruled our way. You managed to upset the apple cart, destroying everyone's expectations in giving us a verdict in the case."

He smiled as I continued with a series of questions.

He answered each one without batting an eye. He cherished, respected, and protected his Wallenberg case decision as his judicial "shining moment and shining hour."

MW: "Just why exactly did you stick your neck out when the Secretary of State, the entire State Department, and John Robert's urged you to 'duck the issue and wash out the case?' They wanted you to consider it a political question and buck it back to the White House, thus ending and quashing our effort to gain his freedom? Why were you so bold? What gave you the backbone to stand up against everyone in Washington for Wallenberg and to support our effort to rescue him from the Soviet Gulag? Can you tell me more?"

JP: "I felt it was my duty and my job. To be a judge is to love mercy, do justice, and walk humbly with my God. My mother, Maude Daniels Parker, 'Maudie,' first taught me those words. She said to learn them by heart on my first day of kindergarten. Those words have stuck with me ever since. I was appointed to do those three things as a federal judge — to follow that code of ethics and honor. I can do no less. I saw a chance for justice in your case, and I took it. Judges in real life, and despite what you learned in law school, can rule almost any way they choose. They have freedom of choice. We can change precedents that have lasted hundreds of years. For example, the decision in the Brown v. Board of Education and the school desegregation cases."

"In Wallenberg, I decided that I would force my federal district court to reach out actively with a global reach for human rights violations by states and governments, including foreign nations like Russia or Iran. Also, our own U.S. government when they grossly violate human rights, as in your Wallenberg case. If governments do not correct their misbehavior, including Presidents, we have a check and balance system with an independent federal judiciary in place to criticize and curtail Presidential wrong behavior."

"I had no choice but to rule in your favor. Just like Wallenberg, whom you chose to represent." Wallenberg once said, "I have no choice. I must go and rescue the Jews in Budapest. What else could I do?" I loved his bold idealism. He could have stayed home and dated Ingrid Bergman."

Judge Parker continued, "Wallenberg was a practical idealist, a genius with courage. Like you, Morris, you saw a great cause, and you created an argument out of an old and obscure law. You were tenacious, you would not let go, and eventually, you won. You achieved a great victory, and I am glad to share in it. We are both practical idealists. You wrote the brief, argued his case, and championed his cause in his hour of crucial need."

"How did you arrange for your TV appearances on February 2, 1984?" the Judge asked. "I saw you on the ABC morning news at 7:00 a.m. on the day when you and Wallenberg's brother went up the steps of the federal court at 9:00 a.m. to file your brief. You made Wallenberg's half-brother the plaintiff. And when I saw you testify before the U.S. Senate on TV, you lit a fire and caused the light of the world to shine into his prison cell. That's when the real action started," he added.

I answered by telling him how friends in Philadelphia were helpful in contacting the ABC-TV local station. "I was a member of the Big Brothers of Philadelphia. One of the board members had a public relations firm, Kalish and Rice, that was aggressive and Jewish. They told me we are going to the moon. They delivered ABC, CBS and the New York Times as useful publicity. By the time they finished, most Americans knew about Wallenberg's terrible predicament and detention."

JP: "Gaining national publicity was the right thing to do. It was a step forward for Justice and the scales of Justice, so beautiful but blindfolded. It was your duty. This lawsuit is what God measured you for in the first place. I sensed your passion from your opening argument, and I applauded it in my decision."

JP: "Wallenberg was rejected, abandoned, and forgotten by our Embassy in Russia. That is a moral outrage, Foggy Bottom at its worst." He straightened his red tie and the French cuffs of his white shirt. He sat quietly, listening to my additional questions. "You educated me, Morris, throughout the trial. That is what a trial lawyer is supposed to do. Through your supporting brief, I came to learn that Wallenberg was a Swedish diplomat chosen to serve the interests of the U.S.A. in rescuing endangered Jews and then coldly abandoned by our government. I fight for fairness and taking responsibility for one's actions. How could my U.S. government seduce and draft him to go into an unprotected position in Hungary, save 100,000 innocent Jews of Budapest, and then leave him unguarded, to shift for himself, when the Russians came to kidnap him? As you argued in your brief and my federal courtroom, he was an accredited diplomat, protected by diplomatic immunity. They then allowed him to twist in the wind, hidden in a Soviet prison incommunicado for 39 years, until you came to his rescue. The whole story is a scandal and a story of corruption. It's not over yet. The new stink of ongoing corruption centers on the White House. President Reagan had his chance to do something right and decent, and he dropped the ball, urged by Roberts to abandon Wallenberg to "duck the issue." I have a deep source within the White House walls that keeps me current and posted. The Russians were upset. They refused to honor your complaint and come into court, so I ruled against them in my default judgment. Instead of coming into court, they went to the White House to meet with John Roberts, who gave them a deal. Did the Russians have something on Roberts, a kind of blackmail about which we don't know? Was he compromised? His behavior was irrational and evil."

Judge Parker was still very current and clear on the facts. His mind was as sharp as ever. It was only the pain in his legs that caused him to retire early. I wished he was still on the court, ready to protect the favorable verdict of $39 million in damages and an order to the

Russians to present Wallenberg alive in his courtroom. "I sense he is still alive," said the Judge. "I have my own reliable sources in our CIA, and they tell me he is alive. Yours was not just a daring adventure. You are on to something important, historic, and authentic. I will try my best to make sure the White House and State Department politicians, who want to protect the Russians from embarrassment, do not get their hands on my verdict. They will try to kill it or shift it over laterally to another federal judge once I am gone.'

JP: "It is just two months since I rendered my verdict for you and your client on October 18, 1985. I wrote my opinion very carefully. Some of my ambitious colleagues are looking for advancement up to the appellate court. They are political opportunists, willing to sell out on their core values and principles in exchange for a higher post in the federal court system. They are willing to give up judicial integrity for promotion to the Federal Court of Appeals. Frankly, I would rather remain a federal district court trial judge, appointed for life, as in your case."

JP: "For some reason, one member of the White House staff has cold feet about the Wallenberg case, and the embarrassment it has caused for Gromyko and Lavrentiy Beria, and other dictators and criminals at the top of the Russian government. Roberts wants to appease the Russians and bury the case in the archives. The Russians are angry as hell. They think I was acting out of order in accepting the case and ruling against them. Well, that is too damn bad. They were the ones acting way out of order in kidnapping Wallenberg and refusing to allow him to return home to his family in Sweden. They had no business holding him in the first place. No trial. No hearing. Treated like a dog. Even the worst criminals at least get a trial. They were afraid of something, and we still do not know quite what it was. Wallenberg deserved to be set free in 1945. He should have received the Nobel Peace Prize and other medals for what he accomplished and sent home from Moscow. Instead, the Soviets brutalized Wallenberg. Nothing was done for him until you came along 39 whole years later. This judicial decision was an easy one for me to render."

JP: "I wasn't appointed to the l court to cover up the Soviet's gross misbehavior. Keeping Wallenberg on ice for 39 years is still criminal. Russia thumbed its nose at my decision. I would have held them in contempt if it were not for pressure from both the State Department and the White House for me to stop any further action. That interference was unethical. I should have been holding them as convicts in a criminal prosecution, as a follow up to giving you a verdict of civil punishment of 39 million dollars. My colleagues on the federal court applaud what I have done." He sighed and took a sip of water from the glass next to him on the table. Then, he was silent for a moment.

JP: "This case is not over. Some people think I will be snoozing like an old dog turned out to pasture. But I will keep both of my eyes wide open. There may be more shenanigans. The President was ready to meet with you when his staff manipulated him. He knew he had a duty to demand the prisoner's release as a political war prisoner, but he dropped the ball."

MW: "Our relations with Russia in the winter of 1985-1986 were at a freezing point. Reagan denounced Russia in 1983 as the 'evil empire.'[11] We were confrontational. What could be a better time for this President to demand Wallenberg's release under the U.S. Hostages Act? The President was looking for additional faults of 'hooliganism' as ammunition, and yet on demanding Wallenberg's release, giving them another poke in the eye, he pulled back."

"I have no answer for White House shenanigans," said Parker.

---

[11] Reagan called the Soviet Union the evil empire in 1982 during a speech at the British House of Commons. He said it again speaking to a convention of the National Association of Evangelicals in Florida on March 8, 1983. See *Reagan refers to U.S.S.R. as "evil empire" again* at https://www.history.com/this-day-in-history/reagan-refers-to-u-s-s-r-as-evil-empire-again

We did not realize as we sat there in chambers that afternoon that our government was about to play a cruel and corrupt game by having the Executive Branch intervene and tamper with Judge Parker's final decision in the Wallenberg case. The lateral shifting of the Wallenberg case from Judge Parker's closed calendar to the open schedule of Judge Foxwood Robinson is both illegal and without precedent. Judge Robinson became complicit in a behind-the-scenes deal in exchange for his own raw ambition and judicial advancement. He was a federal district court judge in the same district as Judge Parker. He was about to be elevated from the District Court to the Court of Appeals in exchange for quashing Parker's brave judgment. The case moved laterally, within the District Court in a moment of utter judicial corruption instigated by the White House and U.S. Department of State.

The lateral movement of cases from one active federal district judge to another is never allowed, especially after the 60 days for an appeal passes. Only a written appeal to a higher court was permitted. The Soviets never took that initiative to appeal the case. Instead, they hired an American law firm, Baker and McKenzie, to do their dirty work. This law firm colluded with the State Department and with John Roberts at the White House. They knew that Wallenberg was still alive and in danger. Our government simply hung him out to dry. I was outraged by what they did with the Parker final decision. They violated the basic tenets of the separation of powers; our State Department sent him to Hungary to rescue the Jews. He was our de facto diplomat. We had a duty to bring him home. My government said "No." The hottest rim of hell is reserved for those who in a time of moral crisis, suspend judgment," according to Dante in "The Inferno." That rim is reserved for John Roberts and his cronies.

It was getting close to 5:00 p.m. It was time to go. I thanked Judge Parker for our visit and wished him a smooth recovery from his leg's constant pain. Parker proved to be right about both Judge Spottswood Robinson and John Roberts. They were both ambitious and unprincipled, and would do anything to advance their careers. A few months after Parker's retirement, the Wallenberg case was mysteriously shifted laterally to Judge Robinson's calendar, without the retired Judge's approval. Robinson rudely and illegally dismissed the verdict without a hearing or any notice to me as counsel. He erased the decision. He had no business even hearing the case and should have known Parker's judgment was final. Someone from outside the judiciary was messing with the system. A few weeks later, Spottswood Robinson got his "payment," a swift elevation to the U.S. Court of Appeals District of Columbia Circuit, with Senate approval, the advancement for which he was gunning for the whole time.

John Roberts served President Reagan for another few months. He never explained to me why he arbitrarily canceled my meeting with President Reagan. It would have been a successful and fruitful conversation and would have brought Wallenberg to freedom at age 72. Today, Roberts is Chief Justice of the Supreme Court of the United States. He almost lost his confirmation as people learned about his treachery in the Wallenberg case. He still refuses to answer a plethora of letters from citizens wanting to know why he killed Wallenberg's open gate opportunity for freedom while serving as White House Chief Counsel in the Reagan White House. We should demand an explanation, even at this late date. Why wait for his retirement or death?

He may take the secret of his treason and unpatriotic acts with him to his grave. After his years in the White House with Reagan, Roberts never admitted he worked with the Russians. He practiced trial law for a few years with the Hogan & Hartson law firm in Washington, D.C. A few years later, he was named to the United States Court of Appeals for the District of Columbia Circuit, also called the D.C. Circuit. After that, Roberts obtained the awesome power of Chief Justice of the United States Supreme Court. He refuses to answer my questions on why he behaved as he did. Fred Fielding had lunch with me a few years ago. He knew that Roberts' behavior in canceling my meeting with the President was the smoking gun.

There are a series of confidential memos to the President in 1984 at the Reagan library in the California secret archives discovered by my law associate Phil Collins. In these memos, now available to the public, Roberts admits everything. Fielding was part of the cover-up. Fielding now confesses, and he admits Roberts had a failure of nerve and his own agenda for suppressing my meeting with Reagan. "Whatever goes around, comes around."

The truth will be exposed one day. I am patient and still believe in God and his ultimate control of the cosmos and our destinies. I believe good men and women triumph in the end. But now I am 83, and Wallenberg is 110. It is May 1, 2020, the same day 36 years ago in 1984, when the Russians were first served with legal papers in our Wallenberg case. It is also Law Day, a special day ironically, when the Rule of Law and Due Process are celebrated not violated. May Day or Law Day comes and goes. And still no honest word on Wallenberg. Dear God, hear our prayer and give us the privilege of bringing home his remains from Russia to a hero's welcome and proper burial.

Speaking with Chief Justice Roberts

Chief Justice Roberts was on my radar for a lucky conversation for a long time. For 35 years, ever since I learned from E.J. Kessler of the *Jewish Forward* that this weasel sabotaged my scheduled visit with President Reagan in 1983 to discuss Raoul's rescue from the Soviet Union. Well, lucky for me and unlucky for him, I was able to corner him and force out some mumbled apologies. His cowardly behavior in advising President Reagan, "please duck the Wallenberg release issue and do not meet with Morris Wolff as scheduled for the morning of November 11, 1983." His now-famous handwritten "duck the issue" note to President Reagan is in my Wallenberg file.

I confronted him in his chambers. I met him by surprise; at least it was to him. He did not expect me. I crashed his rooms and Supreme Court security under the pretense of visiting Supreme Court Justice Ruth Bader Ginsburg. Justice Ginsburg is Jewish and a landsman civil rights advocate who started at Harvard Law. She graduated from Columbia Law because her husband, for business reasons, had to move from Cambridge, Massachusetts to New York City, as it shows in the excellent biopic movie of her life.

Ruth was a fighter and a genuine article with core civil liberties values and principles. She has pioneered the fight as a lawyer-litigator for women's "equality" and "women's rights." She has integrity, which Roberts lacks. Roberts, by contrast, is an agile opportunist with no discernible core values. He sways with the wind, and his record on the Supreme Court shows this last-minute agility to line up with the majority. Roberts is smooth. He is also a coward, an expedient politician of the lowest level. He is what in the law would be called a "naked opportunist" and "careerist," one who will step on anyone's face on his way up the ladder to success, whatever that word might mean to him at the moment.

Roberts cares only about his advancement up the invisible ladder of prestige, greed, money, and status. He takes good care of his political leadership position on the Supreme Court, as witnessed by his behind-the-scenes manipulations in shifting as needed in a slick and unprincipled way, like algae on lake water. Roberts cares about only himself and those he can use to achieve his ambitious and selfish goals.

Roberts has been a significant roadblock in my long effort to rescue and save Wallenberg. This story's verification unfolds by an independent and fearless investigative reporter, E.J. Kessler, in the *Jewish Forward*. (See her article that came out at the time of my U.S. Federal District Court victory for Wallenberg in 1985.)

The impromptu gate-crashing conversation with Roberts in the Supreme Court building finally took place in 2018. It had been hanging fire and on the back burner since November 11, 1983. On that date, a young White House counselor to the President, Roberts, killed my scheduled meeting with President Reagan. At that time, Reagan was ready to endorse my lawsuit seeking Wallenberg's freedom. Wallenberg was alive and 72, a young age for the great hero. I was scheduled by my friend Faith Whittlesey, Reagan's assistant, to meet with President Reagan in the White House. Today is November 11, 2019, as I finally complete this chapter, 36 years to the day when I was on the President's Oval Office calendar. I was on Ronald Reagan's schedule to gain his support for confronting the Russians and achieving the rescue of Raoul Wallenberg, a kidnapped Swedish diplomat. I was there to urge the President to invoke the Hostages Act of 1868 in a public declaration and a private diplomatic note to the Russians. This appeal would have forced the Russians to set Raoul Wallenberg free. It had to be a forceful challenge at the presidential level.

For decades, the Soviets moved Wallenberg through a series of solitary and lonely prison cells with horrible sleeping conditions on an iron bed. He somehow stayed alive by tapping on the walls and keeping up communication through a 26-letter alphabet that he invented and maintained with fellow prisoners. His code name was

"The Swede from Budapest." Returning prisoners reported to me, and they knew Wallenberg was in custody. He often led men in outdoor saunas, rubbing their bodies in the arctic snow for invigoration and yoga health.

Wallenberg lived on minimal food in solitary confinement. The Russians restricted his contact with other prisoners. How he stayed sane and alive all those 39 years is a mystery and a miracle. He invented an alphabet documented by Professor Harvey Rosenfeld in his bio "Wallenberg: Angel of Rescue." He tapped on the walls to remain alert and active in "lucky Morse code conversations" with other prisoners. He made social contact through the prison walls with the 26-letter alphabet he created and shared with others. He also led the men in snow baths outdoors in Siberia when housed there. I received this information through secret verbal reports from German ex-prisoners who shared a gulag cell with Wallenberg in Russian prisons in Mordovia, Moscow, and Siberia. Wallenberg was illegally kidnapped from Hungarian soil on January 17, 1945, and not seen since that dark day.

President Reagan held the key to Wallenberg's freedom. Roberts knew from CIA reports that Wallenberg was still alive. At first, Roberts was supportive of my upcoming meeting with the President. He also knew of the then soon to be filed (February 2, 1984) lawsuit against the Soviets and the comprehensive Wallenberg rescue effort. He knew Wallenberg had been selected for his dangerous mission by the War Refugee Board of the U.S. government with promises of protection. Roberts knew that it was an American responsibility to bring Wallenberg home. It was our duty because our government sent Wallenberg to Hungary. (Read my book *Whatever Happened to Raoul Wallenberg?* on the American moral and legal responsibility of rescue.)

I first met with a young John C. Roberts on November 4, 1983, and spoke with him for an hour in the White House in preparation for my Oval Office meeting with Reagan. Roberts' job was to screen all prospective visitors as the President's Counsel. As I left my meeting with Roberts, he said, "I will see to it that the President visits with you. Without fail, the President will demand Wallenberg's release in his conversations and meetings with Premier Andropov. Raoul Wallenberg is our responsibility. He is our de facto U.S. diplomat. We sent him into danger in Hungary during World War II to save the Jews from genocide. We must use our power to bring him home."

Roberts was devious and deceptive, and he lied to my face. He would do just the opposite. Roberts tied the hands of the President by taking me off the appointments calendar. I did not realize his lack of sincerity and honesty. He had already abruptly and secretly canceled my meeting with President Reagan. Roberts did everything he could to stonewall and sabotage any efforts to reschedule it.

President Reagan received a full briefing from Faith Whittlesey on my plan to go to the federal district court and fight for Wallenberg's freedom. He was on board and saw my visit with him as a great photo-op moment for support from Jews and Hungarians among his supporters. I wanted to meet with the President to secure his assistance in getting Wallenberg out of Soviet custody and returned home to his family. Reagan was enthusiastic about the recent positive news that Wallenberg was miraculously and by the grace of God still alive. The President personally placed me on his schedule for a one-on-one meeting with Faith present. He told Faith Whittlesey that he wanted to act decisively without delaying Wallenberg's return home for a hero's welcome. But Roberts, under short-sighted and unprincipled pressure from McFarland and others high up at State, reversed the meeting and got Roberts to fiddle with the President's appointments for November 11. Roberts blocked my scheduled Presidential meeting. I was counting on President Reagan to use his power and prestige and to demand Wallenberg's release.

Instead, the Reagan meeting was sabotaged, canceled abruptly at the last minute by Roberts. It was ripped from the President's agenda without Reagan ever knowing it. I did not receive any explanation, nor was I told why we lost the last real chance to rescue Wallenberg. I was in the dark, never to know why the abrupt cancellation took place.

Wallenberg was still spry and a young 72, despite his years in custody. He stayed fit with daily exercise. He was in good health, according to reliable sources. We were optimistic, and our crusade for Wallenberg's release had gained momentum even before I filed the lawsuit. Roberts sabotaged my meeting without telling the President.

Over the years, my good friend Justice Antonin Scalia tried on several occasions to schedule a meeting for me with Chief Justice Roberts in his Supreme Court chambers. He respectfully or disrespectfully declined — a coward at heart in facing the truth.

I met Justice Scalia during my year as a professor of international law at the University of Hawaii Law School in 1998. I had lunch with him at the Supreme Court Dining Room for Justices several times during my two-year stint as a scholar at the Woodrow Wilson Center in D.C. In 2007 and 2008, Justice Scalia and Chief Justice Roberts were active members of the Supreme Court's conservative arm. Justice Scalia set up a three-person luncheon at the Supreme Court dining room for us in 2007. Roberts ducked out at the last minute. Perhaps he sensed lunch might become an embarrassing confrontation. I was disappointed. How could he insult his fellow Justice Antonin Scalia by reneging at the last minute? How could he be so rude? We set the date for two weeks in advance! Justice Scalia tried to apologize for his colleague's behavior.

Antonin Scalia and I had great chemistry. We enjoyed a close friendship for 15 years. He liked that I was a man with a mission in Wallenberg, and like Scalia, a fighter and a scrapper. We both loved to argue. We met as tennis opponents in a scheduled singles tennis match in Hawaii. We were Constitutional law professors with a yen for tennis. We became friends who confided with trust in each other. We enjoyed spending time together. He offered to do the necessary to make sure that Roberts and I met for a 'lucky conversation' while Justice Scalia was still alive. Unfortunately, he died in 2016, two years before my chat with Roberts. Tenacity finally won the day.

I met with Justice Ruth Ginsburg in Washington, D.C., at the Court in June 2018. As a Jewish woman and human rights activist, she wanted to know more about my work for the Wallenberg family in the field of human rights advocacy in Russia. She indicated by phone, "I will try to get you in to see Roberts. He should face up to his responsibility in this matter. Did he cancel your meeting with the President? Why? What was his excuse? I am interested. You deserve an answer from the horse's mouth."

She was angry. "Let the facts speak for themselves. You may need to subpoena the White House appointments book of President Reagan. The records should be made available to you as a scholar researching the President's permanent papers." Ruth Ginsburg is a talented lawyer and jurist with a gifted mind. She is 85 and quite ill when I write this chapter (10/11/19) but fighting gamely to hold on, write opinions, and keep her seat on the Supreme Court. "I'm going to go out with my boots on," she recently told me.

In June 2018, after my friend and tennis partner Antonin Scalia passed away, Roberts suddenly was willing to meet with me and to have "a little chat." This meeting happened after Ruth Bader Ginsburg barged into chambers with me and said, "John, you need to speak with this man. His name is Morris Wolff, and he is one of my colleagues from professorship days. He was at the University of Pennsylvania Law School when I was teaching at Columbia. We got to know each other as colleagues at law professor meetings before I joined the Supreme Court." He has done some great and talented work in the Wallenberg case in getting a $39 million judgment against the Russian bastards who kept Wallenberg illegally in jail. You must explain your bizarre behavior when you canceled the meeting with President Reagan on the Wallenberg matter."

She did not seem to respect this man. She continued: "I know John, you will tell the truth." She looked over at me and smiled with a grin towards Roberts. No one else was there. Ruth speaks plainly; she calls it the unvarnished truth. "I have seen enough gobbledygook in my day," she said as she left the two of us alone.

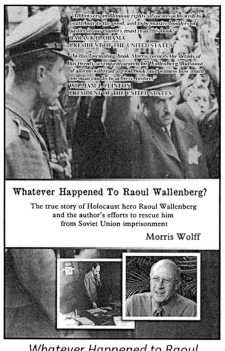

Whatever Happened to Raoul Wallenberg by Morris Wolff

Justice Roberts was sweating as he sat in his soft plush leather chair with his unexpected guest. He knew that I would write about his decision and choice to countermand a Presidential order and arbitrarily cancel my meeting with the President without notice. I noted his sabotage in my book on Wallenberg.

Roberts said, "I have read your book on Wallenberg. Quite fascinating! I was aware that you severely criticized and questioned my behavior. I canceled your visit with President Reagan. I tried to do what I thought was best for him. A lot was going on at that time. We were trying to warm up to the Russians, end the cold war, and to avoid insults and confrontation."

Roberts congratulated me on the writing of *Whatever Happened to Raoul Wallenberg?* "I like your writing style and lack of ambiguity. You seem to go for the jugular," he said. I took his comments as a compliment. During my interview, he made little effort to defend his actions or to apologize. He was quite calm and collected. He opened up and gave me in detail "his side of the story." I opened up our lucky conversation by thanking him for agreeing to meet with me. We decided to have lunch and walked together to the Judge's Private Dining Room from his office. The maître d' seated us at a small table in the Supreme Court's private dining room. I had earlier had lunch with Justice Scalia in this same room. Roberts opened our conversation by remembering our mutual fondness for Justice Scalia and his warmth, his rapier-like wit, his great popularity among the justices, and his keen intelligence and a quick mind.

Roberts reminisced, "Justice Antonin Scalia loved to debate and converse with everyone with a law degree, no matter how old or young. He was an extrovert, where I am an introvert. He loved to put his friends and foes on the hot seat. Tony was outgoing and a social butterfly. He loved being with people. Scalia told me with great relish about his famous "tennis match" with you in Hawaii and how you let him win a few games. Tony loved the Washington social scene, merry-go-round, and was fascinated by the social life. He loved people and enjoyed a good argument with anyone. He was feisty and more open than I am. I am more of an introvert. He tried to get me to open up over time. He told me there was nothing to fear from laughter, from sharing the truth and enjoying life."

Roberts continued to open up as we warmed to each other, and I carefully listened. "Tony wanted to televise our sessions. He thought the Supreme Court should open up to the public and the media. He did not think the Court should be an elitist ivory tower to quote his words. "We are the people's court," Tony would say. "We must be open to the public." This openness is especially for those who cannot be here in person to see and watch us do what he called the people's business. He wanted to open things up, and have more ventilation."

"Tony loved to meet and debate with students at distant law schools. Scalia loved to travel, especially to Hawaii, in the wintertime. That is how you met him out there in the middle of the Pacific Ocean at the University of Hawaii Law School. He told me how you were hand-picked by the Dean to play tennis with him. Tony said you were drafted and had no choice. You were merciful in keeping the game fun and not making it a deadly competitive Battle of the Titans! He never forgot your kindness. He said he learned the Yiddish word 'rachmunis,' or 'rachmones' for compassion from Jewish lawyers like you."

That's true," I replied. "Justice Scalia and I learned a lot from each other over time. The Dean of the Law School for Hawaii drafted me for that tennis match. At his faculty meeting on a Tuesday afternoon, he told me to show up at 9:00 a.m. the next morning on the university tennis courts. I arrived a few minutes early. At the dot of nine, there was Justice Scalia, promptly on time, and ready to go just like an eager little puppy dog, wanting to know, "who are you, anyway? Are you any good as a tennis player? What is my tennis ranking, and why was I chosen to play with him?" He was a little nervous and wanted to show his best, which was nothing much in terms of his tennis game. I told him that it was an honor to play the game with him. During our friendly competition, I gave him some suggestions or tips to improve his prowess. He was pleased with my teaching and explanations."

"We became good friends, not just tennis friends. I was amazed that he invited me to eat with him at the Supreme Court. I came from time to time for lunch in this dining room as his guest. I tried to get him to make a meeting with the three of us. Our levels of warmth and compassion were quite similar — he is a warm Italian at heart, and my being 'a compassionate Jewish questioner,' according to Tony. We bantered that day in Hawaii for a while, and then we began hitting back and forth, just warming up. I quickly realized that we were at very different levels. He was an ardent beginner; I played varsity tennis at Amherst College for three years and later won tennis championships.[12]"

Soon it was noon, and the dining room was beginning to fill up. Chief Justice Roberts and I were getting to know each other by talking about something other than the sensitive subject at hand. That subject was how he had shafted Wallenberg and left him to rot by deleting me from the President's schedule. Bantering on innocuous topics like tennis or people is a useful technique in any warm-up to any negotiation. When you do not know the man on the

---

[12] I won the men's singles in the Iowa senior games in 1980. I also won the All Florida Seniors and the Villages Seniors men's doubles for gentlemen 80 and above championship in 2017.

other side of the table, it is vital to establish some warmth and common ground. It is a warm-up technique of great value.

During medical product sales and negotiations in China, I used it, where I negotiated in French because the translators could not do their job speaking English and Chinese. The Minister of Health had learned French, and so we carried on successfully in French. He learned French during years of exile in Paris with Mao Tse-tung. I knew French and Spanish as tools of conversation in strange places. Now, in this dining room of frigid and wary relations, the good memories of our mutual friend Tony Scalia was to be our selected middle ground. It was a good icebreaker leading up to what we had come together to discuss. I furnished my Hawaiian tale on Justice Scalia. "He was dressed to the nines, properly dressed for the tennis occasion in all white. He had on a French tennis shirt by Rene Lacoste, replete with the little green alligator, smart white shorts, and long white knee socks. He looked like the Good Humor ice cream man. He had a brand-new tennis racket and two cans of unopened tennis balls."

Roberts said, "How was Tony's tennis game? Was he any good? I cannot see Tony as a tennis great, or even as any kind of athlete. He was more of a bookman, an intellectual."

I replied, "Tony was an eager and passionate player. He had more energy and enthusiasm than skill. We enjoyed laughing and the fun of it all. Our tennis game was the doorway to a great and loyal friendship."

We ordered lunch. Both of us had a cup of soup and a side salad of mixed greens, tomatoes, and sliced cucumbers. We were in a quiet private part of the dining room. After clearing the dishes, Chief Justice Roberts turned to the main reason for our meeting.

"I am sorry I have chosen to avoid you. I never answered any of your phone calls or letters. That includes letters from others that came across my desk asking, 'I knew exactly your role in trying with ardor and passion for rescuing Wallenberg.' You took on the case pro bono. My hat's off to you on that. I got letters from school children worldwide and survivors asking me why I interfered with your meeting. I turned a deaf ear, mainly because of other matters on the President's desk that conflicted with your request on Wallenberg. I was ashamed of what I failed to do and my lack of courage. The State Department fought for no action and no meeting. Yet we failed as a matter of policy. Our administration's position in the Wallenberg matter of ducking the issue turned out to have been dead wrong in retrospect. We sent him there, as you often said. It was our duty to bring him home. Period. Full stop. It was a time to be courageous, and I remained silent."

"The President wanted to challenge the Russians. He was devoted to the rescue of Wallenberg. The Soviets, through diplomatic channels, were full of threats. They said, "You must drop or decouple the Wallenberg matter from any other item on our agenda. The President was angry. He immediately replied, 'Why the hell did we make him a citizen? I want to bring him home. Let's put pressure on the Soviets to do the right thing.'"

Roberts: "That became a dilemma both for me, as the President's counsel, and for McFarland at the State Department. There was a specific treaty on the uses of outer space between the U.S. and Russia. This treaty was pending and under secret negotiations at the time. The Soviets insisted we take Wallenberg's rescue off the table or leave it on the table unresolved. Otherwise, they would trash the treaty to prevent the use of outer space for bomb development, and we'd be right back in the cold war.[13]"

Roberts: "I went immediately to talk with President Reagan. I was on the horns of a dilemma. I knew Morris that you were correct and right on the law. We had to choose between pushing for Wallenberg's release or getting the balky Russians to come to the table and sign the peaceful use of outer space agreement. We chose

---

[13] For a full discussion of these agreements, see U.S.-Soviet Cooperation in Space (https://www.princeton.edu/~ota/disk2/1985/8533/8533.PDF), Washington, DC: U.S. Congress, Office of Technology Assessment, OTA-TM-STI-27, July 1985

the latter. We should have demanded both. Yes, the President did have a duty to demand Wallenberg's release as a diplomat, with immunity and as an American citizen held without due process by a foreign government. That is made clear under the U.S. Hostages Act of 1868 that you with clarity and correctness urged us to follow in your letter to President Reagan."

"Wallenberg was already an American citizen, as you made clear in your letter, by an Act of Congress. He was entitled to full protection. President Reagan honored Wallenberg in a Rose Garden ceremony on April 4, 1983. That was six months before your request as his lawyer crossed my desk and exactly one month before I said yes to your scheduled meeting of November 11, 1983. It was four months before you filed your lawsuit against the Soviet Union in federal court in Washington, D.C. I followed it all. I felt bad about my action in rejecting your letter and canceling your appointment with President Reagan."

I sat silently for a moment, collecting my thoughts. I was overwhelmed by Chief Justice Roberts's openness and honesty. I wanted my response to be diplomatic and in a tone that would sustain our continuing conversation. I said, "Justice Roberts, you rejected my scheduled meeting and buried my letter to the President! You knew that was an unlawful act, an obstruction of justice by you as the President's lawyer and chief legal counsel. You were entrusted with responsibilities as legal counsel to the President to report all matters to him. You evaded that duty. You violated that relationship of trust."

He shifted uncomfortably in his seat. He said, "What I chose to do in disobeying the President's directive was an indictable offense with a possible prison sentence to follow. I knew full well what I was doing. I knew the risk but took it anyway. I was myopic. I thought that your meeting's cancellation was necessary to maintain a certain serenity between Russia and the United States. I hoped for an environment where we could negotiate and reach out to each other to warm up relations. We were at the height of the Cold War, and things were tense. A wrong move might have led to an all-out nuclear conflict, plus we had the outer space meeting on the front burner. Hindsight is an easy vantage point from which to view things. Was I following the tradition of Nathan Hale as a patriot, or was I a reckless fool? I feel I did the right thing at the time. I am sorry about the consequences for Raoul Wallenberg. These were unintended consequences of what I considered something important on the level of global survival. The rapid change in leadership and instability in Russia caused our State Department to be very concerned about the Wallenberg matter."

Morris: "How could you possibly arrogate to yourself that piece of Presidential power and make that decision? The President had to sign off on that decision of yours as a matter of law and foreign policy. You had no power under law to make that decision. That was a decision for the President alone to make. You were obliged to make it clear despite his moments of forgetfulness or early Alzheimer's to tell the President exactly that! You had no other lawful choice. It was his decision and not yours. It was simply not enough for you to say, 'Wolff is right, but Mr. President, let's duck the issue.' That is what you said and in writing no less! It is on the permanent record of the White House Papers. I have a copy." I showed it to him. Roberts nodded in consent, remembering what he had written in the classified memo back then.

Justice Roberts: "I wanted him to duck the issue for political reasons. I made it very clear, and I told him that you were completely right on the law. And that the President had a duty to comply and follow the law, I did not say the law was ambiguous. I just implied there were extenuating political consequences and circumstances."

Morris: "Were you being pressured by someone over at the State Department to back off from the Wallenberg freedom issue?"

Justice Roberts "Absolutely true. John McFarland, our National Security Adviser, and the State Department bureaucrats were pressuring me every inch of the way. I thought only about the fragile world situation and a possible worldwide arms reduction and peace and detente with Russia. I may have been wrong, but I chose to go that way."

"President Reagan already had Alzheimer's and forgetfulness. We took advantage of his disability. He didn't remember from one day to the next. We ran the country for the last two years of his last term. I took the Wallenberg matter off his agenda and canceled your meeting with him. He failed to remember it, and I chose to let it slide. What I did might have been wrong, illegal, and unethical, but right and correct for our national security at that time. However, it was Hobson's choice."

"President Reagan was my only client. It was my duty to tell him to follow the laws and treaties, including the Protection and Rescue of Diplomats under the Vienna Convention of 1961. Sometimes good decisions are hard ones. I have had trouble living with this one."

"What was I to tell the President? I told him about my respect for your legal acumen. I said to him, 'Morris Wolff is right. He is correct about your legal duty to demand the release of Wallenberg as an American citizen and as an international diplomat protected by both U.S. and international law.' "

Morris: "I can see now how difficult the timing of all of this must have been for you and President Reagan. It was a complex situation. You felt there was already more than enough to negotiate on the President's menu. We were already discussing arms reduction, plus the Strategic Defense Initiative (SDI). The Russians were howling. They did not want our acceptance of the SDI."

Justice Roberts: "Your lawsuit was right on. I read your complaint and briefs with care, especially your argument for jurisdiction in a U.S. federal court based on the Alien Tort Claims Act. Your lawsuit was brilliant and creative with a winning argument. You made a valuable new law, and you quieted the skeptics and naysayers. You proved it could be successful."

Morris: "I wish I could have met with you after the meeting with Reagan was canceled, Justice Roberts, when you were White House counsel, instead of getting the brush off. You were wrong not to communicate with me directly. 'It can be done,' says the plaque on my grandfather's wall. We could have won this one for the Gipper and Wallenberg."

Justice Roberts: "I agree with you there. Together with working openly and in harmony, and not at arm's length, we would have gotten the job done. We would have found a way to accomplish Wallenberg's rescue without embarrassing the Russians, let them save face, and still work towards arms reduction and world peace. We should have had you, Morris, on our team negotiating that year with the Russians in Moscow. You knew their cagey frame of mind and strategies. You had more global experience negotiating for years with the Russians in your AIESEC student exchange program than any of us. That was our mistake. We needed your experience and savvy."

Morris: "I fought for Wallenberg's freedom with a singleness of mind and a dedication of purpose. Nothing else mattered, and it became a consuming passion for me. Raoul Wallenberg was only 32 when the Russians kidnapped him. He deserved to live and enjoy those 40 years in the sweet air of liberty and freedom from 32 up to age 72. He earned that freedom. And with our help, the 20 years after were his as well. Had his brother come to me sooner, we could have rescued him. The timing was the only thing we had. I took immediate action the same day I got his brother's plaintive 4:00 a.m. phone call from Sweden begging for my help. I went right away that Saturday morning downtown to the University of Pennsylvania to the Penn library. I found the applicable laws in a musty old law book that is marked Jefferson 1789. Librarians found the book for me in the Rare Book room of that great and famous law library."

Justice Roberts: "I am glad we had this meeting. I should have made it happen a long time ago. Justice Scalia was right when he said to take things head-on. I wish he were here with us. He would be glad that we finally got together. I appreciate your overcoming my defensiveness and fear to meet. Please keep your word and stay in touch."

We shook hands. Feeling quite empty and not at all exhilarated, I simply said good-bye. Presidential decisions can be quite complex, with many different issues involved. But the man himself must make those crucial decisions to meet or not to meet.

Some of my "Lucky Conversations" occur years after they are vitally needed. Sometimes they arrive on time; sometimes, their delay is part of a more significant part of synchronicity and destiny. Time mellows many things. We could have changed history if Roberts made the correct choice and left my meeting with President Reagan alone. What possible harm could there be in working together towards the eventual rescue of Raoul Wallenberg? Raoul was 72 and still vibrant. Now it is too late. "There is a tide in the affairs of men which seized upon the moment leads on to glory," as William Shakespeare said. We failed to 'seize upon the moment,' and Roberts was the roadblock.

At least I received an answer, a lame excuse, from the horse's mouth. At 83, I may begin to grow in wisdom, patience, and tolerance. I may gain perspective and sometimes see "the larger picture" from a nearby hillside. I might even mellow. Yet some moments never change when you are a hardcore advocate as I am for saving the life of a man-saint like Raoul Wallenberg.

There is absolutely no excuse for Robert's expedient actions, and it was tantamount to an act of sabotage. Self-interrogation occurs at every step along the highway. Over the next ten years of my journey, I must stay in touch with the basic map of all the routes traveled and those still out there that one can continue to take.

Lucky conversations are my keepsakes and lifetime souvenirs. Sometimes they are exhilarating and, at other times, deeply disappointing. This meeting with Roberts was one of them. I have no respect for Roberts, either as a jurist or a human being. At a time of moral crisis, he suspended judgment and went to the sidelines to "sit this one out," as he put it.

These face-to-face meetings, and the sharing of ideas, are peak moments in my life. Sometimes my stories are about sudden exploration and adventure like crashing the Phillies World Series of 1980 or meeting President Kwame Nkrumah by chance on the tarmac in 1960 at the airport in Ghana. Or finding myself walking for a fun hour with Jackie Kennedy and kicking the autumn leaves in Central Park on my birthday on November 30, 1993. Or by crashing John Robert's office with the help of Justice Ruth Ginsburg and confronting him about his sabotage of Wallenberg's potential freedom.

My Biggest Influence, Leo Wolff

My favorite person growing up was my Dad, although, at times, he could be quite severe and scary to a young boy. He believed in using a strap to enforce discipline. This trait was an unfortunate holdover he picked up as a young man at the Jacobsen Hochschule in Germany, in 1913, where an equal number of Christian and Jewish boys came to learn together on scholarships.

He came to America against his will. He loved his school, where there was no discrimination. Friendships formed, and some of these friendships survived the Holocaust.

Coming to America was his mother's timely and prescient decision. No one cared more about my education and development and my future than this man. He sacrificed his own life and recreation time for making a great life for his five children. He was my inspiration.

Dad was a self-made immigrant from Germany, with two dollars in his pocket aboard the SS Cincinnati. He loved music, horseback riding, and rare moments of fishing, golfing, or otherwise having fun with us. He was a bright and complex man, filled with ambition, uncommon energy and idealism, and an abiding dream to create something great.

He was headstrong, highly intelligent, and humble about his excellent people skills. Our lucky conversations were by appointment only. Leo Wolff decided when other people spoke to him. Our discussions began in September of 1943 when I was seven years old, in Philadelphia, during World War II when food, goods, and clothes were scarce, and money was meager. Our lucky conversations continued to the day of his death, March 2, 1969.

My German-Jewish father believed deeply in the value of education. He won a scholarship (equal to a Rhodes Scholar) to the finest all-boys boarding school in Germany. The school taught strict adherence to being on time and to Prussian order and obedience.

My Quaker education focused on civil disobedience, becoming a radical, and pursuing human rights. He had a strict boarding school in Seesen, Germany, as his formative educational resource. I had a Quaker School, where pacifism, human rights, open discussion, tolerance, and seeing "the inner light in others" was key to their teachings. Quakers believe it is better to discuss and share ideas and be open-minded: "better to light a candle than curse the darkness." My father thought, "I am the father and the boss." Discussion is a one-way experience until a child reaches 13-years-old, the Bar Mitzvah time, and often not even then.

Dad often reminisced about early days in Niedermarsberg, Germany, and the Jewish School to which he was sent on a scholarship miles away in Seesen, Germany. Also, Dad talked about play days with his friend Percy Thorner on Paulinenstrasse and how they broke into the sauerkraut factory and stole sauerkraut from the wooden barrels and goods from the export shelf.

Segregation of the Jews happened even by 1912 and anti-Semitism was growing. The Wolff children could play as young children after school with their Christian friends but not attend school with them. He went to a segregated school for Jewish children before winning a full ride boarding scholarship to the Jacobsen Hochschule in Seesen. He loved the Jacobsen School, started by a German Jewish wealthy idealist. In the summer of 1959, as an exchange student to Cologne, I went back to visit the little country village where Dad was born.

The Jacobsen School was designed for integrating Christians and Jews with quotas to educate equal numbers of outstanding Jewish and Christian young men together in a happy and productive environment. This platform was an effort to defeat the disease of antisemitism at an early stage of development. A Jewish idealist started it with money, a Bill Gates of his era in the 1870s. The school was devoted half to Jewish boys and the other half to Christian young men at the middle through high school levels. Jacobsen was trying to establish an integrated elite of future leaders. He realized that anti-Semitism was rampant in Germany. Perhaps a joined elite group of well-educated graduates could stem the tide of anti-Semitism in Germany. Dad described school life at Jacobsen.

Leo Wolff, circa 1911, in his gymnasium uniform.

Dad: "We slept side by side in separate steel beds in open dormitories."

Morris: "What was it like?"

Dad: "It was rigorous. They woke us up with switches on our feet every morning at 5:00 a.m. Then, run in the snow to get exercise and wake up. Brutally cold morning showers, hands, fingernails inspected, completion of our daily homework, and our lessons' inspections.

Morris: "Did you get any free time?"

Dad: "Never, there wasn't any. No one knew any free time. It was all work "Arbeit Macht Frei" and all that propaganda of encouragement. The same words of encouragement were hung, ironically, above the iron and steel gates at the concentration camps' entrance. But I loved the school and the learning part. We had good teachers."

"I wanted to stay and complete school. I did not choose to go to America with the rest of my family. It was 1912, and I was 15, a very formative year in my education. I wanted to be a medical doctor, a specialist who could heal my mother's dislocated hip and her terrible limp. She was in pain, and it was my task to get training and to fix it."

"It was my destiny to be able to complete the 7th and 8th grade. I never got to ninth, either there or anywhere. My mother decided that our family would migrate to the USA in 1912, and so we took a boat — the SS Cincinnati — and we arrived at Ellis Island. They tried to change our last name to have one "f" instead of two, but my mother was adamant. That is our name, "Wolff." Do not change it, and the man at the desk corrected his error immediately. That was your determined grandmother at work."

"We came as a family of eight children with your grandpa Solomon and grandmother Llena Herzstein Wolff. That was two years before 1914 and the outbreak of the Great War. Our relatives wrote letters and asked us, actually begged us, to come back home and fight for the fatherland. Jewish boys fought for Germany in WWI and gave their lives, but not in World War II with Hitler killing the Jews left and right. My mother refused our cousin's naive request. No son of mine goes back to Germany ever. We are Americans now, and don't you forget it." She became an avid American patriot, raising the American flag every morning at our home at 19th and York Streets in North Philadelphia. She debunked the cousin's misguided and naive request to return. She urged him instead to drop everything and to come immediately to America. But he stayed and died in the Holocaust with many of my cousins and relatives from Niedernberg, Hanover, Hamburg. We had a lot of family members there. They were all killed in either the camps or by bombs dropped in a blitz on Hamburg."

"A stupid return to serve the enemy would have been misplaced patriotism. No Jew should have been fighting for Germany in either war."

Behind him on the wall was the large oval picture of his mother, Lena, the woman who had brought all eight children, and Solly, her husband, to America. She did it by sheer dint of determination, energy, and clear focus. She had despaired of Germany (fortunately) in 1910 and grabbed her children Rosa, Minnie, Leo, Morris, Amanda, and Derva and departed on the SS Cincinnati.

Dad: "My mom had a terrible limp. It got worse over the years. She worked with her right hip severely dislocated. She was in constant pain, but she was stoic. She sucked up her pain and never whined. She expected the same of us, stiff upper lip and "immer geradeaus" (always straight ahead). She walked to work each day, rain or shine, snow or sleet, in our country village of Niedermarsberg no matter what, just as I am going to go to work now."

"We are working people. It is the center of our lives. But as my beloved mother of memory walked to work each morning, the young men on the corners — the good for nothing loungers — would lie in wait. They teased and taunted her. They pointed out her infirmity and called her 'Gimpel Lena,' or Lena with the limp. They were miserable young punks. They chose to make life miserable for the physically impaired. And yet from wicked and evil and undeserved pain and humiliation comes the good. She won her freedom and mine too."

"Those punks were the spark. They are the ones who got my mother fully fed up and quite done with Germany. She loved her little millinery shop. She was the finest women's hat maker in that entire region before World War I in Germany. One day, in 1910, she came home from work, sat down dead tired, took off her hat and black gloves, made her ritual cup of tea, and said, 'We're going to America. I have had it. That's it.' There was no arguing with her. Once my mother Lena decided something was to be, once she made up her mind, that was it. I was allowed to stay one more year for my Bar Mitzvah at the synagogue on Paulinerstrasse. I studied Hebrew and memorized my portion. We were orthodox Jews, and later Reform Jews once we got to America. Everyone else in the family packed up for America. I stayed an extra year with my uncle and aunt, Tante Yulshin, to complete my bar mitzvah. I wanted to stay in Germany."

"Sometimes I think about that strange choice. We could not see what was coming to Germany. It was just 1912, just before the First World War from 1914 to 1918. I loved Germany. I did not want to go to America. I was a maverick, a contrarian, thinking this was a good time to break from my family and stay in Germany. My aunt and uncle doted on me; made me feel super special. I became their only child during that year. So sometimes I wonder, 'what if I had stayed?' I would have married and prospered and become part of the German Jewish elite, based on my completed education. I would have been a doctor, able to heal and fix my mother's infirmity. That was my dream and plan. Doctor Leo Wolff with a lovely home and vibrant garden in Cologne on the River Rhine with a big family of my own. Middle-class bourgeoisie. Allowed to practice medicine right up to 1939 and then taken away to be a doctor in the army and then killed. And you, my little son Morris, born in 1936, would have been a cinder in the Holocaust. By 1943, the Nazis gassed all of the Jewish children. Then the Nazis threw their bodies in the rivers."

My Dad stopped a moment in his reverie about fate and coincidence and dislocated hips and mothers determined to get out and go to America. My grandmother smelled and sensed something evil in the air. She had good instincts. The meanness of those cowardly bullies left their mark. They were my family's early exit managers and did not know it.

My Dad continued, "So much of life is pure chance, pure luck, such as my finding your mother. I pursued her 'til she said yes. I was 32, and she was a 19-year-old beautiful raven-haired young girl. I stalked her; followed her as she walked to school. I was smitten and was 13 years older, an older man pursuing a beautiful young girl. The police could have arrested me for harassment and invasion of privacy. But I won the prize. I never regretted my ardent efforts in chasing and pursuing her. I love her to this day though I don't know how to live with her."

"When you see something you want, go for it. Aim high. The only sin in life is a low aim, so I went for Carolyn, and God was good to me."

My Dad was ambitious, a gifted breadwinner. He got off the boat with two dollars in his pocket and worked his way up from a drug store soda jerk to a window designer for women's specialty shops, to become a self-trained dress salesman. He later created ownership of his nationwide dress company, the Form Fit Dress Company. "You look your best in a Form Fit Dress," as mentioned before, was his cheerful motto. I loved him dearly and enjoyed being with him. I also hated him when he hit me with a belt as part of his strict discipline concept. He motivated me to persevere and overcome adversity, be ambitious and honest, and work hard and not settle for second best. "The only sin in life is a low aim," he repeated this maddening phrase over and over.

My father worked 24/7 to provide for five hungry children and his beautiful wife, Carolyn.

His first women's dress business failed. He declared bankruptcy. He picked himself up by the scruff of his neck and got back in the game. Leo Wolff and Company of 1334 Cherry Street closed that pivotal year 1933 and re-opened in the year of my birth, 1936. It was a good omen. Dad was only 39, ready to start over again. His dress "Bizness" in our hometown of Philadelphia was no more. Only debts remained, which he chose to repay "100 cents on the dollar" since they had all been loans from close friends. He did not want to screw any of his friends or embarrass himself, even though the law gave him a legal way out. "I have to look them in the face daily."

A three-man smashing success replaced his one-man failure. Wagmeister, Freedman & Wolff opened on Broadway, "the great white way" under the banner of Form Fit Dress of New York City. A catchy jingle supported the new enterprise: "You'll look your best in a Form Fit Dress." Out with the old; in with the new. Happy days were here again.

Label from a Form Fit Dress

Dad's past failures were valuable in the new venture. Form Fit Dress Co. of 1385 Broadway received the benefit of his know-how, hard lumps, pains, and savvy. The bright lights of New York beckoned, and a back-breaking commute from Philadelphia was the price. Our family never moved to New York. Mom said, "No way. My family and my people are here. We stay here." And that was that. Dad adjusted with an incredible travel schedule back and forth to New York twice a week. Then he traveled to Washington, D.C. for one week. The next week to the Pennsylvania coal mining cities of Altoona, Scranton, Wilkes Barre, Pottstown, Tamaqua, and Mahanoy City, hawking his half-size women's dresses. This activity was still known in the trade, in Yiddish, as "the schmatte business." All his needlework staff was loyal, hardworking first-generation immigrant Jewish and Irish women, sent by fellow Jew David Dubinsky, President of the ILGWU. Dad had little time for conversations, but he made time for talks with his four sons, Carl, Richard, David, Morris, and daughter Ruth.

My hero, Leo Wolff, became an incredibly successful dress salesman. As an immigrant, he inspired us with pep talks. He was upbeat and had no room for pessimists or naysayers. He told us over and over, "opportunities for success in America are boundless. The streets are paved with gold in America." He was born in a barn next to the cows. His family escaped before the Holocaust destroyed six million Jews in Europe. Had he stayed in his little village of Niedermarsberg, meaning under the Mars Mountain, and not left Europe with his mother, father, four brothers, and three sisters, I might have been born in that little farm village in Germany on November 30, 1936. I would have been from day one a useless cinder in the Holocaust, of no market value to the Nazis. My grandmother knew best. "We're getting out of this stinking place," she announced one day. "I smell trouble." And away to Hamburg, she went with the family, got on the SS Cincinnati, and sailed to Philadelphia's freedom.

Dad worked all the time. If he was at home, he never sat idly. Dad did not watch TV but read the books that I gave him. He was always on the move, straightening out the furniture or an already straight painting over the fireplace, looking over our homework, computing our weekly allowances, and developing his idea of our plans for careers for our future.

From Dad, I inherited my energetic DNA resilience and determination that "I Can Do It." Dad was highly motivated, ambitious, and focused. His dedication to my mother was strong  even though there were many arguments. It was very confusing for a watchful and caring 9, 10, or 12-year-old to watch and feel helpless to correct or improve. I knew what to do but was powerless to do it. Dad's love for my mom was unpredictable, stormy, and passionate. Dad instilled in me hardcore values that have seen us all through demanding challenges in life.

Growing Up with a Tough Dad

My Dad sacrificed everything for us, his wife, and his children. "My children are my only hobby," he would say. "I give them everything." And he did precisely that. He gave up his life, his rest, and recreation for us. We were indeed his one and only "hobby." What a challenging hobby indeed. I believe we were a constant and stressful pressure on his mind and his heart 24/7.

His four sons — Carl, Richard, Morris, and David — were given a tremendous early advantage in life with a virtual rocket boost towards the upper atmosphere of opportunity in being inspired by our Dad and his sacrifice.

By giving up his own life, he created a "high platform" for us later to take off into the atmosphere of success and meet celebrities and other famous people. One does not get to work in the White House stratosphere, the U.S. Department of Justice, and the U.S. Senate, working for Bobby Kennedy and President John F. Kennedy by merely putting in a paper application. You get there through hard work, an excellent education, high values, strategic contacts, great ambition, focus, and the cushion of an elevated platform, a launch pad created at first by the devotion of selfless parents.

Each of my three brothers launched meaningful and successful careers. They each took off from Dad's "high platform" created by his blood, sweat, tears, high energy, ambition, intelligence, and stamina. We got his DNA and his game plan of life for establishing a self-made man.

Education was everything, and my Dad treasured and valued scholars, learning, and books. He read ardently and was self-educated. His formal education was cut short due to his mother's decision to bring her family of eight children from the small farm in Niedermarsberg, Germany (Westphalia), to the "new land of opportunity." Our immigration was America of 1912 when immigration was still wide open until the McCarran Act of 1924 shut the doors to most Europeans. "We got here just in time," he said, "Opportunity was wide open for anyone willing to work hard and save."

Fortunately, here they were in the Promised Land long before the catastrophic Holocaust. My grandmother had good instincts about survival and timing. My grandmother's brothers and sisters stayed in Germany. The Nazis took them to the death camps, and most of them died in the Holocaust's burnings. Some escaped and somehow made it to Denver, Albuquerque, and Bath, Maine. No rhyme or reason to the paths of migration. Albuquerque and Denver were still cow towns, part of the Wild West. It was still wild in 1912.

When it was time for university, Dad went with us by car, a seven-hour drive from Philadelphia to Amherst College, where he would focus on getting each of us, one by one (during the 1950s) admitted. He would "present us," telling us to sit in the back of the office as he made his pitch. It was a "pitch" that amused and still impressed the Dean to see a father so willing to stand up for his boys. He would tell the positive side of each one of us, and he would sell us like goods, pointing out to the Dean 'how lucky Amherst would be.' He would sell our "merits" for admission to the Admissions Director Dean Eugene ("Dean Gene") Wilson. Dad took over the interviews, as if we were a valuable shipment of fine goods just in, of his best and latest dresses. He was very persuasive, and when he extolled my virtues to the Dean, I wondered about whom he was talking. The word "gung-ho" comes to mind.

My Dad was always selling, and I appreciate now, many years later, just how much time, effort, love, and devotion went into those "Amherst College" business trips. He won every time. He went up to Amherst for four crucial sales. "Always best to go in person if you have something to sell," he told us. "Go face to face. Let them see you and your passion. Trying to sell by phone is impossible. You always lose. Let them see you; let them see that you cared enough to come. We each gained Dean Wilson's approval, and he came to love my Dad and how he "was always in our corner."

Despite his hectic schedule, working hard all day, and stealing four hours of sleep on the sofa each night, my Dad found time for me. He created our carefully scheduled private time "lucky conversations" every Sunday night at 8:00. They often coincided with Eddie Cantor and Sid Caesar's Colgate Comedy Hour, so I resented his insistence that they take place at that time. I was an outspoken maverick, quite unconventional, and admittedly "different."

I never fail to speak up when I have something on my mind. That got me in trouble many times at home, the middle child looking for attention, afraid no one would hear him. When I felt that I had something to say, I never ate my words.

That got me in trouble many times at home and school. I loved to pick arguments, verbal arguments with others. I was litigious even before I became a lawyer, always willing to scrap. I was headstrong and left-handed, the only one among five children and the middle child. My Dad and I had verbal wars and tons of arguments. Our tempers interacted, and I always lost. "If you don't like the rules of the house and living here, then find someplace else. You don't have to live here," he would say when provoked. We often bumped hard with significant differences of opinion on most things. And yet we respected and loved each other and each other's minds and intelligence. I could tell. I deeply admired this man, although, at times, he frightened me. I always tried to please him.

That process of "butting heads" with my father made me resilient (a rough, tough pussycat, according to my mother). Years later, my mother told me she saw through the front I needed to develop to survive. Challenging my father's point of view at times gave me outspokenness as a life-time quality, toughness, ambition to make something of myself, a will to succeed, and a desire to win at everything, whether it was beating my father at golf or winning a tennis tournament. These traits or qualities have remained with me at age 83. I am still idealistic and litigious, willing to fight for my ideas and ideals and human rights.

Dad believed in obedience and regimentation, based on his dogmatic and repressive experience at the Jacobsen Hochschule, his strict boarding school in Germany. It was all he knew. Dad and I developed a "modus vivendi," but we rubbed, and he punished me a lot. We did not get along at all for the first 13 years. Then, with my Bar Mitzvah, came a change in me. I decided I had much to learn from my father. I realized he was doing his best to raise five children, and I could not interfere with my radical ideas about equality and a child's right to be heard. I also decided we needed some distance to grow and that I would not be regimented or "trained." I had to move away for college at Amherst and remain away for law school at Yale. I was not coming home to law school at Penn, even though they wanted me to and made that clear during invitational lunches and made me feel wonderfully comfortable during visits with Professor Mishkin at the Penn law school.

Plus, I knew if I came home from law school, they would suck me into being a 'marital arbitrator' for my parents, sitting them down at each end of the dining room table, and listening to their complaints about each other. Allowing oneself to be subjected to this can be very painful. It can have lasting consequences, especially about trusting marriage. It is a no-win situation. Apparently, I did help to keep them together. My Mom told me that after Dad died that my role as peacemaker was key to their remaining married. I was glad to hear that, and I loved them both and wanted them married to each other, if at all possible.

At age 13, I decided not to allow them to draw me into the family business. I could see my two older brothers going that way, and I wanted no part of it. I wanted to chart my own course as a lawyer or something other than medicine. Law, Fairness, and Justice interested me. Law became a field that held interest because of its focus on human rights and due process. It became apparent that my Dad was not grooming me for inheriting one-third of his dress business, even though I loved traveling with him at Easter time to visit his customers in Scranton, Allentown, Altoona, and Mahanoy City.

I still liked my one-on-one Sunday night private time with Dad. Initially, we knew it as "allowance night." Each one — Carl, Richard, David, Ruth, and then Morris — came to a one-to-one meeting in his bedroom, standing briefly at his Chippendale desk. He would pump us for a detailed report plus general information vitally important to him about our school behavior during the past week. What did you learn? Give me some of the highlights? And also, he asked about our "comportment," otherwise known as adolescent behavior. Comportment was a pretty big word for eight-year-olds. It meant had we been good or bad? Did we get reported to Principal Bessie Husted? Nope. Did we have only A's on our new report card? Yep. Had you been sent home from school at any time for poor behavior? Nope. How was your behavior on the playground? Do you get along? Are there any bullies? How do you handle them?

A man of few words at that Sunday nighttime, but the conversations were alive with electricity, nonetheless. There was no room for mistakes, ambiguity, error, or bad behavior. Teachers were to be worshipped and obeyed. My parents gave each teacher lovely gifts each Christmas to cement the Shoemaker School relationship with their college-bound able young geniuses.

My Dad asked, "How much of your money did you spend this week? On what? Why? Was that a necessity or a luxury? Do you need it? Why not save that ten cents, rather than waste it on ice cream? Little children in Hungary go to bed each night hungry. Why not send it to them?"

He inculcated the value of selflessness and thrift at an early stage. Our conversations were brief, succinct, and to the point. We had a weekly budget, and seven cents for soup once a week was a special treat. Or a full hot lunch with meat or fish and two veggies was fifteen cents. We never got a slot in the budget for that extravaganza. We packed and took our lunch from home in a brown paper lunch bag, with a half sandwich of cream cheese and olive on pumpernickel bread, a half a kosher pickle, and an apple for dessert. We learned thrift at an early age. I had a paper route and a greeting card route by age nine, selling Christmas cards in boxes in October and November, and Easter Cards in March and April even though we were Jewish. I soon found out what religion our neighbors were. I skipped ringing the doorbells of the Jewish homes for obvious reasons.

My traveling with Dad was my precious "one-on-one time" with him. Each son had a particular individual avenue for accessing Dad, our own special time together. He had limited time. Eldest brother Carl played tennis. Richard went fishing with him, and I got to travel with him on the road selling half-size women's dresses to a series of predominantly Jewish-owned small family shops. We were four boys: Carl, Richard, David, Morris, and our baby sister, Ruth. Four boys in a busy family who were claiming and competing for bits and pieces of his time. He loved us all the same, or so it seemed. But he did favor Carl for going into the dress business and for a fundamental attitude of "yes, Dad" obedience. The great white father when Dad was absent.

"Da business," Dad's horrendously competitive national business, sucked out his life and led to an early death. He had more life inside had he retired. "Da schmatte business" claimed most of his downtime even on weekends when he was home. It seemed he worked 24/7, all the time, day and night, with a tiny five minutes out.

During my adolescence, I traveled with Dad during Christmas and Easter vacations. It was my way of spending quality time with Dad, carrying his sample bags, lightening his load, and keeping him company. Dad seemed to change as we left the driveway. He softened during those trips away and became more human and less distant, less aloof. Dad put away his role as the harsh disciplinarian. He became less bossy and demanding. Dad let his hair down, such as it was, and stopped telling me what to do. He allowed me to be myself, and we were like pals. Dad didn't have to role-play. He became fun to be with until he got home.

One time on a business trip to Wilkes-Barre and Scranton, I persuaded him to go to the movies, something entirely out of character for my Dad. My father did not trifle with films, but I did. It was unheard of for my Dad to have fun and relax in the evenings after work — my father reserved nighttime after dinner for writing up orders.

Morris: "Put that stuff away," I admonished him for being a workaholic. "We are going to the movies, to the picture show." This time my pleadings worked! I got him away from his work for one evening of relaxation and fun. After dinner, we walked together, proud father and son, down the street to the dazzling red, white, and blue blinking lights of the Rialto Theater. We bought two tickets for

"The Lemon Drop Kid," a 1944 comedy starring Bob Hope and Virginia Mayo, my dream girl. I watched my father relax and laugh from deep in his belly. He was at peace, free of all responsibility. It was like being in our own movie world together. It was just the two of us in the dark looking up to the silver screen, with the rows of people eating popcorn with the black and white movie flickering magically in the dark, beamed up to the giant silver screen.

It was 1950, the middle year of the 20th century. Peace had come briefly to America, but a new war broke out at the 38th parallel in Korea. It was just five years after the end of World War II in 1945. I was 14, and my Dad was 53. That night is my favorite memory of being in conversation with my Dad. Watching Bob Hope in "The Lemon Drop Kid" was the magic of a major film. My Dad and I, together at the movies on a fun night out, away from it all.

That was the only time I cajoled my father into relaxing for a few hours on a business trip. All the other times, he was all business with his precise regimen, habits, and practices entirely in place. He kept notes on all his customers, which he reviewed carefully before entering one of the hundreds of stores he had in his files. He knew the egos, the foibles, and the weak spots of each owner and sales associate. Dad knew them all by their first names, along with the names and ages of their kids. Knowing this information was a warm-up point, an icebreaker. He would pick out the favorite son and ask, "How is he doing in school?" knowing he was doing damn well in advance.

Dad was a charmer, and when the "Big honchos" or bosses or owners turned Dad away, he innocently claimed, "I didn't come here to sell dresses. I came here to give the salesgirls a well-deserved box of Barricini candies." Dad would then whip out a box of candy wrapped in white tissue paper, with a large white satin bow, and ceremoniously open the box in front of everyone at the nearest cosmetics department counter and start handing out chocolates. Dad created excitement, fun, laughter, and friendships. He genuinely cared about these hard-working salesgirls. Dad knew that the women must get excited about selling his goods by getting them excited about him. Soon, he opened his sample bags, began selling his dresses, and took orders for a new shipment. His dresses always sold off the racks first. The manufacturer made the dresses with good taste for a particular set of women.

He kept in his vest pocket little 2x3 white reminder cards. They were his "must do" list and "no-no" notes. He would remind himself which styles of dresses had sold best before and at which store, what colors, and what kind of Barricini candies to buy the saleswomen in the different small specialty shops and department stores in all of the towns he visited. He also had to remind himself of store owners' specific likes and dislikes in each city and the dates of their children's weddings and births.

I wonder how my dear father would have done as a salesman and owner of a successful dress manufacturer during the coronavirus. Many of his customers would close. Owners of all his stores would find it challenging to stay open. Macy's would be going bankrupt, and others like J Crew that went bottoms up bankrupt on May 5, 2020.

Besides many Jewish-owned stores throughout the Pennsylvania coal region, these stores would have collapsed before his eyes after years of loyal purchases. These were loyal and profitable customers back in the day. They included great stores like Kauffman's of Pittsburgh, a major customer. Stores, such as the national chain JCPenney, would have killed Dad to see these stores collapse and crater out.

Dad was always proud to have me with him in those long-ago days of the 1950s. I was a prop he could use as a "warm-up' subject before the main act or event. I loved to ease the strain on his back by volunteering to carry the sample bags at all times. That made me feel good and that I was doing something of value, especially when I saw how heavy the bags actually were. I lifted them and thought of his being alone and coping with loneliness and lifting these heavy bags.

In every town, he worked me in as part of the opening act. He used me to divert away for a minute from the opening line of his sales pitch, indicating my latest tennis or chess match victory. He bragged about how my school elected me again for another term as the class or student council president or member of my tennis team. Having me there cut the remorseless loneliness of the solitary nights away from home. He would get homesick when away and call home and then write letters to my mother at night while alone in the hotel, suggesting how to "bring up our children while I am away." As if she did not know. She was a great and competent mother. Sometimes he got home before the notes, but there they were for posterity written in his perfect German script on the hotel stationery of one-night lonely visits in faraway cities, time robbed away from family and cozy evenings with his children. I felt I did not know him until I got the chance to travel with him. Then things opened up. He became warmer, easing up on control. No need for him to be "boss." He could just be himself and not have to assert control.

Dad had a standard practice, and he followed it with religious fervor. He rarely veered away from it. Mornings started with a small traveling alarm clock playing a gentle wake-up melody. Dad carried the clock with him and called it "Susie." It would begin an abrupt intervention on a good night's sleep, sharply at 5:30 and again at 6:00 a.m. I can still hear that little traveling alarm clock ringing with my dad saying, "Rise and shine. Up we go. It's another beautiful day in the great USA, where the streets are paved with gold, and our dress customers await our arrival with eager and open arms." He gave pep talks to himself and me every day.

Dad would then kneel briefly by his bed and say a quiet prayer and a recitation of the 23rd Psalm followed by another "you can do it; you can do it" self-pep talk. Then it was off to his shower, and a shave, then looking after drying off in the mirror to clip the ends of his mustache, no goatee, always clean-shaven and young-looking. Then into his long one-piece BVD over the shoulders and under the crotch underwear, covering both upper body and bottom, followed by a clean well-starched white shirt, his gray pants, then a carefully knotted conservative red and blue striped tie, followed by red and blue suspenders, his suit vest, gold watch fob, and matching gray suit jacket. He always was proud to be "a three-piece suit man" conservatively dressed to the nines. After he finished dressing, it was time for two eggs, bacon, and a tartine of butter and jelly and then hitting the road.

Dad would wipe his mouth and comb his mustache and then said, "Let's go! There is money to be made. We have five hungry chicks to feed." He made a motion toward the door, giving an order in his Germanic-Prussian style. "Carry the bags," a command that I both followed and enjoyed. I did not want to burden him — better, an adolescent of 14 or 16 to carry the family goods.

We descended in a small elevator from the second-floor dining room after consuming his standard second breakfast of a small glass of orange juice and another half grapefruit when it was in season with a red cherry. He cut the grapefruit into sections leaving it in its skin. He would eat each small segment and then squeezed the grapefruit until nothing survived but the yellow rind. "A grapefruit every day keeps the doctor away." He was giving us early training in healthy eating. He believed in fresh fruit and hot oatmeal as our away breakfast feasts back in 1950, before healthy eating even became fashionable — an active and caring father.

I can still hear his words of self-encouragement. He was his cheerleader. Dad muttered to himself, "You can do this; Yes, Leo, you can do this. Up and at 'em!" After he squeezed his half a grapefruit delivered to our room into one glass of juice, it was on to his version of a healthy breakfast of rye toast with two soft-boiled eggs in separate white cups. He would take a sterling silver knife, cut off the soft-boiled egg at the tippy tops and ceremoniously devour them using a small spoon in the egg holders.

Dad was relaxed and cheerful at breakfast, wanting to always engage in conversation with me. There was no morning newspaper to block us off from one another. I was allowed to have coffee, a special treat. I could also order pancakes or waffles with bacon, anything I wanted. Breakfast away was like a party. Dad was not harsh or bossy when we were on the road. He did not act bipolar. Dad was a calm and relaxed friend rather than hypomania. He eased off, and the moods disappeared. His behavior became consistent, and any basis for fear vanished.

He would sometimes turn from a manic beast Mr. Hyde into a calm and refined Dr. Jekyll as we left for our three days on the road and started our 100-mile journey home. There was always the chance of a blow-up once we arrived. He had to take charge even though he had been away for just three days. My mother kept a clean and perfect house. After a long trip, Dad, for no reason, would walk into the living room and start moving chairs and sofas around, showing all of us he was the man in charge.

Finally, my exasperated mother exploded with "Leo, get out of here. Stop moving furniture. Fix yourself a drink. Stop fixing and moving things around. Get yourself a shot of straight Haig scotch and sit down. There's nothing wrong with the furniture."

Sometimes his crazy antics would escalate into a full-scale battle royal. We children ran to our rooms, leaving a beautiful and carefully planned Shabbat dinner with white tapers on the table. It was tragic and painful. I wanted to rescue my father from himself. All had been well before he got there. All were happy and calm until he walked in the door on a Friday late afternoon just before the Shabbat holy dinner. Holy became holy hell. He regularly sabotaged his own pacific and tranquil home life. I was conflicted. I hated this behavior and how he abused my mother by criticizing her for no reason and moving the furniture. I did not know how to feel like an adolescent son faithful and loyal to both parents.

I loved this great and unique self-made man. I knew his bon vivant fun side from our treasured trips on the road together, and I loved being with and near him despite his volatile and stupid outbursts. Dad was a perfectionist, and he hated slipshod work. But he was nuts. He did not suffer fools gladly or otherwise. I knew how to appeal to his better angles gently with a mix of tact, diplomacy, and respect. I could converse with Dad alone and bring out his best. I became his unexpected personal and private consultant and, at times, his life coach, that started at age 9 through age 33 when he began to die on our worst Valentine's day ever. I was his unpaid pro bono counselor and lawyer. I did not want this job at any price.

Sometimes at night, I would hide under the covers and pretend to be asleep. He would come into my room to chat, usually in tears or close to tears.

Morris: "What is it, Dad. What are you doing in my room?"

Dad: "It is about your mother. I do not know what to do with her. I don't know how to win her love or to please her. What should I do?"

That is hardly a question to pose to a 13-year-old boy, eager to do well in the eighth grade.

Morris: "I am trying to get some sleep. It is after midnight. Can't this wait 'til tomorrow?"

These nightly conversations tore me apart emotionally. Why me? Why not Carl or Richard? They were older and wiser. My Dad knew I was the most caring and sensitive one, easy to reach. An easy mark, as others realized later. These invasions of my mind and my sleep made my blood boil. I was angry. There was nothing I could do to fix or change things. This suppressed anger would bubble up years later in my married life until I realized what was happening precisely with psychiatric help. I have a terrible temper. I began to learn how to control it. It was not a thing of the past. My anger was in the present time; a gift from my father. It lurked and lingered in dark pools under the thin skin. My emotions and anger were my own Achilles heel.

This invader of my nights was the same man telling me how to live my life. Now he was coming to me and asking me how to live his, how to please my mother. He also sensed correctly that I was her favorite and that I would somehow have some deep understanding of how to charm, court, and please her. This same man who sometimes beat me as a 9-year-old with a large black belt and buckle when I would question his judgment. Now I was his adviser. These occurrences were a delicate and confusing balance that sometimes did not balance. It was unfair, and I was all about fairness and justice. I might go in short order from Dad's consultant to whipping boy in a mercurial and unpredictable 24-hour period.

I ended up temporarily in therapy, spending weekly 50-minute sessions trying to figure out this complex relationship, its residual impact on my life, and my treatment of and connection to women. It took 30 years for me to finally resolve the anger, forgive my father, and find a good woman to share my new life in happiness and deep contentment. She is an angel, and I genuinely appreciate her coming gently to share my life. We are happily and joyfully married.

While talking to me at age 12 as his unpaid marriage consultant, Dad held his hands to his face. He would sniffle and cry, "I'm so ashamed," and then he would apologize for waking me up and walk out, leaving me wide awake and messed up. Dad wanted to be heard and not fixed. I became a mediator for the two of them, which was a compromising position for me as a precocious child trying to please them both. I was injured, but not permanently, by the imposition of their problems on me. I should have been carefree and out playing tennis and not playing a junior version of Sigmund Freud. My wife, Patricia, has helped me with these misplaced feelings of having failed my parents by not saving their marriage.

These were "pull you all apart, and into little pieces" matters that adults should not discuss with a 12- or 13-year-old adolescent working through his own confusing issues of adolescence. Years later, when I enrolled at Yale Law School, I received a frantic call from my mother. "Come home. Your father is throwing things again." That is all she said. I got in my car and drove seven hours to Elkins Park. "What's the matter?" I said. "Your father is throwing things." I sat down between them at the dining room table to mediate the argument. Now they wanted my unformed legal skills to help. "We want a divorce," they said. I replied, "I am not yet a lawyer; I am just a law student." I wanted out of their neurotic relationship and their constant battling before it left a permanent scar on my psyche.

And yet I served as their mediator for the next two hours, listening to their barrage of complaints, listening to both sides of the story, and taking matters under advisement. "I have nothing to say at this time. I will take these matters up with you again when I get home for Easter vacation. You do not need to settle anything right now. Give time to cool things down and begin to heal."

We revisited the issues of good communication when I returned home. Things healed to some degree, and a papered-over reconciliation took place. They apologized for involving me in their problems. Their apology made me angry. It was my first losing case as an arbitrator-mediator.

Both parents were loving and devoted. They dedicated their lives to their children but not each other. They had an incredible drive to achieve for their children and unmatched flawless success. My mother was a schoolteacher. She loved children and was a wonderfully gentle and loving mother. Dad was a self-made man who rose from nothing but a small bed in a one-bedroom for eight, with the smelly cows huddled in the very next room, giving warmth to the children for winter, stationed on the other side of the white stucco wall. They were a tough match, not easily recommended by Match.com.

I had a rare chance to get to know my father on a 24/7 basis when we took business trips together to Pennsylvania's coal regions that lasted for three or four days. Dad and I would journey on the so-called "Central Pennsylvania Circuit" of Jewish family-owned department stores.

My Dad always bought a box of candy to charm the saleswoman and made life happy for them in the steel and coal towns of the Keystone State. We would swoop in, through the horseshoe curves of Pennsylvania. We visited Altoona (Hotel Altamont), the coal hills of Scranton (Hotel Casey), the state capital of Harrisburg (Hotel Penn Harris), and other medium and small towns depending on where they loved him for 20 years. They relied on his judgment of which dresses to buy. He made successes out of untrained salesgirls who cherished his knowledge of what sells in Pennsylvania department stores.

I received valuable training and on the job education. I learned how to sell an idea to a jury. I saw Pennsylvania, and most of all, I got to see my father in action: smiling, confident, and successful. We would relax at breakfast together before a day's work. The only tension was at home and not on the road. He was Mr. High Energy, indefatigable. I inherited his stamina and energy.

I feel his spirit with me here right now, looking over my shoulder, sometimes correcting my grammar or suggesting and selecting a different choice of words, an expert at making welcome suggestions. He was like a coach, a good coach. He always had my back.

He was my Dad, a giver, and a donor to me of a good life with many gifts. He is right here with me, happy to see me well-married to precisely the kind of woman he predicted years ago would make me happy. He really knew what I needed in a wife. He had it nailed, and I don't know how, but he did.

Thanks, Dad!

My Final Conversation with Dad

My final conversation with Dad was on a cold winter's day around Valentine's Day, February 14, 1969.

When I woke up that morning in my warm bed at home, I had a premonition that something terrible was about to happen to my father. My home in Germantown was only 30 minutes from Dad's house in Elkins Park. My intuition told me something was desperately wrong with my father, and he was covering so no one would know. I could feel it in my bones. His energy was coming to an end, dying out. It was an annoying, troublesome feeling that would not go away; things were not right. Later that day, the telephone rang. It was my mother. She called me at my office in downtown Philadelphia. I was about to go to court before Judge Leo Weinrott in the Philadelphia Court of Common Pleas.

"You must come now. I know it's 9:00 a.m., and I know you must be in court at 10. I cannot reason with your father. He wants to go out in this storm to sell dresses. Please come and talk sense into him." Mom was hysterical. I was the only son remaining in Philadelphia. My brothers had fled to Dallas, Houston, and New Jersey. Like the TV detective Charlie Chan, I was the "honorable son number three," the only one who could talk sense into my Dad. Why me? There were three others?

"Morris, drop what you are doing. Come home at once. Come quickly. You must restrain your father. He is packing his sample bags and making plans to go out in this blizzard, this snowstorm to drive to upstate Pennsylvania, to the coal region, to visit his favorite customers. He won't listen. Come home; help me restrain him. He's acting crazy. If he sets out on this trip this morning, he'll kill himself skidding off the highway somewhere in the dark into a snowbank."

I called Judge Weinrott and told him my predicament. He had "adopted" me as one of his favorite young lawyers and made me a Mason a year earlier. He was the only judge where I could get away with this continuance. I drove through the snow to our family home in Elkins Park and entered my father's house. I was there to persuade him not to go out in a blizzard, traveling to his favorite towns and cities on a hazardous day. He anticipated my arrival. He knew my mother had called me, as she always did when there was a crisis. I was the pre-selected peacemaker. My older brothers evaded the opportunity and responsibility, saying, "Leave it to the lawyer in the family." I had a sense of foreboding. I couldn't put my finger on it. The feeling was about my Dad and a message about his "final days." Leo Wolff was only 72.

We had an overnight blizzard. God tried to ensure that my father would not leave his warm and cozy weather-protected home in Philadelphia to travel to the anthracite coal country. He tried to persuade me that he had to take this trip on behalf of my two oldest brothers to sell women's half-sized dresses for their company. He was supposed to be in Florida with Mom. Something told me to see my 72-year-old dad and make damn sure he stayed home. He was stubborn and bull-headed. He wanted to be on the road.

I arrived at our family home. I tried to take his car keys away. Dad was about to start on a dangerous business trip in the snow selling his treasured women's dresses. He didn't need the money; he needed the action, the feeling of self-worth, and the adulation, respect, and love from the department store salesgirls who loved him and looked forward to his charm, his visits, and his humor, and a box of Barricini candies. Dad did not care about the blizzard. He was packed up and ready to roll, and he was going. His public and their stroking awaited him. His ego was soon to be slaked and satisfied. There is nothing I could do but cry inside myself.

My Dad was determined, resolute, and of one mind. There was no doubt. "I'm going anyway." These were his first words. "I decide what I choose to do. It's my life and not yours. I do not take my directions from you or anyone else. I'm going, and that's it. None of you can stop me." Dad had the determination, and he spoke in self-encouraging ultimatums.

There was no way to talk this headstrong man out of something he was determined to do. He had asked my mother to marry him 39 times until she finally said yes. If he wanted to do something, he did it. He made himself into an American, learning fluent English in two months without a German accent. Upon arrival as an immigrant from Germany, my father determined that he would do it all independently. His own father was weak, and his mother was too busy. My Dad was the modern edition of 'a very determined and focused self-made man.'

If Leo went after something, he got it. That was his style, aim dead straight ahead. He would not accept interference from anyone. That's how he landed my mother, through overbearing persuasion, hustle, intense courtship, and annihilation of all of his competition and opposition. At 32 and already a business success, he overpowered a 19-year-old beauty with promises and gifts during the Great Depression. Once he proposed to my Mom, he thought that he owned her; Dad had no idea what to do with my mother, this gift from heaven. The challenge for Leo was in the chase and not the possession. He could have been a much better husband; it was not his forte. No one had trained him. He had no role model. We could sense and see this fact as his children, and there was nothing we could do about his incompetence as a husband even though many evenings he came crying to me for advice. What could I do? I was 12 when his nightly visits began. I was busy with my own life and growing up into manhood. He would sit at the end of my bed and cry. Why me, oh, lord?

My mother usually had a calming effect on his impulsive behavior. This time, she could not prevent my father from going out in the ice and snow to present his samples and sell his women's dresses to his customers. He was ready to drive to all the little and big towns in central Pennsylvania's anthracite coal belt, where he had loyal customers who loved him and trusted his judgment. He told them exactly what to buy for each season of the year, and it differed from city to city and town to town. He had different populations to deal with, some chic and some working class. And he would tailor his sales pitch to what worked in a specific region. I know. I went with him on these trips during Christmas and Easter vacation and watched his magic from the sidelines. He was a master. I learned the skills and strategies to be a courtroom lawyer by watching and listening to him sell. Dad should not even have been at home in Philadelphia or thinking about going on the road in the first place. He belonged in Florida in February. He and Mom had just purchased a new home under sunny skies and warm clime, a condominium in North Hollywood. They had planned to settle down for the winter.

At least we thought so. When springtime came, Dad could hit the road again in Pennsylvania and see his favorite customers and buyers, Abe Shapiro, at the Globe Store in Scranton, and Aaron Feller, at Feller's Fashions in Harrisburg. These visits made him feel important, vital, and alive. It was a tonic or a drug. He was growing older, but at least waiting for him in Florida would be his fishing pal Herman Grollman, owner of Grollman's Dry Goods Store off Easton, PA. Herm called him that morning and implored him to come south. But now this bull-headed and stubborn old man would soon be gone towards his death in the blizzard and snow.

I came to see my father in an attempt to persuade him to stay home, to talk him down from his dangerous and foolhardy mission and final adventure. I failed and Dad went as planned. This conversation was our last one. Our last time physically together. It is hard to call it a lucky conversation, but it was fortunate for I grabbed a piece of his last healthy moments on earth.

I found my Dad zipping up his two black massive sample bags. Each one carries 10 to 12 dresses. I often carried these for him when we made trips together during Easter vacation from college and high school. Those pleasant days of good eating and adventure were long gone. I now had my own family, my private law practice, and my independence. I got away from the dress business as an adult on purpose. My brothers were caught in it and had to listen to his dictatorial claptrap. He held them under his spell and thumbs. They did not get along in business and ultimately sued each other, as if in their own "death wish," destroying the monumental company and the assets that my Dad created.

Now on a snowy day, in the middle of a blizzard, Dad was about to set out, "come hell or high water," on his last business trip. He was well-dressed, immaculate in his three-piece, well-tailored, conservatively grey business suit with a gold watch fob, a red and blue tie, and gold tie pin all neatly in place. When I pulled up in the driveway, he already had on his made in England Burberry overcoat, his Stetson brown felt hat, and was ready to roll.

He tried to persuade me. "Look, Morris, this is my life. Retirement in Florida is not for me. My life is selling dresses to my customers in the coal region." He was about to zip up his sample bags when I arrived and tried to halt the proceedings. Next, he wanted me to carry the bags to the car. I refused. "I'll do it myself," he answered. We argued for a half-hour. I tried to step in front and prevent him from going. He would not stop for anything short of a lasso or a bullet. Finally, he picked up the heavy black canvas bags of half-sized women's dresses and somehow traversed the slippery ice at the front door. He opened the door, put the bags inside his brand new metallic blue Cadillac, and drove away. He was leaving for four days to drive in dangerous conditions from one town to the next.

Ironically, it could have quickly become a stay and play at home day for lovers. It was Valentine's Day, and this crazy and dedicated man was going out onto dangerously icy roads during a week of predicted heavy snowstorms. And it was not for himself. It as for my two older brothers, Carl and Richard, who had taken over the business, and had asked Dad to retire. He simply couldn't. It was in his blood.

"Leo, this is simply crazy," said Herman Grollman, his fishing buddy, in a last-ditch phone call, as Dad stood in the doorway, sample bags in each hand. "Leo, why don't you stop your plans, get on a plane, and get yourself shipped back to Florida. I'll meet you at the airport. We'll go fishing in the sunlight and warm weather right near here. Yankeetown, Florida, right now has the very best fishing in the whole state." Herm lost the argument. Leo was resolute.

My Dad loved life and being alive. He loved the fun and was a "bon vivant." He loved dancing and classical music, especially Chopin, Bruch, and Mozart. Had he known his death was coming so soon, I am sure he would have gone back to Florida that day and followed my advice and that of Herman, one of his major customers and best friend.

Leo still wanted to get sales and to create something big for his two oldest sons. Their business is suddenly slow, and Dad's contacts were both special and valuable. No one could sell the way Leo Wolff was able to do. He was the top salesman in the industry.

He was not ready for his retirement. The second home in Florida was for the future, not now. In his mind, he was expecting to live many years longer playing golf and making up with my mother for the years of lonely nights in hotels away from loved ones "on the road." Usually, he was gone from Wednesday morning to Friday night, when he always came home in time to celebrate the Shabbat dinner of matzo ball soup and chicken with his five children and wife.

Our final conversation went something like this:

Morris: "Dad, you are crazy. No way you are going to go driving out in this snow alone. You are going to get even sicker, catch pneumonia, and die. Is it worth it? There is another blizzard, a second one predicted, and it is already arriving for the Lehigh Valley and the central Pennsylvania coal region. If I could go with you, it might be different. I could carry your sample bags and help out. But I can't because I am busy at my law office. I wish it were the old days when I was 13 and I went with you during Easter vacation, 20 years ago. Then it was fun. We talked. I practiced my Bar Mitzvah portion as we drove in the car with you listening. You would tell me to enunciate and "throw my voice." I loved traveling with you, just the two of us, and staying at different hotels every night, but this is different. I can't come with you. I can't carry your sample bags. I can't just pick up and leave my clients. I have a family and my own business to look after."

Dad: "I don't want you to go with me. I understand you're busy. I am proud of how hard you work. You have inherited my traits of ambition, hard work, and a sense of responsibility. Morris, stay right here at home and take care of your family and by growing your law practice. I am making this special trip just to help your two older brothers, who need my help. Their dress business is struggling. It's a rat race of competition these days, and they need more accounts and more sales volume. I am transferring my long-time Form Fit Dress accounts and goodwill over to them. They need to tap into the fountain of goodwill that I have accumulated with clients over the years."

Dad: "I must hit the road. I have to go to help Carl and Richard. They have taken over my business, and they need my help. I can only help by going on the road for them. I flew up from Florida, especially to put in a few days, and remind my customers that I am still alive and selling, selling, and selling. I work for my boys, your brothers, Carl and Richard. Their business is in trouble because they don't have enough sales. Old accounts are drying up. My chemistry with some of these older buyers is not replaceable. I am the only one who can bring in these old tried and true customers of mine in the coal regions. I will be home in three days. It is no big deal that I'm going to see them."

I used to compare my father to the salesman Willy Loman in Arthur Miller's play "Death of a Salesman." He was like Willie, a salesman, a man out there alone riding on the crest of a dream, a permanent smile, and an ocean of self-confidence. Dad was a lot more successful, having put four sons through Amherst and one through Harvard business and another through Yale Law. Dad was a dynamo, the last of an era of self-made men who pulled themselves up by their bootstraps, with a ton of self-will, self-confidence, and a deep sense of "I can do this." He would face moments of non-acceptance, rudeness, and tons of humiliating turn downs and rejections from potential customers, but he carried on bravely, always heading always toward the next sale. I learned to be a fighter from my Dad. He taught me how to persevere and never accept a kick in the balls as the last chapter of injustice, whether it was being. For example, when I didn't receive acceptance to Harvard Law School or fighting corrupt police officers in Sumter County, Florida. He taught me to be unyielding in matters of justice, due process, and decent behavior. His DNA became my DNA, and I am proud of this inheritance. For my dad, the next conquest was always just over the next horizon. He was determined to set out on the morning of a bleak and cold February day. My mother and I tried to block his effort.

"Don't go, Dad," I implored. "The roads are too icy. It is dangerous out there. You are going to kill yourself."

"I have to go," he answered. "I have no choice. I am doing it for my boys. My father continued placing the dress samples in the bags and zipping them up. He loved this routine of getting ready, and he was not about to let me interfere. He was determined to go. There was no doubt about that. He even sold himself on the idea, and that was that. He was a super salesman. He was a good man who always served his family first. He sacrificed for us, cutting the best parts of the roast beef for everyone at the table and then taking the remaining scraps. He loved his family, and despite all the teasing and tears, he adored his wife.

Morris: "Go back to Florida; that's where you belong. Your fishing buddies at Yankeetown are calling for you to come back. Go and enjoy the sunshine. Play some golf."

Dad: "Look, I am not asking you to go on this trip; I will do this myself. I don't need you. I can drive and carry my sample bags — no big deal. I am 72 and able to take care of myself. Your brothers need me. I am going out today to help them. Today I am a Tribute Dress Company salesperson and not Form Fit Dresses. The money goes to them. They have named the company Tribute, as a tribute to me. Get it? I feel honored, and they need help to turn their business around. I can save it. I am here for them, just as I have always been here for you when you need me."

I wish I could have gone with him to protect him, carry his sample bags into the little stores along his route, and keep him company.

I distracted Dad briefly with the conversation. He loved to talk about himself and his background. "Never forget your roots," he would say. "You come from very humble beginnings. Your grandpapa slept in a simple room next to the cows, smelling them all during the winter." Dad rose on a meteoric trajectory from a small farm on a dirt road in Germany to create the Form Fit Dress Company of New York City, in the heart of Manhattan. His little one-person company had grown from Philadelphia to the big time situated in the high-rise garment district on the classiest thoroughfare. There was his national dress company in the lights at night.

I told my daughters, "Grandpapa Leo went broke twice and rose from the dust again to create his empire, and his motto, "You look your best, in a Form Fit Dress." The jingle caught on and persuaded stores across the country like Pizitz of Birmingham and Kauffman's of Pittsburgh, two large Jewish-owned stores along with Gimbels and Macy's, to buy his carefully tailored dresses, always in good taste. Dad never really knew and understood my mother. I did, and that ticked him off. But for a dress sale, he had an uncommon understanding of the feminine psyche and the essence of what made women tick and buy. He knew what women wanted in the boudoir and shopping in the classiest department stores across America. These were the 1950s. People were getting rich. The middle class had spendable cash, and at $8.75 through $14.75 wholesale, who could go wrong with a new dress or two for Sunday church or weekday work?

Now on a snowy day, in the middle of a blizzard, Dad was about to set out, come hell or high water, on a business trip. He promised that this was his final business trip selling dresses to his loyal customers in the coal region. He planned to drive from town-to-town on dangerously icy roads during a week of heavy snowstorms. "Crazy," said his friend Herman. "Put him on a plane and ship him back to Florida. I'll meet him at the airport. We'll go fishing in the sunlight and warm weather here at Yankeetown, best fishin' in the whole state." Instead, Leo, stubborn as hell, went out in the snowstorm.

Morris: "Dad, you do not need this. You have put in your time. Now you are retired with golden years ahead. You have given us all so much of yourself. Go back down to Florida with your buddy Herm and with Mom to your new place at Canongate. Go fishing. Have fun."

Dad: "I have no choice. Selling is my job, it is in my blood, and it has always been. It gives my life a raison d'etre, real meaning, and I love my customers. Gerson Weiss in Scranton and the Globe Store in Wilkes-Barre and Fellers in Harrisburg. They are all waiting for me."

My effort to stop him failed. My instincts told me this trip would kill him. The change in temperatures between February in Florida and Philadelphia was severe. He would carry his heavy sample bags himself and alone in a blizzard — almost a death wish. I wondered. I would not be there to help him.

He stopped zipping and looked me in the eyes. We made eye contact, but there was no change in his resolute manner. He began to sniffle, and then a full-blown crying jag. He was under pressure of his own making. No one was forcing him to go. He took off his rimless glasses and wiped them carefully with one of his old handkerchiefs from the Jacobsen Hochschule. He was a romantic, sentimental man. He believed that carrying a 60-year-old handkerchief brought him special luck and retrieved his own austere mother's strength and determination. He held up and showed me the cloth. "Look here. See the number 33 sewn in red numbers at the edge of this handkerchief? Your grandmother, Lena, sewed that number in each handkerchief, and again in my white dress shirts, pajamas, and underwear. That was a requirement of every student, number identification plus clean nails, and good manners. I remember her taking me to the train on a cold day like this and seeing me off to boarding school. She did this when I was just 12. I earned a full scholarship, and she was sending me off to Jacobsen Hochschule (high school) boarding school in Seesen, Germany, far from our little house where the cows slept in the next room during the winters. I treasure this little white handkerchief, and I keep it close to my heart. It reminds me of my mother's strength and determination. I have to go. I have to do this for your two older brothers. They are in a financial jam, and they need sales."

Had he known his death was coming so soon, I am sure he would have gone back to Florida. But this was his work. He was not ready for retirement even though he had already purchased a home in Florida, expecting to live many years longer playing golf and making up to my mother for the years lost while away "on the road."

I had my law practice and my family to look after. From my modest home in Germantown, I had come out, feeling, and somehow knowing this would be the last time I would see my Dad alive. I was right. The next time I saw Dad, he was dead and in a mahogany coffin. He caught pneumonia on that final business trip and never got past the killer bacteria. He barely got back to Florida to reunite with my mother. He spent his last three days in the sunshine. He collapsed and died on the golf course during a round of golf, with the scorecard in his hand. It took a lot to take him out.

Dad died on March 2, 1969, from pneumonia and a massive heart attack. Had he gone to Florida, as we begged him, he would have lived.

Mom: "I told him to retire, but he was a stubborn man. Always about helping his sons first. I told him, don't go north, Leo. We have no reason to go north in the dead of winter. Maybe he had a death wish. Perhaps he did not feel valued or needed in retirement. The only thing that gave him meaning was his work and his loyal customers. They somehow reminded him that he was important. He was drawn to them like a moth to a flame. It wasn't just for your brothers. Leo had to work for his own ego and importance, and feelings of vitality and self-worth."

Morris: "Did you love him, Ma?"

Mom: "Yes, I always loved him. He just never really knew it or trusted my love. Perhaps seeing his parents as a model in his childhood convinced him that human love was not real, not to be trusted. He was emotional but did not trust emotions. He was honest and kind. He had integrity and relished his good reputation. He was clean and reliable with ambition and good habits. I will miss him." He always had to have the last word, even on his epitaph."

Morris: "What was his epitaph?"

Mom: "Never give up. Never give up." He did everything his way, even during his final act. He died with dignity; he died alive and never knew a sick day. Just full throttle 72 years of hard drive and work and then peep, the light switch goes off, and he is dead. He died the way he wanted to die, still riding shotgun in the saddle, in full control of his world and his mission in it. I miss him already. In heaven, he's upstairs selling dresses to the shop girls and bringing his box of candies and telling his latest stories and jokes. He's all right. He's going to be working upstairs full throttle. That's the only speed he knows."

Leo Wolff, circa 1964

Epilogue

In this, my second book, "Lucky Conversations," I write about my meetings with a diverse group of people who have made a significant impact on my life. They each had something unique to offer me. They gave me new information about life and "savoir-faire," how to live it well, new wisdom and life lessons, plus encouragement to live life to its fullest. As Hall of Famer 3rd baseman Mike Schmidt of the Philadelphia Phillies put it: "Always do your best to hit the ball very hard. Make sure you run out every ground ball. It may be a base hit, and if you get to first base, that's the only way you can ultimately score."

My meeting with Carl Sandburg in May of 1944 at the National Book Award Luncheon at the Waldorf Astoria in New York, at the ripe old age of eight, left me with these great words of encouragement as a young poet and writer. "The moment you get an idea, even if it's just the first line or two of a possible poem, write down the fragments large or small and come back to them. The idea or the song, the lyric, or the fragment of the song or of the poem will complete itself while you're away." He went on: "The mind keeps working on ideas. Write something new every day. Keep a diary and come back to old ideas. You'll find something in the woodshed every day that you can turn to gold or music."

Then to the 1960s, when I met with President John F. Kennedy alone in the Oval Office on April 11, 1963. He took a very careful look at my resume and what I had accomplished in building a permanent headquarters for AIESEC in Geneva and starting the AIESEC student exchange program in Ghana and Nigeria in West Africa.

President Kennedy sat there rocking in his chair gently. He read every inch of my resume. He was smart. He actually wanted to know, "Who is Morris Wolff?" Kennedy and I had a genuine conversation, not just the flap-crap dialogue that most politicians repeat to everyone who comes to visit.

"We need more men and women in public life who know how to have a real conversation, ones that help get the nation's business done," Kennedy said. "Your students in AIESEC know how to converse in different languages. These friendly discussions begin the small steps towards international understanding and 'hands off the stranger,' which ultimately will lead to world peace. So let's work together to make it happen during our lifetime."

"You are busy creating lifetime opportunities for others. You had the courage to go to Africa's new nations and make the less fortunate feel welcomed and included. Keep being a change agent for the good." Our visit concluded, but his words live on.

Later, on my birthday, November 30, 1993, God gave me a romantic "magic moment" meeting on a sunlit autumn day in Central Park. I took a one-hour walk kicking the leaves and watching the squirrels with Jackie Kennedy. I almost bumped into her on my way to my law office on the East side of the Park that morning and decided to take the day off. I told her that I had worked for Attorney General Robert Kennedy, "Oh Bobby, "he was my favorite of all the brothers. He took care of me religiously after the President died, and I went to pieces."

I was amazed by the courtesy patience of famous busy people. On a snowy winter day, December 11, 1983, I had a five o'clock meeting scheduled with Secretary of State Henry Kissinger alone at his private New York office on 5th Avenue. As I waited in the outer chamber of his office, he walked in at three minutes before five with a tray with two Lenox china teacups and a full tea set serving with cupcakes and cookies. We had an English tea party that broke the ice and put me at ease. We had tea together before discussing business. Dr. Kissinger was of pivotal value. He set up meetings with Kropotkin and KGB officials to locate and rescue Holocaust hero Raoul Wallenberg. Kissinger's report on his meeting with Kropotkin, Khrushchev and other top Russian operatives almost gained Wallenberg's release, and is reported in my first book, "Whatever Happened to Raoul Wallenberg?"

On October 15, 2020, I received a call from Secretary Kissinger about the Wallenberg case. He was in his office in New York, where we met in December 1983 to discuss the Wallenberg case. Today, Mr. Kissinger wanted an update about the Wallenberg case. Also, our discussion included presidential legal power to unleash nuclear weapons. Mr. Kissinger wanted my opinion as an international lawyer and law professor on the wisdom of the present law giving the US president sole authority on the decision to unleash atomic weapons in a global attack.

Also, my lucky chance meeting with Prime Minister Patrice Lumumba of the Congo and President Nkrumah of Ghana at the airport in Accra, Ghana in the hot and humid month of August in 1960, and reaching an agreement on the spot to extend the AIESEC Peace program for college students to several nations in Africa. I often wonder if these were meetings by chance or by destiny. I was in the right place at the right time and tried to do the most that I could do with the opportunity.

Bobby Kennedy, my first boss at the Department of Justice, gave me the chance to sit at the table of legal strategists. They actually drafted the historic Civil Rights Act of 1964, which changed America and ended legal segregation. My employment was as his lawyer by US Senator John Sherman Cooper, from Kentucky, who gave me access to the Senate floor debates. I sat by his side and advised him and other Senators on the legal compromises needed to get the bill passed by Congress and enacted into law on June 17, 1964.

The part I most enjoyed was the "gate crashing" exciting moments with the world champion Philadelphia Phillies when they beat the Kansas City Royals for the World Championship, and I got to meet all of the victorious champions in their locker room after the victory. And I got a full Phillies uniform that night as a lifetime memento.

I have met and spoken with many famous people — from poets to painters to boxers to Presidents — and from First Ladies Jackie Kennedy Onassis and Eleanor Roosevelt, on up to His Holiness, the

Dalai Lama. We set these people apart, and we call them "celebrities." They earn that status, and yet their humility and unpretentious nature are what truly distinguishes them as great human beings.

This was my major discovery. I was at ease with each one and never felt intimidated or out of place. I enjoyed each conversation and treasured the memories. I hope you will gain a pleasant, unforgettable memory and have the same great experience when you meet your next "celebrity." I suggest you don't stand there. Walk up and say hello. Let them know precisely who you are. Tell them the one thing you like most about them. That will be an excellent way to start a conversation, albeit "a lucky conversation!" Go with the flow.

They are people just like us, or at least they were at one time. Once we have consorted with celebrities, we can never go back. We want more. We want the tingle all over again. Some of us stand by, on the edge of an opportunity. We may even watch a celebrity (meaning an interesting person) walk by. They may have wanted to meet you! So next time stop them and say something nice. I assure you everyone loves an honest compliment.

That is what my law partner did when we both spied Jackie walking towards us. On November 30, 1993, he just kept walking towards our office on the Eastside. I peeled off and took advantage of the moment. I walked up, stood in front of her with social distance, and said hello. It was the start of a beautiful friendship.

So, what do I suggest? Be an opportunist when the occasion presents itself unexpectedly. Find an excuse, a hook to get that other person interested in talking with you. Walk up and say hello as I did with Nkrumah and Lumumba at the airport in Ghana. It works. They love to meet people too. The people we met in the pages of this book were all stopped by me. Some by chance. Some by appointment, but in each case, I took the initiative. We know by a quick face recognition precisely who they are and what they do.

Like rock stars, I got to know the effervescent and bubbly star Charo, the music group The Eagles, Mick Jagger, and Elton John by just taking the right airplane. We all loved music, so we had something significant in common. We created a moment to sit and chat at length. These lucky conversations were created by the "chance meeting" of sitting cheek to cheek next to them on a plane ride. We decided together to move beyond a superficial hello, and created an opportunity to dig deeper, learn real things about each other. That was easy with the gregarious and beautiful entertainer Charo on a plane flight from Reno to Philadelphia in 1985. I was coming back to Philadelphia, where I was serving for two years as the first Dean of the Nevada College of Law at Reno, and she was coming from a musical appearance at the Reno casinos. She is a lady and able to entertain anyone. She is still my very good friend.

Going deeper can happen only when both people are interested. That happened to me in my unexpected conversation with Malcolm X on the steps of the Justice Department during the Civil rights debates of 1954. He took time with me and did not rush away. He wanted to create an argument, a civilized discussion about the value of law as compared to demonstrations. We had a keen interest in knowing the other. Our "lucky conversation" had depth and profound meaning for me. We discussed an important issue: humanity and the right of every person to have the guarantees of liberty which our founding fathers had placed in the United States Constitution.

With others, like Muhammed Ali, I did not have that same chance "to go deep." With Robert Frost, it was a profound, full hour in-depth and serious discussion. He was patient; totally relaxed. He welcomed me and spent the hour ruminating and quoting other poets and himself as well. It was not a sound bite. We learned together about the roots of his most famous poems, *Birches* and *The Road Not Taken*. And he spoke like a poet, in rhyme, and with lyrics.

Through this book, we walked through a "museum with many rooms filled with portraits of famous and good people." I have tried to create beautiful paintings of their lives. We have had a chance to stop and look together at a series of diverse and fascinating people.

These are high achieving people with significant differences. They have been creative and have made things happen. We visited a Fine Arts Museum, a pantheon of the famous.

We visited the "American Poets Corner" with Robert Frost and Carl Sandberg. What makes them celebrities? How did they perform miracles, carving as if out of thin air a durable series of books of great poems? Poems like *Mending Wall* by Robert Frost with its lines "something there is about a wall that wants it down." The poem is about the needs or uses of boundaries between two neighbors in Vermont and their tendency to welcome limitations. We explored the will to survive and rise above human loneliness in the gutsy and determined "survive and thrive" lives of two magnificent first Ladies Eleanor Roosevelt and Jackie Kennedy Onassis.

Meeting famous people, and enjoying a lucky conversation, is a rare possibility for everyone. Maybe you will be encouraged by this book to step up and say hello when a celebrity you want to meet and chat with walks by. Think quickly. Find something catchy to say that stops them in their tracks. That requires a "hook" and on the spot creativity, courage, and curiosity.

Just imagine that they were put there by God at this very moment just to meet you. Don't disappoint them. Just give it a try. Email me and tell me the results. I can't wait to hear from you. Tell me all about it. Your accounts may become "Lucky Conversations-Volume Two!"

moewolff657@gmail.com

Von Dardel v. Union of Soviet Socialist Republics, 623 F. Supp. 246 (D.D.C. 1985)

U.S. District Court for the District of Columbia - 623 F. Supp. 246 (D.D.C. 1985)
October 15, 1985

623 F. Supp. 246 (1985)
Guy VON DARDEL, on his own behalf and on Behalf of his half brother, Raoul Wallenberg, and Sven Hagstromer, Legal Guardian of Raoul Wallenberg, on Behalf of Raoul Wallenberg, Plaintiffs,
v.
UNION OF SOVIET SOCIALIST REPUBLICS, Defendant.
Civ. A. No. 84-0353.
United States District Court, District of Columbia.
October 15, 1985.

*247 *248 Anthony D'Amato, Northwestern University School of Law, Chicago, Ill., Joseph W. Dellapenna, Villanova University School of Law, Villanova, Pa., Jerome G. Snider, Davis Polk & Wardwell, Washington, D.C., Guy Miller Struve, Jo R. Backer, John G. Rich, Whitney L. Schmidt, Davis Polk & Wardwell, Murray S. Levin, Alan K. Cotler, Erik N. Videlock, Martha A. Toll, Pepper, Hamilton & Scheetz, Philadelphia, Pa., for plaintiffs.

MEMORANDUM OPINION

BARRINGTON D. PARKER, District Judge:

In this proceeding declaratory and injunctive relief and damages are sought against the Union of Soviet Socialist Republics ("Soviet Union" or "USSR") for the unlawful seizure, imprisonment and possibly death of Raoul Wallenberg, a Swedish diplomat. The complaint is brought on behalf of Wallenberg by Guy Von Dardel, his half brother, and Sven Hagstromer his legal guardian. Guy Von Dardel and Sven Hagstromer are Swedish citizens. Hagstromer was appointed guardian of Wallenberg's legal interests by the District Court in Stockholm, Sweden.

The plaintiffs allege that in 1945, Raoul Wallenberg was arrested in Budapest, Hungary by representatives of the Soviet Union and that since then he has suffered imprisonment and possibly death. At the time of his arrest he was acting at the initiation of the United States government in an attempt to save the Jewish population in the Budapest ghetto from deportation to Nazi extermination camps. If these allegations are true, they violated Wallenberg's diplomatic immunity, the laws and treaties of the Soviet Union and the United States, and the law of nations.

BACKGROUND[1]

During the course of World War II, the United States Government, in an effort to save from extermination by the German Nazis the thousands of Jews then domiciled in Hungary, sought the assistance of Sweden, a neutral nation. This was an effort that the United States could not undertake alone. Because the United States was at war with Hungary, its diplomatic presence was withdrawn. Raoul Wallenberg agreed to join the Swedish Legation in Budapest, and to otherwise cooperate with the efforts of Sweden and "to act at the behest of the United States." Joint Resolution of Congress declaring Raoul Wallenberg to be an honorary citizen of the United States, Pub.L. No. 97-54, 95 Stat. 971 (1981) ("Joint Resolution").[2]

*249 Granted full diplomatic status by Sweden, and funded by the United States, Wallenberg arrived in Budapest, Hungary, in July 1944. While stationed there, he served as Secretary of the Swedish Legation and was entitled to full diplomatic immunity. In the next six months, until his arrest by Soviet officials, Wallenberg saved the lives of nearly one hundred thousand Jewish persons providing them with funds and other means of support provided by the United States. While in Budapest he became the counterforce to the notorious German Nazi Adolf Eichmann. His efforts to save Hungary's Jews from extermination were described in a Senate Report:

He printed and issued thousands of Swedish protective passports of his own design. He purchased and rented scores of houses in Budapest, declared them to be Swedish Embassy property and equipped them with Swedish flags, and protected and cared for the refugees he gathered within these safe houses. Risking his own life time and time again, Wallenberg followed the "Death Marches" and went daily to the deportation trains where he literally pulled people out of the clutches of the Nazis. And, when the Nazis decided to blow up the ghetto in Budapest and all its inhabitants with it, Wallenberg confronted the Nazi leaders (Adolf Eichmann), threatened to see to it personally that they were hanged as war criminals if they proceeded with their plan, and thus prevented its execution.

S.Rep. No. 97-169, 97th Cong., 1st Sess. at 2 (1981) ("Wallenberg Senate Report").

Hungary was later overrun by the Soviets and in early 1945, Wallenberg was arrested by their occupation forces in Budapest. From that time forward, his precise whereabouts and his status within the Soviet Union have not been ascertained. In a note dated August 18, 1947 and delivered to the Swedish Embassy in Moscow by Soviet Foreign Minister, Andrei Ya Vyshinsky it was asserted that "[a]s a result of a thorough investigation it has been established that Wallenberg is not in the Soviet Union and he is not known to us." Affidavit in Support of Plaintiffs' Motion for Default Judgment Guy Miller Struve, cocounsel for plaintiffs (June 17, 1984) Ex. D ("Struve Affidavit").

Ten years later, however, in response to renewed diplomatic inquiries based on the testimony of persons released from Soviet prisons that Wallenberg was still alive, Deputy Foreign Minister Andrei A. Gromyko admitted that Wallenberg had been a prisoner in the USSR. He further stated that while imprisoned, Wallenberg had died of natural causes on July 17, 1947. In a note dated February 6, 1957, delivered to the Swedish Embassy in Moscow, Gromyko described the detention of Wallenberg, and the misinformation which made the detention possible, as "criminal activity," and attempted to fasten the blame for it upon Viktor S. Abakumov, a former Minister of State Security who died in 1953.

Raoul Wallenberg was apparently among other persons detained in the area of the military operations of the Soviet forces. At the same time it may be considered indubitable that the subsequent detention of Wallenberg, and also the incorrect information about him which was given by certain former leaders of organs of state security to the Ministry of Foreign Affairs of the USSR over the course of a number of years, were the result of criminal activity of Abakumov. As is known, in connection with the grave crimes committed by him, Abakumov, acting in violation of the laws of the USSR and striving in every possible way to inflict harm on the Soviet Union, was condemned and shot by order of the Supreme Court of the USSR.

The Soviet Government sincerely regrets what has occurred and expresses its deep condolences to the Government of Sweden and also to the relatives of Raoul Wallenberg.

Affidavit, *supra,* Ex. F, pp. 2-3.
However, between 1954 and 1981, a steady flow of reports from former Soviet prisoners indicate that Wallenberg did not *250 die as claimed in

the Gromyko note. To the contrary, the reports suggest that Wallenberg remained alive and in the defendant's custody after 1947. Joint Resolution, *supra.*

There is insufficient evidence before the Court to support a definitive finding as to whether at this time, Wallenberg is dead or alive. While the USSR has continuously represented that Wallenberg died in 1947, those representations are inconsistent with and at odds with credible and uncontroverted evidence presented by the plaintiffs in this proceeding and they are rejected. On the basis of the record presented here, the Court finds that the Soviet Union has always had knowledge and information about Wallenberg; that it has failed to disclose and has concealed that information; and that otherwise, defendant's representations are suspect and should be given little, if any, credit. If alive, Wallenberg would be 72 years of age and he would have been held in custody for nearly 40 years. The complaint in this proceeding was filed with this Court in February 1984. A request for documents relevant to the issue of jurisdiction was filed along with the complaint. The summons, complaint and discovery request, together with a notice of suit and Russian translations of the documents, were regularly processed through the United States Department of State. The packet of documents was then delivered to and served upon the Soviet Ministry of Foreign Affairs in Moscow in accordance with the Foreign Sovereign Immunities Act ("FSIA" or "Act"), 28 U.S.C. § 1608(a) (4). On May 1, 1984, a certified copy of the diplomatic note evidencing service of the documents was filed by the Department of State with the Clerk of this Court.

The defendant's time to answer or otherwise respond to the complaint expired on June 1, 1984. The Soviet Union did not respond to either the complaint or the document request. On April 19, 1984, the Soviet Ministry of Foreign Affairs returned all of the documents to the United States Embassy in Moscow, together with a note asserting absolute sovereign immunity from suit in non-Soviet courts. Struve Affidavit, *supra,* ¶¶ 4-6 and Ex. B.

Under the circumstances, it is appropriate to consider the plaintiff's application for a default judgment. In the discussion which follows, the Court will address first, the questions of jurisdiction, venue, and statute of limitations. It will then address the merits of the litigations and an analysis of the issues arising under the substantive law. This Court's factual findings are supported by a satisfactory, substantial, and well documented record.

JURISDICTION AND VENUE

Several sections of Title 28 United States Code allow this Court to exercise jurisdiction over this action. Under Section 1330(b) of the Foreign Sovereign Immunities Act, personal jurisdiction is present when the defendant may be found in the United States, through its agents and instrumentalities, and because defendant has been duly served with process pursuant to 28 U.S.C. § 1608(a) (4) (Struve Aff., *supra*, ¶ 3 and Ex. A). Because this is a civil action arising under the "laws, or treaties of the United States," subject matter jurisdiction under FSIA is appropriate pursuant to Sections 1330(a) and 1331. *Letelier v. Republic of Chile,* 502 F. Supp. 259, 266 (D.D.C.1980). Additional reasons to support this conclusion are discussed ante at p. 11. Finally, this Court may exercise subject matter jurisdiction over this proceeding under the Alien Tort Claims Act, 28 U.S.C. § 1350 because it is a "civil action by an alien for a tort only, committed in violation of the law of nations or a treaty of the United States." *Tel-Oren v. Libyan Arab Republic,* 726 F.2d 774, 813-14 (D.C.Cir. 1984), *cert. denied,* ___ U.S. ___, 105 S. Ct. 1354, 84 L. Ed. 2d 377 (1985), opinion Bork, J.; *Letelier,* 502 F. Supp. at 266.

Venue is appropriate in the United States District Court for the District of Columbia because the defendant is a foreign state, 28 U.S.C. § 1391(f) (4).

The Foreign Sovereign Immunities Act, 28 U.S.C. § 1602

This Court has subject matter and personal jurisdiction under the Foreign Sovereign *251 Immunities Act. Under the Act, a foreign state is generally immune from the jurisdiction of federal courts, 28 U.S.C. § 1604, subject to a number of exceptions and limitations set forth at §§ 1604 and 1605. Section 1604 provides that the immunity afforded by the Act is "[s]ubject to existing international agreements to which the United States is a party at the time of enactment of [the] Act." Section 1605(a) sets forth several categorical exceptions to immunity, including situations in which the sovereign defendant has waived immunity, § 1605(a) (1), situations involving certain commercial activity or property in the United States, § 1605(a) (2)-(4), and certain noncommercial torts committed by the foreign state or its agent, § 1605(a) (5).

The Act provides the district courts with subject matter jurisdiction over civil cases against foreign governments where immunity is not appropriate under its terms. 28 U.S.C. § 1330(a). Moreover, where the requirements of subject matter jurisdiction have been met and proper service has been made, the Act operates to create personal jurisdiction over the foreign government defendant. 28 U.S.C. § 1330(b).[3] The absence of immunity thus establishes both subject matter and personal jurisdiction over a case against a foreign government. *See, e.g., Yessenin-Volpin v. Novosti Press Agency,* 443 F. Supp. 849, 851 (S.D.N.Y. 1978).[4]

In 1976, Congress had a twofold purpose for enacting the Foreign Sovereign Immunities Act: (1) to liberalize the law of immunity by adopting and codifying the doctrine of "restrictive" immunity, and (2) to assure consistent application of the law of sovereign immunity by eliminating the participation of the executive branch of the government so as to "assur[e] litigants that ... decisions are made on purely legal grounds and under procedures that insure due process." H.R.Rep. No. 94-1487, 94th Cong., 2d Sess. 7 (1976), *reprinted in* 1976 U.S.Code Cong. & Ad.News 6604, 6606 ("House Report"). To accomplish these objectives, the Act established a set of legal standards governing claims of immunity in civil actions against foreign states. These standards were explicitly intended to incorporate established principles of international law regarding the immunity of sovereigns. House Report, at 14, 1976 U.S.Code Cong. & Ad.News at 6613.

According to the drafters of the FSIA, "sovereign immunity is an affirmative defense which must be specially pleaded, [and] the burden will remain on the foreign state to produce evidence in support of its claim of immunity." House Report, *supra,* at 17, 1976 U.S.Code Cong. & Ad.News at 6616. Thus, the burden of demonstrating that immunity exists rests upon the foreign state. *See, e.g., Arango v. Guzman Travel Advisors Corp.,* 621 F.2d 1371, 1378 (5th Cir. 1980). In the absence of an appearance by the defendant, however, the Court must make an independent determination that it has subject matter jurisdiction. *See, e.g., Letelier v. Republic of Chile,* 488 F. Supp. 665, 667 (D.D.C.1980).

The plaintiff cites five independent reasons why the USSR should not enjoy immunity in this case. The Court has taken note of all these arguments but finds the first four far more compelling than the last. The reasons are as follows: First, by virtue of its decision to default, the USSR failed to raise the defense of sovereign immunity. ***252** Second, the FSIA incorporates preexisting standards of international law, under which a government is not immune for certain acts in clear violation of the universally accepted law of nations. Third, the FSIA is limited by treaties to which the United States is a party; the USSR cannot claim immunity under the FSIA for acts which constitute violations of certain of those treaties, to which the USSR is also a party. Fourth, the USSR waived immunity in this action, and is therefore not entitled to raise it as a defense, pursuant to 28 U.S.C. § 1605(a) (1). And, fifth, the actions of the USSR constitute non-commercial torts within the meaning of 28 U.S.C. § 1605(a)

(5); immunity for commission of such is therefore inappropriate under the Act. A fuller discussion of the first four is set out below.

A.

Under the FSIA, sovereign immunity is an affirmative defense that must be pleaded and proved by the sovereign defendant. These obligations were made clear in the documents which were served upon the Soviet Union. Included among them was an explanatory notice of suit and the full text of the FSIA, both with Russian translation. The transmittal note from the United States Embassy accompanying the papers underscored the procedures:

Please note that under United States law and procedure, neither the Embassy nor the Department of State is in the position to comment on the present suit. Under the laws of the United States, any jurisdictional or other defense including claims of sovereign immunity must be addressed to the court before which the matter is pending, for which reason it is advisable to consult an attorney in the United States. (Struve Aff., Ex. A.) Moreover, because of prior involvement in FSIA litigation, the procedure is one with which the Soviet Union is fully familiar. Indeed in several reported cases in which the USSR has been a defendant since the passage of the Act, it has appeared through counsel for the purpose of contesting jurisdiction.[5] *See Bland v. Union of Soviet Socialist Republics,* 17 Av.Cas. (CCH) 17,530 (E.D.N.Y.1982); *Harris v. VAO Intourist, Moscow,* 481 F. Supp. 1056 (E.D.N.Y.1979); *United Euram v. Union of Soviet Socialist Republics,* 461 F. Supp. 609 (S.D.N.Y.1978); *cf. In re Estate of Petro Seminiw,* 78 Ill.App.3d 570, 33 Ill. Dec. 731, 397 N.E.2d 64 (1st Dist.1979); *In re Estate of Bari Nabif,* 69 A.D.2d 904, 415 N.Y.S.2d 901 (2d Dept.1979).[6] However, in this proceeding, the USSR has chosen to default and to raise the issue of immunity not by a motion filed with the Court, but merely by a communication addressed to the United States Embassy in Moscow.

In *Letelier, supra,* 488 F. Supp. 665, 669 n. 4, this Court raised the question of whether such a diplomatic assertion of immunity, in lieu of "a formal appearance or the filing of a pleading," could suffice to raise the defense of sovereign immunity. In that case, the foreign state defendant sent a diplomatic note to the Department of State challenging the jurisdiction of the Court. The Court declined to rule on the sufficiency of this method of raising the affirmative defense of immunity, because the

Court found that it had subject matter jurisdiction "even assuming it has been pleaded properly." *Id.* at 670 n. 4.

The degree to which a foreign state is entitled to immunity under the Act is necessarily determined by the procedures set forth by Congress. Congress explicitly intended that sovereign immunity remain an "affirmative defense which must be specially pleaded, the burden [remaining] on the foreign state to produce evidence in *253 support of its claim of immunity." House Report, *supra,* at 17, 1976 U.S.Code Cong. & Ad.News at 6616. This allocation of the burden of proof was, in fact, one of the bases for Congress' decision to structure the Act as a presumption of immunity subject to a group of exceptions. *Id.*

In the present case, defendant has not only failed to plead immunity as an affirmative defense, but has chosen to raise immunity in a manner explicitly precluded by the Act. Prior to passage of the FSIA, the defense of immunity could be raised by diplomatic approaches to the Department of State. *See, e.g.,* House Report, *supra,* at 7, 1976 U.S.Code Cong. & Ad.News at 6605-06; *Ex Parte Muir,* 254 U.S. 522, 532-33, 41 S. Ct. 185, 187, 65 L. Ed. 383 (1921). It was the express purpose of the FSIA to remove the executive branch from the determination of such issues. By raising the issue of sovereign immunity in a diplomatic note, the USSR has knowingly chosen a procedure that is no longer available under United States law. As such, it cannot be recognized as an adequate pleading of the defense of immunity. *Ex Parte Muir, supra,* at 533, 41 S. Ct. at 187. Having failed to raise immunity as an affirmative defense, or to provide even a bare allegation that its acts do not fall into one of the exceptions to the FSIA, defendant has deliberately chosen to forego whatever entitlement it might have had to immunity under the terms of the Act.[7]

B.

The Foreign Sovereign Immunities Act, like every federal statute, should be interpreted in such a way as to be consistent with the law of nations. *See, e.g., MacLeod v. United States,* 229 U.S. 416, 434, 33 S. Ct. 955, 961, 57 L. Ed. 1260 (1913). Congress explicitly anticipated such an interpretation, stating its intent that the Act "[incorporated] standards recognized under international law." House Report, *supra,* at 14, 1976 U.S.Code Cong. & Ad.News at 6613.

Historically, when a nation has committed a clear and egregious violation of a well-established and universally recognized standard of international law, courts have recognized the need for an appropriate exercise of jurisdiction. In *Bernstein v. N.V. Nederlandsche-Amerikaansche*

Stoomvaart-Maatschappij, 210 F.2d 375 (2d Cir. 1954), the court deferred to a press release issued by the Department of State in which the Department took the position that in cases seeking reparations for confiscations of property by Nazi officials, American courts should not be restrained by doctrines of international law that, under more routine circumstances, would require a court not to exercise jurisdiction or reach the merits of a claim. 210 F.2d at 375-76. Moreover, the doctrine of sovereign immunity has historically been based on principles of "grace and comity." *Verlinden B.V. v. Central Bank of Nigeria,* 461 U.S. 480, 486, 103 S. Ct. 1962, 1967, 76 L. Ed. 2d 81 (1983). As such, the doctrine is inherently limited and appropriately disallowed where the foreign state defendant has acted in clear violation of international law.

In *Banco Nacional de Cuba v. Sabbatino,* 376 U.S. 398, 84 S. Ct. 923, 11 L. Ed. 2d 804 (1964), the Supreme Court held that the act of state doctrine barred consideration of the validity of a Cuban confiscation of property located in Cuba, basing its decision largely on the fact that there is some division in the international community regarding state expropriation of the property of aliens. ("There are few if any issues in international law today on which opinion seems to be so divided ..." 376 U.S. at 428, 84 S.Ct. at 940). In dissenting, Justice White urged that the act of state doctrine should not shield acts which are clearly violations of international law, even where (unlike the present case) such acts would otherwise be subject to the act of state doctrine:

*254 The reasons for nonreview, based as they are on traditional concepts of territorial sovereignty, lose much of their force when the foreign act of state is shown to be a violation of international law. All legitimate exercises of sovereign power, whether territorial or otherwise, should be exercised consistently with rules of international law, including those rules which mark the bounds of lawful state action against aliens or their property located within the territorial confines of the foreign state. 376 U.S. at 457, 84 S. Ct. at 955-56.

The concept of extraordinary judicial jurisdiction over acts in violation of significant international standards has also been embodied in the principle of "universal" violations of international law. *See, e.g.,* Restatement of Foreign Relations Law of the United States (Revised) § 404 (Tent. Draft No. 2, 1981) ("A state may exercise jurisdiction to define and punish certain offenses recognized by the community of nations as of universal concern"). The concept of universal violations is not limited to criminal jurisdiction, but extends to the enforcement of civil law as well. *Id.* at Comment *b.*

Congress was fully aware of these doctrines of international law in 1976 when it adopted the FSIA, and meant to incorporate them into the statute.[8] The statute should be read, then, not to extend immunity to clear violations of universally recognized principles of international law. The violation of the diplomatic immunity of Raoul Wallenberg is such a violation. The ancient and universal consensus on diplomatic immunity places it squarely within even the most restrictive interpretation of the coverage of the Alien Tort Claims Act, 28 U.S.C. § 1350. *See* discussion at 258-59, *infra*. As such, the Congress in 1789 opened the district courts of the United States to suits by aliens claiming tortious violations of diplomatic immunity. Congress has also enacted statutes designed to protect internationally protected persons, including diplomats, 18 U.S.C. §§ 1116 and 1201, as to which a private remedy has been implied. *See* discussion at 257-58, *infra*. If the FSIA was interpreted to bar suits against foreign governments under § 1350, or to preempt the private rights created by §§ 1116 and 1201, it would act *pro tanto* to repeal these statutes.[9] Statutory interpretation that would effect such a repeal is not favored, *e.g., United States v. United Continental Tuna Corp.*, 425 U.S. 164, 168-69, 181, 96 S. Ct. 1319, 1322-23, 1329, 47 L. Ed. 2d 653 (1976), and is therefore rejected by this Court.

C.

Section 1604 of the FSIA provides that immunity is "subject to" international agreements to which the United States was a party at the time of its enactment. Thus, where the substantive provisions of the Act would operate in a specific case to interfere with any such international agreement, such provisions must be preempted to the *255 extent necessary to permit the full operation of such agreement.[10] In this proceeding, both the United States and the Soviet Union are parties to two international agreements, the operation of which would be frustrated by any decision granting immunity to the Soviet Union: the Vienna Convention on Diplomatic Relations, April 18, 1961, and the 1973 Convention on Internationally Protected Persons.

The Vienna Convention and the 1973 Convention are both designed to protect diplomats from offenses against them. In order for the conventions to operate effectively, the perpetrators of such offenses must be subject to liability for their acts. To the extent that the FSIA would shield the Soviet Union from such liability, it is in conflict with the terms of the conventions and thwarts their effective operation. Under § 1604, the immunity granted by the FSIA must be limited so as to avoid such a result; in the present case, the Soviet Union must be denied immunity.

This result is particularly just since the Soviet Union is a party to both conventions. Under the Vienna Convention the USSR is pledged to protect the very rights it is violating. Under the 1973 Convention it is pledged to punish the very crimes it is committing. Moreover, the Soviet Union's unlawful treatment of Wallenberg was ongoing even as the Conventions were drafted and signed. Thus, it knowingly accepted the validity of legal standards that it knew at the time were being violated. Against such a backdrop, the denial of immunity against claims seeking relief for such violations does not seem unjust.

D.
Under § 1605(a) (1) of the FSIA, foreign states may waive immunity "either explicitly or by implication." According to the House Report, an example of an explicit waiver under the FSIA might be found in the form of a treaty obligation under treaties of friendship, commerce, and navigation. Neither the statute nor the legislative history, however, makes clear how immunity can be implicitly waived.[11]

The United States courts have not yet fully explored the proposition that by ratifying an international agreement a foreign state implicitly waives a defense of sovereign immunity against claims seeking compensation for acts which constitute violations of such agreements. In *Frolova v. Union of Soviet Socialist Republics,* 558 F. Supp. 358, 363 n. 3 (N.D.Ill.1983), *aff'd,* 761 F.2d 370 (7th Cir.1985), the court in dictum rejected plaintiff's argument that because the Soviet Union's refusal to permit plaintiff's husband to emigrate violated international and Soviet law, it had impliedly waived immunity. In *Siderman v. Republic of Argentina,* No. Civ. 82-1772-RMT (C.D.Cal. March 12, 1984), however, the court found jurisdiction over the Republic of Argentina for claims related to the torture of one of the plaintiffs "by applying the `Law of Nations' concept." A number of legal scholars have examined this principle in the context of *256 human rights violations,[12] and have concluded that a sovereign may implicitly waive its immunity for such violations when it ratifies human rights agreements. R. Lillich and F. Newman, *International Human Rights: Problems of Law and Policy* (1979); Comment, *The Foreign Sovereign Immunities Act and International Human Rights Agreements: How They Co-Exist,* 17 U.S.F.L.Rev. 71 (1982).

These conclusions are directly relevant to the present case, which involves violations not only of international human rights agreements but also of treaties codifying the fundamental principle of diplomatic immunity, which has been universally recognized as binding since before the times of Blackstone and de Vattel.[13] By explicitly agreeing to be bound by the terms of those agreements, the USSR has implicitly waived its immunity in this action alleging their breach. As Lillich and Newman have noted with respect to the United Nations Charter,

it would be most difficult to conclude that the Charter provisions on human rights cannot legitimately be given effect by the courts in appropriate cases. Indeed, it would be contrary to the letter and the spirit of the supremacy clause of the Constitution if the courts did not attempt to carry out a treaty provision to the fullest extent possible.

R. Lillich and F. Newman, *International Human Rights, supra,* at 76. Any other result would rob each of those agreements of substantive effect, and would render meaningless the act of the Soviet Union in signing them.

The Alien Tort Claims Act, 28 U.S.C. § 1350

The Alien Tort Claims Act, 28 U.S.C. § 1350, was enacted in 1789 by the First Congress of the United States. The section provides that the "district courts shall have original jurisdiction of any civil action by an alien for a tort only, committed in violation of the law of nations or a treaty of the United States." The statute vests this Court with subject matter jurisdiction over this proceeding and the right to determine liability for injuries resulting from violations of the diplomatic immunity of Raoul Wallenberg. The Court of Appeals for this Circuit recently considered the application of § 1350 in *Tel-Oren v. Libyan Arab Republic,* 726 F.2d 774 (D.C.Cir.1984). That case involved a terrorist attack on an Israeli bus by members of the Palestine Liberation Organization. Plaintiffs, survivors of the attack and representatives of some of those killed, asserted jurisdiction under 28 U.S.C. §§ 1331 and 1350.[14] The District Court dismissed the case for lack of jurisdiction, and plaintiffs appealed. The Court of Appeals issued three opinions which affirmed the decision of the District Court, but each opinion stated separate grounds for reaching that result.

Judge Harry Edwards adopted the interpretation of § 1350 previously adopted by the Second Circuit in *Filartiga v. Pena-Irala,* 630 F.2d 876 (2d Cir.1980), whereby proof of a tort in violation of international law as that law is currently understood establishes both a cause of action and jurisdiction in the District Court. Judge Robert Bork proposed a more narrow reading of the statute, arguing that the doctrine of ***257** separation of powers should be seen to limit the effect of the statute to those violations of international law that were recognized as actionable in 1789

or to those which, though more recently established, explicitly enta[ ]
private right of action. Judge Roger Robb concurred on the ground th[at]
political question doctrine precluded judicial consideration of the clai[ms]
raised by the plaintiffs because the legal issues surrounding terrorism ar[e]
complex and imprecise. It is clear that even under the narrowest of these
standards proposed in *Tel-Oren,* or adopted in other forums § 1350
provides this Court with subject matter jurisdiction to determine the
liability for the injury that has resulted from the violation of Raoul
Wallenberg's diplomatic immunity.

A.

In *Filartiga v. Pena-Irala,* 630 F.2d 876 (2d Cir.1980), a former
Paraguayan police official was sued by the father and sister of a young
man whose death by torture he was alleged to have caused. The District
Court dismissed the case, saying that although official torture violated
emerging standards of international law, it was obliged by dicta in prior
Second Circuit opinions to rule that § 1350 does not reach a state's
behavior towards its own citizens.

On appeal, the Second Circuit reversed. Judge Kaufman wrote that the
"law of nations," as used in the statute, is a developing body of principles
which must be interpreted "not as it was in 1789, but as it has evolved and
exists among the nations of the world today." 630 F.2d at 881.[15] Looking
to the sources of international law enumerated by the Supreme Court
in *The Paquete Habana,* 175 U.S. 677, 700, 20 S. Ct. 290, 299, 44 L. Ed.
320 (1900) "executive or legislative act or judicial decision" and the works
of expert "jurists and commentators," 630 F.2d at 880 the court found that
"the limitations on a state's power to torture persons held in its custody"
constitute a principle on which the opinion of civilized nations is so united
as to raise it to a norm of international law. 630 F.2d at 881. *See also* 630
F.2d at 887-89. The court concluded that the cause of action "is properly
brought in federal court." 630 F.2d at 887.

In *Tel-Oren,* Judge Edwards adopted the approach of the Second Circuit.
He stated that § 1350 provides jurisdiction in federal district court where a
plaintiff alleges a tortious violation of a principle of international law on
which the community of nations has reached a consensus. This is true even
where no other basis of jurisdiction is present, and regardless of whether or
not a "right to sue" on that violation is independently granted by
international law. 726 F.2d at 772-82. Applying these standards to the facts
in *Tel-Oren,* Judge Edwards found that, however reprehensible the actions

nts may have been, no consensus existed among nations arrant an extension of the *Filartiga* approach to the law of lude disapproval of non-state acts of violence or terrorism. 91-96.

esented here easily satisfy the criteria set forth by Judge . An accredited diplomat has been detained and held ..imunicado for more than 35 years; his whereabouts have been concealed; and the defendant may have caused his death. There can be no clearer violation of the law of nations. Under the analysis of Judge Edwards, this proceeding is appropriately before this Court.

B.

Judge Bork concurred in dismissing *Tel-Oren* on the ground that plaintiffs had failed to meet a more stringent test than proposed by Judge Edwards and relied upon by the Second Circuit. Under Judge Bork's analysis, plaintiffs would have to show not only a violation of the law of nations, but also a source of a right to sue under federal or international law. 726 F.2d at 801, 808. Judge Bork stated that only by limiting § 1350 to cases in which *258 the law of nations clearly envisions judicial involvement would the doctrine of separation of powers be properly served. In cases such as *Tel-Oren*, where the rule of decision under international law is insufficiently developed, he creates a presumption against jurisdiction which can only be overcome by showing that plaintiffs have been provided with a cause of action under federal or international law. 726 F.2d at 1808. The facts and allegations of the present case appear to satisfy the requirements set forth by Judge Bork. First, in discussing the unsettled nature of international legal standards regarding terrorism, Judge Bork acknowledges that related areas have been the subject of international consensus through written conventions. 726 F.2d at 806-07. Among the conventions he lists is the 1973 Convention on the Prevention and Punishment of Crimes Against Internationally Protected Persons, Including Diplomatic Agents. Diplomatic immunity is an area in which international legal standards have long been clearly stated, and the Convention complements preexisting international accords on the treatment of diplomats.

In the course of his analysis, Judge Bork notes that he is "guided" by the language of the Supreme Court in *Banco Nacional de Cuba supra*, p. 254, in which the Court established a sort of sliding scale with respect to judicial application of international law:

[T]he greater the degree of codification or consensus concerning a particular area of international law, the more appropriate it is for the judiciary to render decisions regarding it, since the courts can then focus on the application of an agreed principle to circumstances of fact rather than on the sensitive task of establishing a principle not inconsistent with the national interest or with international justice.

726 F.2d at 804. The rules of diplomatic immunity are so well established that judicial determination of a violation of diplomatic immunity poses little or no threat to the doctrine of separation of powers. It is, therefore, fully consistent with the rationale underlying Judge Bork's opinion to permit the federal courts to apply the law of diplomatic immunity. However, even if his opinion is read to require an explicit showing of a cause of action granted under international law in any case that may touch on foreign relations, plaintiffs' allegations fall within one of the areas that the opinion specifically places within the reach of § 1350.

He stated that the statute is given its more appropriately limited meaning by looking to the "law of nations" as understood in 1789. At that time, the "law of nations" was limited to three primary offenses: "'1. Violation of safe-conducts; 2. Infringement of the rights of embassadors; and 3. Piracy,'" 726 F.2d at 813, *quoting* 4 W. Blackstone, *Commentaries*, 68, 72, and Judge Bork concluded that "[o]ne might suppose that these were the kinds of offenses for which Congress wished to provide tort jurisdiction for suits by aliens in order to avoid conflicts with other nations." 726 F.2d 813-14. The American colonies, having adopted the common law of England, adopted a "private cause of action for which section 1350 gave the necessary jurisdiction to federal courts" in these three types of cases. 726 F.2d at 1814 n. 22. *See also Respublica v. De Longchamps,* 1 U.S. (1 Dall.) 111, 116, 1 L. Ed. 59 (Pa.Ct. Oyer & Term.1784). Thus, the doctrine of diplomatic immunity is so firmly established as to fall within even the very limited interpretation of § 1350 favored by Judge Bork.

C.

Judge Robb invoked the political question doctrine to dismiss *Tel-Oren,* based on arguments similar to those used by Judge Bork in defense of the separation of powers. The opinion cautions against judicial interference in a politically sensitive area where the rule of decision is not adequately defined. 726 F.2d at 827 and *passim.* However, international legal standards with regard to the treatment of diplomats have long been clearly established, and their application should therefore pose *259 little risk of embarrassing the political branches. As Justice White wrote in his dissent in *Banco Nacional de Cuba,* while

> political matters in the realm of foreign affairs are within the exclusive domain of the Executive Branch ... this is far from saying that the constitution vests in the executive exclusive absolute control of foreign affairs or that the validity of a foreign act of state is necessarily a political question. International law, as well as a treaty or executive agreement, see *United States v. Pink,* 315 U.S. 203 [62 S. Ct. 552, 86 L. Ed. 796], provides an ascertainable standard for adjudicating the validity of some foreign acts, and courts are competent to apply this body of law, notwithstanding that there may be some cases where comity dictates giving effect to the foreign act because it is not clearly condemned under generally accepted principles of international law.

376 U.S. 461-62, 84 S. Ct. 957-58. The political question doctrine should therefore not defeat jurisdiction in this case.

D.

Under any one of the three *Tel-Oren* opinions, § 1350 provides this Court with subject matter jurisdiction to consider this case. Plaintiffs are aliens; the causes of action they bring are in tort. There has, without question, been a violation of the law of nations, as defined by legal scholars, confirmed in international conventions to which the United States is a party, and codified in United States law. The requisites of the Edwards/*Filartiga* approach are thus satisfied.

The violations alleged involve an area of international law in which standards and norms have long been well-defined. The underlying rationale of the opinions of Judges Bork and Robb a reluctance, where legal standards are uncertain, to permit the courts to enter politically sensitive areas is therefore met.

Finally, this case satisfies the most stringent of the requirements set forth by Judge Bork. Well before 1789, the protection and well-being of diplomats were understood to be a part of the law of nations, and English (and then American) common law recognized a private cause of action where the law was violated. This right to sue has recently been reaffirmed by the Congress and this Court with respect to acts of violence against internationally protected persons.

STATUTE OF LIMITATIONS

Plaintiffs' claims against the USSR are not barred by any applicable statute of limitations.[16] Plaintiffs contend that Raoul Wallenberg is still alive, and that his unlawful detention is therefore a continuing violation of the laws of the United States, the laws and treaties of the USSR, and the law of nations. In such circumstances, the *260 statute of limitations has not yet begun to run. The tortious conduct by the defendant is an ongoing violation which precludes the running of a limitations period.

In cases involving an ongoing tort, as here, the cause of action does not accrue for purposes of the running of the statute until the last act constituting the tort is complete. *See Page v. United States,* 729 F.2d 818, 821 (D.C.Cir.1984) (citing, *inter alia, Gross v. United States,* 676 F.2d 295, 300 (8th Cir.1982); *Leonhard v. United States,* 633 F.2d 599, 613 (2d Cir.1980), *cert. denied,* 451 U.S. 908, 101 S. Ct. 1975, 68 L. Ed. 2d 295 (1981)).

Moreover, even if Raoul Wallenberg is no longer alive, defendant's concealment of the facts and circumstances surrounding Wallenberg's detention and possible death, since the 1957 Gromyko note, provides two further reasons for this Court to refrain from barring plaintiffs' claims. First, under the "discovery rule" of the District of Columbia, plaintiffs' claims have not yet accrued for statute of limitations purposes. Under this rule, a plaintiff's cause of action does not accrue until the plaintiff learns, or with reasonable diligence could have learned, that he has been injured, *see, e.g., Wilson v. Johns-Manville Sales Corp.,* 684 F.2d 111, 116-18 (D.C.Cir.1982); *Grigsby v. Sterling Drug, Inc.,* 428 F. Supp. 242, 243 (D.D.C.1975), *aff'd without opinion,* 543 F.2d 417 (D.C.Cir.1976), *cert. denied,* 431 U.S. 967, 97 S. Ct. 2925, 53 L. Ed. 2d 1063 (1977), and that his injury is due to wrongdoing on the part of the defendant, *see, e.g., Dawson v. Eli Lilly and Co.,* 543 F. Supp. 1330, 1333-34 (D.D.C.1982).[17]

In this proceeding, the plaintiffs have no way of knowing whether Wallenberg is dead, or, if he is dead, the circumstances of his death and the identity of those responsible. The Gromyko note, in light of the weight of contradictory evidence, cannot provide a reasonable basis for holding that plaintiffs have learned that Wallenberg is no longer alive. Such information remains solely within the control of the USSR.

Second, when a defendant has fraudulently concealed facts giving rise to a cause of action, the statute of limitations is tolled until plaintiffs, employing due diligence, discover or should have discovered the facts giving rise to the claim in this case, evidence that Wallenberg is indeed no longer alive and that defendant was involved in his death. *Richards v. Mileski,* 662 F.2d 65, 68-69 (D.C.Cir.1981). *See also, e.g., Hobson v. Wilson,* 737 F.2d 1 (D.C.Cir. 1984), *cert. denied sub nom Brennan v. Hobson,* ___ U.S. ___, 105 S. Ct. 1843, 85 L. Ed. 2d 142 (1985). With respect to the matter of burden of proof and due diligence, our Circuit Court stated in *Richards:*

When tolling is proper because the defendants have concealed the very cause of action, or their involvement in a cause of action about which the plaintiff might otherwise be aware, they have the burden of coming forward with any facts showing that the plaintiff could have discovered their involvement or the cause of action if he had exercised due diligence. 662 F.2d at 71. *See also Smith v. Nixon,* 606 F.2d 1183, 1191 (D.C.Cir.1979), *cert. denied,* 453 U.S. 912, 101 S. Ct. 3147, 69 L. Ed. 2d 997, 453 U.S. 928, 102 S. Ct. 892, 69 L. Ed. 2d 1024 (1981). The defendant cannot meet this burden. Since 1945, it has concealed the truth concerning the condition and whereabouts of Raoul Wallenberg.

THE MERITS
A.

There are few principles of international law, if any, that are as universally *261 recognized as the principle of diplomatic immunity. The seizure and detention of Raoul Wallenberg presents a clear violation of the law of nations as well as a clear violation of the laws and treaties of the United States and the Soviet Union. Moreover, the record in this action is clear, in that it does not show that the Soviet Union has sought, in any manner, to justify its conduct toward Wallenberg. Indeed, the 1957 Gromyko Note, *supra* pp. 5-6, characterizes his detention and the concealment of his whereabouts as criminal activity.

The history of the diplomatic immunity doctrine is traced from many recognized sources. *See* D. Michaels, *International Privileges and Immunities,* 7, 1971; 1 L. Oppenheim, International Law § 386 (1905); Restatement of Foreign Relations Law of the United States (Revised) § 461 (Tent. Draft No. 4, 1983). The concept was a part of the ancient civilizations of China, India and Egypt, *United States v. Enger,* 472 F. Supp. 490, 504 (D.N.J.1978).

The present day consensus of the international community on the protection afforded diplomats has been codified in a number of international agreements, primarily the Vienna Convention on Diplomatic Relations, April 18, 1961, 23 U.S.T. 3227, T.I.A.S. No. 7502. Article 29 of the Convention states that

[t]he person of a diplomatic agent shall be inviolable. He shall not be liable to any form of arrest or detention. The receiving State shall treat him with due respect and shall take all appropriate steps to prevent any attack on his person, freedom or dignity.

23 U.S.T. at 3240, T.I.A.S. No. 7502 at 14. Corresponding obligations are imposed upon states other than the receiving state under Article 40 of the Convention. 23 U.S.T. at 3246, T.I.A.S. No. 7502 at 20-21.

In the 1970s, the community of nations reaffirmed its commitment to the safety of diplomats by entering into the Convention on the Prevention and Punishment of Crimes Against Internationally Protected Persons, Including Diplomatic Agents, December 14, 1973, 28 U.S.T. 1975, T.I.A.S. No. 8532. The Convention requires signatory nations to take steps to punish the "murder, kidnapping or other attack upon the person or liberty of an internationally protected person," 28 U.S.T. at 1978, T.I. A.S. No. 8532 at 4, as well as other crimes or threats against them. The Soviet Union is a party to both the Vienna Convention and the 1973 Convention. Wallenberg's treatment at the hands of the Soviet Union also violates a number of international treaties and conventions relating to human rights, all of which have been signed by the Soviet Union. Under Articles 55 and 56 of the United Nations Charter, each member state pledges to take action to promote "universal respect for, and observance of, human rights and fundamental freedoms." 59 Stat. 1033, 1045-46 (1945). These obligations are given further substance in subsequent documents. Article 3 of the Universal Declaration of Human Rights, G.A.Res. 217A (III), U.N. Doc. A/1810 (1948), mandates the protection of "life, liberty and security of person." Article 9 protects the right not to "be subjected to arbitrary arrest, detention or exile." Article 10 protects each person's right to a fair and public hearing of criminal charges against him. Article 12 protects the right not to "be subjected to arbitrary interference with ... privacy, family, home or correspondence." The international community including the Soviet Union reaffirmed its commitment to these rights in the International Covenant on Civil and Political Rights, G.A.Res. 2200 (XXI), 21 U.N.

GAOR Supp. (No. 16) at 52, U.N. Doc. A/6316 (1967),[18] and again in the Final Act of the Conference on Security and Cooperation in Europe (Helsinki 1975), Department of State Bulletin Reprint, Sept. 1, 1975.

B.
United States law has long accepted international standards of diplomatic immunity as part of its common law and has *262 recognized a private civil cause of action for a violation of diplomatic immunity. *See Tel-Oren v. Libyan Arab Republic,* 726 F.2d 774, 814 n. 22 (D.C.Cir.1984). In *Respublica v. De Longchamps,* 1 U.S. (1 Dall.) 111, 1 L. Ed. 59 (Pa.Ct.Oyer & Term.1784), the Supreme Court held that the De Longchamps committed "an atrocious violation of the law of nations," when, having first insulted the Consul General of France to the United States, he struck the cane of the diplomat. The Court described De Longchamps' actions as gross insults, and diplomats as "the peculiar objects" of the law of nations. 1 U.S. (1 Dall.) at 111, 117.

In 1976, the United States Congress enacted the Act for the Prevention and Punishment of Crimes Against Internationally Protected Persons, 18 U.S.C. §§ 1116, 1201, 112, 970, 878 and 11. That criminal statute proscribes the murder or attempted murder of an internationally protected person, and permits the exercise by the United States of jurisdiction over such an offense "if the alleged offender is present within the United States, irrespective of the place where the offense was committed or the nationality of the victim or the alleged offender." 18 U.S.C. § 1116(c). An "internationally protected person" is defined as including, *inter alia,* any ... representative, officer, employee, or agent of the United States Government, a foreign government, or international organization who at the time and place concerned is entitled pursuant to international law to special protection against attack upon his person, freedom, or dignity. 18 U.S.C. § 1116(b) (4) (B). Similar prohibitory and jurisdictional language governs the kidnapping of such a person under 18 U.S.C. § 1201(a) (4) and (e).

At the time of his kidnapping, Raoul Wallenberg was an accredited Swedish diplomat. He was thus an "internationally protected person" within the meaning of §§ 1116 and 1201(a) (4) and (e). His kidnapping was therefore a violation of § 1201(a) (4); if he is no longer alive, § 1116 has also been violated. In enacting these statutes, Congress expressly declared its intent to prohibit such acts wherever and by whomever committed, and whatever the nationality of the victim.

Moreover, this Court has recognized a civil cause of action under federal law on behalf of private plaintiffs pursuant to 18 U.S.C. § 1116.
In *Letelier,* 502 F. Supp. at 266, jurisdiction was upheld in a suit brought by the surviving spouses of an exiled Chilean diplomat and his co-worker against those responsible for their murder. The same rationale should apply to § 1201(a) (4) and (e). Under both, plaintiffs are entitled to immediate declaratory relief.

C.

The Soviet Union's treatment of Raoul Wallenberg is unlawful even under its own statutes.[19] The Statute on Diplomatic and Consular Representations of Foreign States on the Territory of the USSR, confirmed by edict of the Presidium of the USSR Supreme Soviet on May 23, 1966, set forth in *Collected Legislation of the Union of Soviet Socialist Republics and the Constituent Union Republics* (Butler ed. 1983), affirms the privileges and immunities due to diplomats, Article 1, as well as the primacy of "international treaty rules" on the subject, Article 3. By its terms, the statute applies to diplomatic or consular representations "on the territory of the USSR." Article 1. The "inviolability" while travelling in the "territory of the USSR" of diplomats representing a "foreign state in a third country" is specifically assured in Article 18. The detention of Wallenberg plainly violates the diplomatic immunity guaranteed by the statute.

Wallenberg's detention is also violative of the Criminal Code of the Russian Soviet Federated Socialist Republic, and corresponding provisions of the Criminal Codes of other Republics of the USSR. Article ***263** 126 of the Federated Socialistic Republic Criminal Code outlaws any deprivation of freedom that was illegal as of the time committed. Article 178 proscribes an arrest or detention which is known to be illegal and which is illegal in fact. Wallenberg's arrest and detention were and continue to be illegal under principles of international law and international agreements which were in force in 1945 and to which the USSR was a party. Moreover, the 1957 Gromyko Note acknowledged the illegality of Wallenberg's detention and of the misinformation that made it possible.

The Soviet Union's treatment of Raoul Wallenberg is unlawful under any standard of applicable law. It has never argued otherwise; it has denied and disclaimed its actions, but it has never defended them.

CONCLUSION

In many ways, this action is without precedent in the history of actions against foreign sovereigns. It involves actions which the Soviet Union has already admitted were unlawful. It involves a gross violation of the personal immunity of a diplomat, one of the oldest and most universally recognized principles of international law. Furthermore, this action involves a deliberate default by a defendant which has repeatedly demonstrated its familiarity with the proper means for raising a defense of sovereign immunity under the Foreign Sovereign Immunities Act.
There can be little, if any, doubt that both subject matter and personal jurisdiction are conferred through that Act. Whatever sovereign immunity the defendant might have had, is, by the terms of the Act, subject to international agreements to which the United States was a party when the FSIA was enacted in 1976 which prohibit defendant's actions regarding Mr. Wallenberg.

Additionally, this Court determines that no applicable statute of limitations has begun to run against plaintiff's claims. Because Mr. Wallenberg is still being unlawfully held by the defendants, or alternatively, he is dead, the statute is tolled by the "discovery rule" and/or the law on tolling applicable when one party has fraudulently concealed facts.
For all of these reasons, default judgment is hereby entered against the defendant.

NOTES
[1] The facts in this proceeding are based on statements of USSR officials, official actions taken by the United States Congress, reports and resolutions of House and Senate Committees and official actions taken by the President. The plaintiffs have filed voluminous appendices in this proceeding.
[2] Mr. Wallenberg became the second person to be voted by Congress an honorary citizen. Winston Churchill was the first. Representative Thomas Lantos of California, a Hungarian Jewish refugee is credited with taking the initiative in making Wallenberg an honorary American citizen. New York Times, April 13, 1985, p. 9.
[3] A court's assertion of jurisdiction over a defendant pursuant to § 1330(b) must also comport with minimum jurisdictional contacts and due process as required by *International Shoe Co. v. Washington*, 326 U.S. 310, 66 S. Ct. 154, 90 L. Ed. 95 (1945). *See World-Wide Volkswagen Corp. v. Woodson*, 444 U.S. 286, 292-93, 100 S. Ct. 559, 564-65, 62 L.

Ed. 2d 490 (1980); *Kulko v. California Superior Court,* 436 U.S. 84, 92, 98 S. Ct. 1690, 1697, 56 L. Ed. 2d 132 (1978); *Hanson v. Denckla,* 357 U.S. 235, 253, 78 S. Ct. 1228, 1239-40, 2 L. Ed. 2d 1283 (1958). *See also Gilson v. Republic of Ireland,* 682 F.2d 1022, 1028 (D.C. Cir.1982). These minimum requirements are clearly satisfied because the defendant maintains a substantial presence in this District.

[4] As a threshold matter, it is noted that the Supreme Court has upheld the constitutionality of the FSIA's authorization of suits by foreign plaintiffs against foreign states. *Verlinden B.V. v. Central Bank of Nigeria,* 461 U.S. 480, 490, 103 S. Ct. 1962, 1969, 76 L. Ed. 2d 81 (1983).

[5] The Soviet Union defaulted without comment in *Frolova v. Union of Soviet Socialist Republics,* 558 F. Supp. 358 (N.D.Ill.1983), *aff'd,* 761 F.2d 370 (7th Cir.1985).

[6] The instrumentalities of the Soviet Union have also appeared when sued under the Act. *See Houston v. Murmansk Shipping Co.,* 667 F.2d 1151 (4th Cir.1982); *Yessenin-Volpin v. Novosti Press Agency,* 443 F. Supp. 849 (S.D.N.Y.1978).

[7] This Court notes plaintiff's further argument that this Court should find subject matter jurisdiction as a sanction for failure to comply with its discovery order but does not find it as persuasive as the others they have offered for consideration.

[8] The fact that the legislative history of the FSIA does not contain a specific reference to these doctrines is not surprising. Congress' primary concern was to codify jurisdictional standards relating to the burgeoning area of commercial litigation against foreign governments. House Report, *supra,* at 6, *reprinted in* 1976 U.S.Code Cong. & Ad.News at 6605. The codification was necessary in order to ensure that these more routine cases did not take on undue political significance through the sometimes inconsistent development of the common law, as influenced by the Executive. *See* discussion at pp. 10-11, *supra.*

[9] In a footnote appended to the end of the majority opinion in *Persinger v. Islamic Republic of Iran,* 729 F.2d 835 (D.C.Cir.1984), *cert. denied,* ___ U.S. ___, 105 S. Ct. 247, 83 L. Ed. 2d 185 (1984), Judge Bork (with Judge Edwards dissenting) rejected plaintiffs' argument that United States courts had jurisdiction over claims for damages arising out of the seizure of the American Embassy in Iran, although this seizure constituted an international crime. 729 F.2d at 843 n. 12 (D.C.Cir.1984). So far as the opinion reveals, Judge Bork did not consider the intent of Congress in enacting the FSIA to preserve existing remedies for violations of international law, as described above, or the effect of 18 U.S.C. §§ 1116 and 1201 or 28 U.S.C. § 1350.

[10] The House Report would limit the immunity of a foreign state under the Act to cases of an express or manifest conflict between the provisions of the Act and those of an international agreement or treaty. House Report, *supra,* at 17, *reprinted in* U.S.Code Cong. & Ad.News at 6616. *See, e.g., Mashayekhi v. Iran,* 515 F. Supp. 41, 42 (D.D.C.1981). Given the clear and unambiguous language of the statute, however, resort to the legislative history is in this instance unnecessary for interpretative purposes. *See, e.g., Greyhound Corp. v. Mt. Hood Stages, Inc.,* 437 U.S. 322, 330, 98 S. Ct. 2370, 2375, 57 L. Ed. 2d 239 (1978); *National Insulation Transportation Committee v. ICC,* 683 F.2d 533, 537 (D.C.Cir. 1982). This reading of the clear language of § 1604 is given further support by the language of 28 U.S.C. § 1330, which gives the federal courts jurisdiction over actions against foreign states with respect to which the foreign state is "not entitled to immunity" under the FSIA "or any applicable international agreement."

[11] The House Report provides two illustrative examples of implied waivers an appearance in court by the sovereign defendant, or an agreement by the sovereign defendant to arbitrate claims in another country. House Report, *supra,* at 18, 1976 U.S.Code Cong. & Ad.News at 6617. These examples, however, are not exclusive.

[12] The importance of looking to the writing of legal scholars in this area of the law was explained by the Supreme Court in *The Paquete Habana,* 175 U.S. 677, 700, 20 S. Ct. 290, 299, 44 L. Ed. 320 (1900). *See also, e.g., Filartiga v. Pena-Irala,* 630 F.2d 876, 879 n. 4 (2d Cir.1980).

[13] *Frolova v. Union of Soviet Socialist Republics,* 558 F. Supp. 358 (N.D.Ill.1983), *aff'd,* 761 F.2d 370 (7th Cir.1985), on the other hand, on one interpretation dealt with a legal right the right to emigrate on which there is not yet such universal agreement among nations. *Cf. Tel-Oren v. Libyan Arab Republic,* 726 F.2d 774, 813 (D.C.Cir.1984) (Bork, *J.* concurring).

[14] The District Court held, and plaintiffs conceded, that with regard "to the role of the law of nations," the jurisdictional prerequisites of § 1331 were equivalent to those of § 1350. *Tel-Oren v. Libyan Arab Republic,* 517 F. Supp. 542, 549 (D.D.C.1981), *aff'd,* 726 F.2d 774, 800 (D.C. Cir.1983).

[15] This position was endorsed by the United States Government in an amicus brief submitted by the Departments of State and Justice (Amicus Br. at 4-5).

[16] The appropriate District of Columbia statutes are applicable to all of plaintiffs' claims, including not only those arising under federal law but also those arising under other sources of law. With respect to plaintiffs' federal law claims, where, as in the present case, Congress has not enacted

a statute of limitations governing a particular claim, the courts will look to the statute of limitations of the forum where the district court sits. *E.g., Johnson v. Railway Express Agency, Inc.,* 421 U.S. 454, 462, 95 S. Ct. 1716, 1721, 44 L. Ed. 2d 295 (1975); *Forrestal Village, Inc. v. Graham,* 551 F.2d 411, 413 (D.C.Cir. 1977). The forum statute of limitations to be applied is that which is applicable to the most closely analogous claim under the forum law, and that which best effectuates the federal policy involved. *E.g., McClam v. Barry,* 697 F.2d 366, 373-75 (D.C.Cir.1983); *Forrestal Village, Inc. v. Graham,* at 413.

With respect to plaintiffs' claims not arising under federal law, the statutes of limitations of the District of Columbia apply as the law of the forum. *E.g., Gilson v. Republic of Ireland,* 682 F.2d 1022, 1024-25 & n. 7 (D.C.Cir.1982); *Steorts v. American Airlines, Inc.,* 647 F.2d 194, 197 (D.C.Cir.1981).

The District of Columbia has several provisions which could arguably apply to one or more of plaintiffs' claims. The statute of limitations for "false arrest and false imprisonment," D.C.Code Ann. § 12-301(4) (1981), and for wrongful death, § 16-2702, are both one year. The D.C.Code also provides a three-year statute of limitations for claims which do not have "specially prescribed" limitations. § 12-301(8) (1981).

[17] Application of the discovery rule in the District of Columbia is not limited to any specific type of tortious injury. Rather, the rule is applicable to any "tort clai[m] in which the fact of injury may not be readily discernible." *Wilson v. Johns-Manville Sales Corp.,* 684 F.2d at 116. *See Burns v. Bell,* 409 A.2d 614, 615 (D.C.App. 1979). The Fifth Circuit in *Dubose v. Kansas City Southern Ry.,* 729 F.2d 1026 (5th Cir.1984), *cert. denied,* ___ U.S. ___, 105 S. Ct. 179, 83 L. Ed. 179 (1984), recently held that the discovery rule applies to all federal causes of action "whenever a plaintiff is not aware of and had no reasonable opportunity to discover the critical facts of his injury and its cause." 729 F.2d at 1030.

[18] The United States has signed but not yet ratified this Convention.

[19] In addition to the laws cited in this section, the Soviet Union is party to treaties the terms of which have been violated by the acts against Wallenberg. *See* discussion at pp. 361-62, *supra.*

Sabotaged by U.S. Supreme Court chief Ex-Hill attorney still fighting for Holocaust Hero

By Sabina Clarke

Editor's Note: The following is Part I of a two-part series about renowned attorney Morris Wolff's crusade to rescue his client Holocaust hero Raoul Wallenberg from a Soviet gulag. Wolff lived on Mermaid Lane in Chestnut Hill from 1975 to 1985. His daughter, Lesley, graduated from Springside School in Chestnut Hill in 1993, where she was class valedictorian, and the University of Pennsylvania. Another daughter, Michelle, attended Springside School and graduated from Harcum Jr. College in Bryn Mawr.

Former Chestnut Hill resident and international human rights attorney Morris Wolff, 74, a '54 graduate of Germantown Friends School and an alumnus of Amherst College and Yale University Law School, returned to Philadelphia in May from his Florida home to address students at Germantown Friends, his former alma mater, exhorting them to become initiators of human rights causes and to participate in changing unjust social conditions.

During his stay, Professor Wolff talked about his ongoing 28-year quest to rescue Holocaust hero Raoul Wallenberg, who has been credited with saving at least 100,000 Jews headed for the gas chambers at Auschwitz. Recruited by our government in 1944 to save the remaining Hungarian Jews in Budapest, Wallenberg was later abandoned and left to languish in Soviet prisons ever since his capture by the Russians in 1945. (On August 5, 1981, in a Rose Garden ceremony at the White House, President Ronald Reagan made Wallenberg an American citizen.)

Morris Wolff's fearless journey to free Wallenberg began in 1983 with a 4 a.m. phone call from Guy Von Dardel, the brother of Raoul Wallenberg. Von Dardel, who had been referred to Wolff by a law professor associate from Chicago, pleaded with Wolff to rescue his brother Raoul and to sue the Russians for his kidnapping and illegal detention. The moment he agreed to take the case, Wolff became the de facto voice of Wallenberg.

Based on Wallenberg's status as an American citizen, Wolff sent a hand-delivered letter to President Reagan urging him to demand Wallenberg's release by the Soviets, citing the U.S. Hostages Act. It was not until years later that he learned Reagan's initial directive to act was sabotaged by the White House and U.S. State Department and specifically by Reagan's Counsel, Fred Fielding, and his Assistant Counsel John Roberts — now Chief Justice of the U.S. Supreme Court.

Wolff recalls, "It was not until 2005 when I was contacted by E.J. Kessler, investigative reporter for *The Jewish Forward* during the confirmation hearings for Chief Justice Roberts, that I saw a memo from Roberts to President Reagan urging Reagan to 'dodge the Wallenberg issue.'

"The memo had been buried in the Reagan Library. So with this new information, I asked to be included on the panel for Roberts' confirmation hearings and question him on issues of integrity and character. I wanted him to tell the public what he knew about the Wallenberg matter and why he did not encourage President Reagan to use the law I placed in front of him to rescue Wallenberg, but I was prevented from doing so because the Chairman of the Senate Judiciary Committee, Arlen Specter, a close friend and a Roberts' supporter, knew I would be a hostile witness."

When he received no support from the Reagan administration, Wolff filed his historic lawsuit, "Wallenberg versus the U.S.S.R.," in Federal District Court in Washington, D.C., on February 3, 1984. He remembers his relief when the judge assigned to his case was Judge Barrington Parker Jr., "He was the grandson of a slave and one of the first African-Americans to enter Yale Law School. He was also a strong supporter of human rights who, despite severe pressure from the White House and the State Department, including a highly improper visit to his judicial chambers by the men in pin- striped suits from State, ordered the Soviets to release Wallenberg and pay damages of $39 million — one million for each year of captivity." Parker, he recalls, called the case "unique and without precedent in the history of actions against foreign sovereigns."

The Wallenberg verdict, handed down on Oct. 15, 1985, was front page news in *The New York Times*, *The Washington Post* and *The Philadelphia Inquirer*, and it went national. This historic lawsuit that no one thought he could possibly win paved the way for a new generation of human rights cases.

Then, after a series of postponements filed in secret by an insubordinate attorney who infiltrated Wolff's team of lawyers and worked to sabotage the verdict on behalf of his firm's main client, Chase Manhattan Bank, there was a four-year delay in implementing Parker's decision. Then, something that has never before occurred in the history of the courts was about to happen. The courts ignored Parker's decision and quietly moved the closed case on Judge Parker's docket to the docket of another judge of equal jurisdiction.

In essence says Wolff, "The case was taken from a judge of equal jurisdiction and destroyed. This, according to an associate of mine, the Honorable Arlin M. Adams, a dear friend and retired federal appellate judge on the Third Circuit Court of Appeals, was 'an extreme example of judicial misbehavior.' In effect, the Executive Branch of our government interfered with the Judicial Branch of our government violating the separation of powers clause in the U.S. Constitution."

To be continued[14]

---

[14] This article is reprinted here in it's entirely with permission of the author, Sabina Clarke, and Pete Mazzaccaro, editor of the *Chestnut Hill Newspaper*. Copyright © 2011 All Rights Reserved.

Ex-Hiller fights shameful U.S./Soviet coverup, Hero victimized by gov't officials at highest level

Playing a role in the saga are such participants as Chief Justice John Roberts, President Richard Nixon, President Ronald Reagan, Henry Kissinger and Leonid Brezhnev. Attorney Wolff's efforts to gain justice for the kidnapped Swedish hero, which began in 1983, continue to this day."

By Sabina Clarke

Editor's Note: *The following is the conclusion of the two part series about renowned attorney Morris Wolff's crusade to rescue his client, Holocaust Hero Raoul Wallenberg, from a Soviet gulag.*

Wolff lived on Mermaid Lane in Chestnut Hill from 1975 to 1985. His daughter Lesley graduated from Springside School in Chestnut Hill in 1993, where she was class valedictorian and the University of Pennsylvania. Another daughter, Michelle, attended Springside School and graduated from Harcum Junior College in Bryn Mawr.

I read with fascination Morris Wolff's spellbinding book, *Whatever Happened to Raoul Wallenberg?* chronicling his 28-year quest representing his client, Holocaust hero Raoul Wallenberg. This true story, packed with intrigue, suspense and high drama, trumps a James Bond thriller.

It involves encrypted cables between Wallenberg and the U.S. State Department, hidden KGB files, White House memos, secret documents, cloak and dagger meetings, daring rescue attempts, bold disguises, cryptic messages, anonymous phone calls and mysterious deaths under suspect circumstances.

It also involves former Russian Premier Leonid Brezhnev, who in 1945 was the Red Army's arresting officer, and after arresting Wallenberg, he stole the 'Wallenberg Diamonds' from the safe in Wallenberg's office. The jewels had been entrusted to Wallenberg by many Jews on their way to the death camps. This fact was later confirmed to Wolff by several reliable sources including John Erlichman, former President Nixon's Chief Counsel.

Through it all, pointed warnings were given to Morris Wolff from powerful people in high places suggesting that he abandon his lawsuit on behalf of Wallenberg. Yet, Wolff pushed on, ignoring all warnings while taking on the U.S. State Department, the White House, the U.S.S.R. and prestigious law firms who all tried to squash his efforts to secure Wallenberg's release.

Aided, at times, by a few brave individuals who also took considerable personal risks, Wolff uncovered concrete information revealing behind-the-scenes machinations aimed at stopping his investigation into the disappearance and whereabouts of Raoul Wallenberg. He recalls his friend Earl Silbert, a former Watergate prosecutor, saying to him, "I think you may want to back off this case. This is not a game of tennis. There are some pretty strong forces working against you —including the FBI, the CIA and other forces at high levels of government."

When warned by President Reagan's former Assistant Secretary of State Richard Fairbanks that the Russians might try to kill him and that he was "interfering with the conduct of foreign affairs" Wolff replied, "Only a bullet will stop me, and you are not about to order that; are you?"

This is a tale of heroes and villains and a fascinating glimpse into our legal system and its shameful derailment precipitated by the interference of the State Department and the White House as well as Russia and Sweden and their Wall Street and Washington, D.C., law firms acting as hired guns for the Chase Manhattan Bank in New York and the Enskilda Bank of Sweden. All were in bed together. All conspired to squash Wolff's case, and in the end, they almost did.

Wolff's quest for justice for Wallenberg has taken him all over the world collecting first-person recollections from Wallenberg's friends and associates and those who were rescued by Wallenberg. With some, Wolff has forged close and lasting friendships.

Now with his new book and some heavyweight book blurb endorsements from former President Bill Clinton, President Barack Obama, Nobel Peace Prize laureate Elie Wiesel, Nobel Peace Prize laureate Anatole Scharansky and others, the Wallenberg story should wind up on the world stage once again, thanks to a May 10, 2011, letter to Wolff from President Obama stating, "Morris Wolff in 1989 went to Israel and enlisted the Mossad, Israel's intelligence agency, in a daring raid to rescue Raoul Wallenberg. On April 30, 2011, we copied that strategy and took out Osama Bin Laden. The use of a carefully planned and wisely implemented strategy is a hallmark of Morris Wolff's legal work in the U.S. Federal Court in achieving a great victory for his client, a hero whom we all celebrate....."

Encouraged by his friend and associate, retired Federal Judge Arlin M. Adams, who has reviewed the procedural facts of the case, Wolff plans to go back to court and seek a reversal of Judge Aubrey

Robinson's decision. (In 1989, Judge Aubrey Robinson dismissed the case and overturned Judge Barrington Parker's legal verdict on behalf of Wallenberg; in 1984, Judge Barrington Parker, who presided over the case initially, ordered the Russians to release Wallenberg immediately and pay $39 million to the Wallenberg family.)

In essence, says Wolff, Judge Parker's decision was ignored. The case was moved, four years later, from the closed docket of Judge Parker to the open docket of Judge Robinson — a judge of equal jurisdiction. This, according to Judge Arlin M. Adams, retired federal appellate judge on the Third Circuit Court of Appeals, was an "extreme example of judicial misbehavior" and something that had never been done before. Simply put, the Executive Branch of our government interfered with the Judicial Branch of our government, violating the separation of powers clause in the U.S. Constitution.

Wolff plans to file a petition with the U.S. Supreme Court seeking a reinstatement of the Parker decision, the collection of the $39 million with compounded interest and the immediate release of Wallenberg — realizing that Wallenberg is almost certainly not still alive. (If he is, he would be 99.) Wolff estimates the current value of the case at $142 million. But for Wolff, who has worked pro bono all these years, the case has never been about money; it is about getting justice for Raoul Wallenberg, a Swedish diplomat who saved more than 1000 Jews from certain death at the hands of the Nazis.

If Wolff succeeds in getting the Wallenberg case heard before the Supreme Court, any monetary award would go towards the creation of the Raoul Wallenberg Center for Altruistic Studies —which was agreed upon by both Wolff and Wallenberg's family from the outset.

Wolff hopes to have the case heard before the Supreme Court, citing Article III, Section 2 of the U.S. Constitution, which states, "Cases involving ambassadors, public ministers and consuls can be brought directly to the United States Supreme Court which shall have original jurisdiction over such matters."

Since Wallenberg qualifies as an ambassador or public minister, his case can be heard directly by the Supreme Court, via petition, with

Chief Justice John C. Roberts presiding. "This", said Wolff, "will provide Chief Justice Roberts with an opportunity to correct his earlier error."

Editor's Note: In 1983, Chief Justice John Roberts, then Assistant Counsel to President Ronald Reagan, advised Reagan in a memo to ignore Wolff's letter seeking Reagan's help in freeing Wallenberg and to "dodge the Wallenberg issue" —despite Reagan's initial directive to act to free Wallenberg.

It was not until 2005, during the confirmation hearings for Chief Justice Roberts that Wolff was contacted by E.J. Kessler, investigative reporter for The Jewish Forward, that he learned why he did not get a response from Reagan and why President Reagan did not use the law Wolff laid before him, citing the U.S. Hostages Act, to free Wallenberg. Until 2005, the Roberts memo had been buried in the Reagan Library.[15]

("Whatever Happened to Raoul Wallenberg?" is published by The Educational Publisher/Biblio Publishing, of Columbus, Ohio. To order the book online for $18.95, visit BiblioBookstore.com or Amazon.com.)

---

[15] This article is reprinted here in it's entirely with permission of the author, Sabina Clarke, and Pete Mazzaccaro, editor of the *Chestnut Hill Newspaper*. Copyright © 2011 All Rights Reserved.

Also Available From Morris Wolff

Whatever Happened to Raoul Wallenberg?
The true story of Holocaust hero Raoul Wallenberg and the author's efforts to rescue him from Soviet Union imprisonment

A fascinating true story of one man's effort to save Swedish diplomat —War Hero Raoul Wallenberg — from the dungeons of the gulag where he was thrown after the KGB kidnapped him from Hungary on January 17, 1945. Author Morris Wolff sued the Soviets for Wallenberg's release and won a 39-million-dollar verdict. Then Wolff went to Israel to enlist the Mossad in a rescue effort and in 1998 enlisted former US Ambassador to Moscow David M Evans. Evans, in the final pages of the book, goes to Kazan and amazingly finds Wallenberg alive in a hospital overlooking the Volga River. Read the details of this great rescue effort and the roadblocks placed in Wolff's path by the governments of Sweden, Russia, and the USA. Wolff wins the US Symphony Peace Award for his efforts at Carnegie Hall in New York in September of 1993 and then doubles his effort to rescue Wallenberg—a bloodhound selfless effort of 27 years with only certain members of the Wallenberg family helping him—while the majority of the family fight vociferously against Wolff's innocent and dedicated effort. The rich bankers in the family fight lawyer Wolff at every step of the way. They have much to hide as collaborators. They do not want Raoul free. This mystery-detective story—all true—will educate, inform, and thrill you!

Order your copy today!
Amazon - https://www.amazon.com/dp/1622495985
Biblio Bookstore - https://bibliobookstore.com/history/whatever-happened-to-raoul-wallenberg-by-morris-wolff